HOW TO WIN WITH AI

Master AI before it replaces YOU

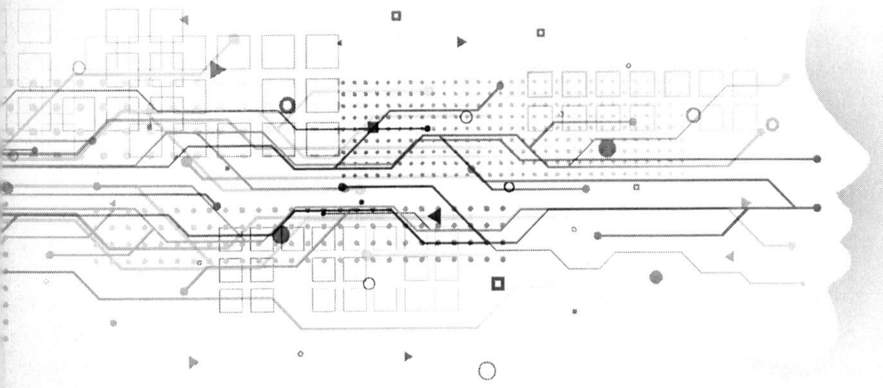

AVINASH MADA

Clever Fox® PUBLISHING
Chennai • Bangalore

CLEVER FOX PUBLISHING
Chennai, India

Published by CLEVER FOX PUBLISHING 2025

ISBN: 978-93-5648-870-0

ACKNOWLEDGMENTS

Thanks to my family

This book wouldn't be here without my family. Dad, Ravi Kumar, your quiet strength and steady guidance have shaped me more than you know. You've taught me that hard work and patience are key, even when things get tough. Nithin, my brother, you've always had my back, whether through laughter or listening when I needed it most. You both have been my support, my safe space, and my reason to keep going. Thank you for being the quiet heroes behind this journey. I couldn't have done it without you.

A note of gratitude for my late mom

This book is dedicated to my late mother Jaya Lakshmi, whose wisdom, love, and guidance continue to shape who I am today. She always saw challenges as opportunities, teaching me to rise above them with courage and determination. I'll never forget the day I dropped out of college at 18 to pursue my digital marketing agency. While many doubted me, she laid a solid foundation, encouraging me every step of the way. Everything I've built has been because of her unwavering belief in me. Mom, thank you for your early support and for always being my guiding light. I miss you more than words can express, and your spirit will forever inspire me.

A special mention of my team

A heartfelt thank you to my Freedom with AI team, and especially to Sai Kiran P. His dedication as a co-author, his brilliance in research, and his tireless efforts to refine my ideas played a pivotal role in bringing this book to life.

ABOUT ME..

I'd like to express my gratitude for taking the time to consider reading my book.

Before I take you deep into the world of Artificial Intelligence, let's get a few things straight. AI is huge; it's like exploring an endless ocean of possibilities and surprises. There are times it'll amaze you with incredible innovations and discoveries. And sometimes, it might make you a bit anxious about the future it's creating.

Picture yourself standing at the shoreline, curious and excited, but also a little cautious about what's hidden in its vastness.

Now, brace yourself as we delve deeper into a new world, where machines can mimic the human mind, outthink us, and adapt with terrifying speed. Imagine a world where your deepest, darkest secrets are no longer hidden, but laid bare, decoded by algorithms that know you better than you know yourself.

A world where control slips through human fingers, as artificial intelligence dominates our intelligence, making decisions that shape the destiny of humanity. This is not the world of science fiction; this is the imminent reality we are on the brink of encountering.

Have you ever considered why humans control most aspects of the planet, despite gorillas being physically stronger? We can even dominate all the gorillas in the world. The reason is our superior intelligence. It's not that gorillas lack intelligence; in fact, theirs is quite similar to that of humans. However, they use it merely for survival, whereas we use ours to multiply, survive, and enhance our way of life.

Believe me when I say this, intelligence is the defining characteristic that establishes humans as the dominant species on Earth. What would happen, then, if we used our intelligence to create a replica of it - Artificial Intelligence. What if AI, excelling in the most complex tasks surpassing the capabilities of the humans, for example

- World's best chess player is AI
- World's best communicator is AI
- World's toughest game "Go board" was beaten by AI
- GPT-4's verbal IQ is 152 and Einstein's IQ is estimated to be 160.
- And the list goes on...

even boasting a higher IQ than Einstein, were to eclipse our intelligence? Could it potentially dominate us and take over our throne as the primary species?

Am I scaring you a bit much? Fear not my friends. This book is not just a chronicle of AI's evolution and capabilities; it's also a guide. By the end, I promise to equip you with a roadmap to navigate the intricate maze of AI's influence on our lives. This plan will help you sidestep the pitfalls and harness the immense potential that AI offers.

Keep this in mind as we journey through this book: AI is moving forward super fast. It's like nothing we've ever seen before, and we need to keep up. If we just sit back and watch, chances are we'll miss out. Today's AI is more than just a bunch of AI tools. They're like artificial beings that can learn, grow, and get better over time.

They keep changing and improving, and we should too.

So, here's the thing as you flip through the pages: nothing is fixed about the future. We've got the power to shape it with the right knowledge and actions. So, let's jump in, keep an open mind, and figure this out together.

INTRODUCTION

As I pen down the first words of this book, I feel a sense of anticipation and warmth, imagining you on the other side of these pages. You see, this isn't just a book about Artificial Intelligence; it's a shared exploration, a conversation between two curious minds separated only by the space of these pages yet connected by the threads of curiosity and wonder.

Before we dive deep into the area of Artificial intelligence, I want you to know that this journey is as much yours as it is mine. At the age of 17, I experienced a setback in my drop-shipping business, losing 10 lakhs. Simultaneously, my father encountered a business loss of 30 lakhs.

Ironically, we found ourselves taking out loans after loans just to cover the interest on our existing debts.

Back then, my CGPA was 4, but our debt was 40 lakhs. I had no faith in getting a job placement. During this time, I wondered what I could do to earn money quickly and ethically.

I saw Kylie Jenner, a 19-year-old girl, on the cover of Forbes magazine. She had earned countless money through Instagram. In fact, she was one of the youngest self-made billionaires in the world.

When I was in school, I used to manage celebrity fan pages, so I realized that I had a basic idea of how to maintain Facebook and Instagram, make posts go viral, and engage the audience.

After realizing that I can turn this hobby into money making skill I started offering social media management and growth services to influencers and international brands, and in the next 6 months, I generated 80 lakhs in revenue. My work was also published in magazines like

Times of India and Indian Express. Instantly, I cleared all the debts my family made.

In the next 3 years, we grew into a complete digital marketing agency by adding 19 members to my team. We also generated several crores in revenue by managing ads worth several hundred crores for our clients.

As life would have it, despite everything going well, we faced a setback. Around 50% of my company's clients were related to crypto and blockchain companies. When Bitcoin crashed 2021, we lost these 50% of our clients, and my company, which had been earning a lot of revenue and was profitable, started incurring losses. There came a point in time when we were struggling to pay salaries to our employees and even to pay the rent.

During such a time, I received a large project. For this project, I needed 8 content writers, but I only had 4. I was not in a position to hire another 4 members. The only option I had was to fire 4 other employees in my company and hire these people in their place. But morally that was a ridiculous idea. So, I was researching how to fulfill this project with just 4 content writers and I came across an AI tool called Jasper.ai.

Given a topic, Jasper would write an article on it, precisely like a professional writer. The way you're excited looking at this current ChatGPT, I was also surprised back then. In fact, I got goosebumps.

I was shocked, wondering how Jasper writes such good content? And that too with human emotions and logical reasoning. I started researching and realized that Jasper uses AI technology.

To put AI simply - it is giving the power of thinking like a human to a software, just like in the movie Robo where the hero Vashikaran gives Chitti the ability for deep thinking.

AI is advancing so fast in the last few years that it's growing from being able to write a blog article to being capable of creating VFX on the scale of Baahubali.

Nowadays, people are using AI for creating content, graphics, editing, presentations, voice-overs, coding, animations, VFX and a lot more. AI is so powerful that soon people with just basic computer knowledge will also be able to create VFX like Avatar or Bahubali right from their bedrooms.

If AI is disrupting so many industries, it means it's going to become something big, I realized.

While deeply diving into my research on Jasper, I found out that Jasper is just a "small drop in an ocean"; in the AI world. The company that provides this AI technology to thousands of companies like Jasper, and that is OpenAI.

My curiosity about OpenAI doubled when I got to know that Elon Musk had invested 500 crores in it. Usually, Elon Musk invests in sectors that he believes will disrupt an industry, so I understood that OpenAI will shake the world in near future.

In November 30, 2022, OpenAI dropped a nuke in the digital world - ChatGPT and rest is history.

Back to my story, we were finally able to fulfill the project using Jasper with just four content writers.

I didn't just focus on content writers but also made robust research on AI tools to improve my team and make my agency more productive and efficient.

Basically, the most time-consuming task in my company is content writing and ad creative designing. So, I thought of making designing as productive as content writing.

Then, I found out and implemented the AdCreative.ai tool. With it, we could make hundreds of ad creatives for my clients within minutes, so my employees were able to deliver double the work in the same 8-hour workdays.

Another time and effort consuming part of my agency is making ad campaigns on Facebook and Google. I learned prompt engineering myself, wrote a mega prompt, and could design any ad campaign in just a few minutes using ChatGPT.

So, what exactly is this prompt engineering?

Just as we code or communicate with a computer in a language it understands in software engineering, similarly in prompt engineering, we need to explain what we want to the AI in a way it understands.

Because of this, the ad campaign process, which used to take 7 to 10 days, was now completed in just under a day.

Literally, we started launching Facebook and Google ads by combining the output given by ChatGPT with our own creativity and experience.

Although the company became productive, we needed new clients. For that, using some more AI tools, we designed a workflow to send personalized emails to thousands of prospects within just a week. Previously, the same task would have required about 30 days of work from 2 employees. Now, one employee can do it in just a week.

In this way, by making my agency super productive, we not only returned to profitability but also doubled our revenue within 6 months without adding any new employees.

If we hadn't used AI tools and had continued with traditional methods, like many agencies, we might have been out of business by now because of competition.

What I believe is that AI may not replace our jobs in the immediate short term, but those who use AI tools to become efficient will compete better, otherwise, we might lose jobs.

The question is, does AI technology have an impact on every individual? The answer is an emphatic yes.

The reason is that every one of the world's top 6 companies, such as Google, Microsoft, Apple, Amazon, Facebook, and Nvidia, is entirely shifting towards AI.

Instead of building a company like OpenAI, Microsoft thought it safer to invest in OpenAI and has invested $10 billion, which means 1.4 lakh crores.

Just to put this into perspective, this is more than the GDPs of 3-4 states in India.

So now there is no question about whether AI is important or not.

It's obvious from the above observations.

The question is how can one compete in the upcoming AI-driven world and what should one do?

According to the World Economic Forum, a total of 170 million jobs will be created and 92 million will be lost by 2030 as tech, AI, and green energy reshape the global workforce. Every new role will be leveraging AI and doing the task efficiently. I realized that without mastering AI there's no survival.

After deep thinking for months about how AI can disrupt every industry and job, I became physically nauseous.

When I made 80 lakhs in 6 months, I became an internet sensation and got featured in the Times of India. A reporter asked me, 'Why don't you create a course on digital marketing? My son is very interested.' I replied that I was recording a course on how youngsters can make money from Instagram. But I left that course halfway through because it wasn't unique; it was the same stuff with different techniques and strategies that you can literally find on YouTube.

So, I abandoned the idea of creating a course because there wasn't a strong motive that I was helping people make huge money or saving them in a crisis.

While researching AI, I found an article where Robin Li, CEO of Baidu, said, 'In 10 years, half of the world's jobs will be prompt engineering,' meaning talking to AI and getting things done in a faster and more efficient manner.

It was at that moment I realized I had the social responsibility to help people master AI, and I ventured into a company called Freedom with AI to share the knowledge and expertise for a better future for all of us.

As a matter of fact, where many course curators charge money to step into a masterclass or webinar, which are mostly pre-recorded, I kept the FWAI masterclass free of cost. This way, anyone who visits understands the importance of AI, and if willing to pay, they get the privilege of joining the world's best and soon-to-be largest AI community. If not willing to pay, they still go back with the learnings and look out for other resources to learn AI. One thing is sure: anyone who attends my masterclass will fear AI and know its importance, which is the exact reason for venturing into FWAI. Learning is obviously a personal choice.

Though I continuously share AI updates, news, strategies, techniques to master AI tools, and many more things on my social media channels, it's still hard to convince people that AI is an inevitable threat if you don't master it. Hence, the idea of writing this book came to my mind, and I decided to fulfill two most important things in the realm of AI:

1. Educate and create awareness about AI.
2. Tell people how to mitigate risks and master AI.

These two important things are nothing but the two parts of the book which you're going to read further.

The only suggestion I have for you before you rush into the subject is that do not skip any point in this book, even if you feel like doing so. Don't do it because unknowingly you might be missing key information that could change your life. What if this book has something for you like the Kylie Jenner moment was for me? Another suggestion is to share the knowledge or wisdom with your friends, parents, relatives because if you're early to master AI, you should also be early to help others become aware of AI. Don't mind me saying this, but AI can be the worst pandemic in the history of mankind if not mastered in the early stages.

Keeping all of that in mind, take a deep breath and turn the page!

"AI can amplify human potential, but only when guided by our wisdom."

CONTENTS

CHAPTER 1

WHAT REALLY IS INTELLIGENCE?

"The measure of intelligence is the ability to change."

– Albert Einstein

Intelligence is at the heart of who we are as human beings. It shapes our identity, drives our growth, and enables us to learn, understand, and apply knowledge effectively. But intelligence is far more than just the accumulation of facts; it encompasses creativity, problem-solving abilities, and the capacity to adapt to new situations. These cognitive skills have been instrumental in our survival, innovation, and the improvement of our quality of life throughout history.

As we embark on this exploration of intelligence, we'll journey from the intricate workings of the human brain to the rapidly evolving realm of artificial intelligence. We'll examine how intelligence manifests in various forms across the natural world and compare it to the artificial constructs we've created. This chapter sets the stage for understanding the complex interplay between human cognition and artificial intelligence, laying the groundwork for the discussions that will follow throughout this book.

In a world where machines are becoming increasingly capable of performing tasks once thought to be exclusively human, it's crucial to understand what truly defines intelligence. Is it our ability to process information, our capacity for emotional understanding, or perhaps our knack for creative problem-solving? As we delve into these questions, we'll discover that intelligence is a multifaceted concept, one that continues to challenge our understanding and push the boundaries of both natural and artificial cognitive capabilities.

The Journey to Human Intelligence

The story of intelligence is as old as life itself, a tale that spans billions of years and countless species. It begins with the simplest forms of life, single-celled organisms floating in primordial seas. These tiny beings, though lacking anything we'd recognize as a brain, displayed a fundamental form of intelligence: the ability to respond to their environment.

A paramecium sensing a chemical gradient and moving towards food or away from danger – this was intelligence in its most basic form.

As life grew more complex, so did the mechanisms of cognition. The development of specialized nerve cells marked a quantum leap forward. These neurons could rapidly transmit electrical signals across an organism, allowing for quicker and more coordinated responses. Imagine a jellyfish, its simple nerve net allowing it to pulse through the water and react to touch. This distributed form of intelligence, while still primitive, was a significant advance.

The next great leap came with the centralization of these nervous systems. In animals like flatworms, we see the first appearance of a brain-like structure – a cluster of neurons that act as a central processing unit. This centralization allowed for more complex behaviors and the ability to learn from experiences. It was the dawn of what we might recognize as a 'brain', albeit in its most rudimentary form.

As we move through evolutionary history, we encounter the vertebrate brain, bringing with it a new level of cognitive sophistication. With distinct regions for different functions, it allowed for more advanced sensory processing, motor control, and the emergence of what we might call 'thinking' in its most basic form. Picture a fish navigating a coral reef, its brain processing complex sensory information to find food and avoid predators.

The mammalian brain represented another quantum leap in cognitive capabilities. With the development of the neocortex, mammals gained enhanced abilities in perception, spatial reasoning, and conscious thought. Consider a wolf coordinating with its pack to take down prey, or a dolphin using echolocation to build a detailed 'sound picture' of its underwater world. These are examples of intelligence that begin to approach the complexity we associate with higher cognition.

But it's with the emergence of primates, and particularly the great apes, that we see intelligence begin to resemble something close to human-like cognition. Chimpanzees using tools to fish for termites, orangutans solving complex puzzles to reach food, gorillas learning human sign language – these demonstrations of problem-solving, tool use, and symbolic communication hint at the cognitive abilities that would reach their apex in humans.

And then there's us – Homo sapiens. Our intelligence represents a leap so profound that it has fundamentally altered the face of our planet. But what makes human intelligence so unique?

At its core, human intelligence is characterized by an unparalleled ability for abstract thought. We can conceptualize ideas that have no physical form, imagine hypothetical scenarios, and engage in complex problem-solving that goes beyond immediate, concrete situations. This ability underpins everything from our scientific endeavors to our artistic expressions.

Our linguistic abilities are another hallmark of human intelligence. While other animals communicate, human language is a system of unprecedented complexity and flexibility. We can discuss the past and future, convey abstract concepts, and even talk about language itself. This ability to share complex ideas has been crucial to our species' success, allowing us to cooperate on a scale unseen in the animal kingdom.

Creativity is another defining feature of human intelligence. Our capacity to generate novel ideas, to innovate, to create art and music and literature – these abilities seem to be uniquely human in their sophistication and scope. This creativity extends to technological innovations that have transformed our world, from the first stone tools to modern computers.

Perhaps one of the most profound aspects of human intelligence is our self-awareness – our ability to reflect on our own mental states, to contemplate our place in the universe, and to ponder the very nature of consciousness itself. This metacognition allows us to examine and regulate our own thinking processes, a crucial component of our advanced problem-solving abilities.

Our intelligence is also deeply social. We possess an advanced theory of mind – the ability to understand that others have beliefs, desires, and intentions that are different from our own. This, combined with our capacity for empathy and emotional intelligence, allows us to navigate complex social situations and cooperate on a massive scale.

Finally, our ability to transmit knowledge across generations through culture sets us apart. This cultural transmission allows for cumulative learning, where each generation can build upon the knowledge of previous ones. It's this feature that has allowed human knowledge and technology to advance at a pace far outstripping biological evolution.

As we stand on the brink of creating artificial intelligence that may rival or surpass our own in certain domains, it's crucial to understand the long and complex journey that led to human intelligence. Our cognitive abilities are the product of billions of years of evolution, shaped by the challenges our ancestors faced and the environments they inhabited. As we move forward into the age of AI, we carry with us this rich heritage of biological intelligence – a standard against which we will inevitably measure our artificial creations.

Unveiling Artificial Intelligence: A New Frontier of Cognition

In the grand tapestry of human achievement, few endeavors have captured our collective imagination quite like the creation of artificial intelligence (AI). It's a pursuit that stands at the intersection of computer science, cognitive psychology, neuroscience, and philosophy, challenging us to unravel the very nature of intelligence itself. As we embark on this exploration of AI, we find ourselves not just as observers, but as creators, shaping a form of intelligence that may one day rival or even surpass our own.

The Genesis of Artificial Intelligence

The concept of artificial intelligence has roots that stretch back into antiquity. Ancient myths and legends are replete with stories of artificial beings endowed with intelligence or consciousness by master craftsmen. The Greek god Hephaestus was said to have created mechanical servants, including Talos, a giant bronze automaton. In Jewish folklore, the golem was an anthropomorphic being animated through mystical means. These tales reflect a long-standing human fascination with the idea of creating life and intelligence.

However, it wasn't until the mid-20th century that the dream of artificial intelligence began to transition from the realm of myth and speculation into scientific reality. The term "artificial intelligence" itself was coined in 1956 at the Dartmouth Conference, organized by John McCarthy, Marvin Minsky, Nathaniel Rochester, and Claude Shannon. This conference, which is now widely considered the birthplace of AI as a field of study, brought together leading thinkers to explore how machines could be made to simulate aspects of human intelligence.

The participants in the Dartmouth Conference were animated by a profound optimism. They believed that significant advances could be made in one or more of these problems if a carefully selected group of scientists worked on it together for a summer. While their initial timeframe proved overly ambitious, their vision set the stage for decades of research and development in AI.

Defining Artificial Intelligence: A Multifaceted Endeavor

Defining artificial intelligence is no simple task. As the field has evolved, so too have our conceptions of what constitutes AI. At its broadest, AI refers to the creation of computer systems capable of performing tasks that typically require human intelligence. But this definition opens up a host of questions: What exactly constitutes intelligence? How do we measure it in machines? What are the boundaries between 'mere' computation and true intelligence?

One useful framework for understanding AI was proposed by Stuart Russell and Peter Norvig in their seminal textbook "Artificial Intelligence: A Modern Approach." They suggest that AI can be categorized along two main dimensions:

1. Thinking vs. Acting: Does the system need to emulate human cognitive processes, or is it sufficient for it to act intelligently?
2. Humanly vs. Rationally: Should the system behave like humans (including our biases and limitations), or should it adhere to theoretical concepts of perfect rationality?

These distinctions give us four possible goals for AI systems:

1. Systems that think like humans (cognitive modeling)
2. Systems that act like humans (the Turing Test approach)
3. Systems that think rationally (the "laws of thought" approach)
4. Systems that act rationally (the rational agent approach)

Each of these approaches has its proponents and has led to significant advances in the field. Cognitive modeling, for instance, has driven research in neural networks and has close ties to cognitive science and neuroscience. The Turing Test approach, proposed by Alan Turing in 1950, has spurred developments in natural language processing and human-computer interaction. The "laws of thought" approach has connections to logic and mathematics, while the rational agent approach has been influential in the development of machine learning algorithms.

The Building Blocks of AI: From Expert Systems to Deep Learning

As the field of AI has developed, it has spawned a variety of subfields and approaches. Some of the key areas include:

1. Knowledge Representation and Reasoning: This involves finding ways to represent knowledge in a form that a computer system can use to solve complex problems. Early AI systems, known as expert systems, used rule-based approaches to encode human expertise in narrow domains.
2. Machine Learning: This subfield focuses on the development of algorithms that can learn from and make predictions or decisions based on data. It includes techniques like decision tree learning, inductive logic programming, and clustering.
3. Neural Networks and Deep Learning: Inspired by the structure of the human brain, neural networks are a set of algorithms designed to recognize patterns. Deep learning, which uses many-layered neural networks, has driven recent breakthroughs in areas like image and speech recognition.
4. Natural Language Processing (NLP): This area is concerned with the interactions between computers and human language. It includes challenges like speech recognition, natural language understanding, and natural language generation.
5. Computer Vision: This field works on enabling computers to gain high-level understanding from digital images or videos. Applications range from facial recognition systems to medical image analysis.
6. Robotics: While not all robotics involves AI, the integration of AI with robotics enables the creation of autonomous systems that can interact with the physical world.
7. Planning and Decision Making: This involves developing algorithms that can make sequences of decisions to achieve a goal, often in complex and uncertain environments.

Each of these areas has seen remarkable progress, but they've also revealed the immense challenges involved in creating artificial intelligence that can match the breadth and flexibility of human cognition.

AI vs. Human Intelligence: A Complex Comparison

When we compare artificial intelligence to human intelligence, we find ourselves in a realm of both striking similarities and profound differences. Like a mirror that's both familiar and alien, AI reflects back to us aspects of our own cognition while also revealing forms of intelligence that are fundamentally different from our own.

Human intelligence, the product of millions of years of evolutionary pressures, is a marvel of adaptability and generality. We can solve a vast array of problems, from the abstract to the concrete. We can recognize patterns, learn from experience, reason about complex situations, and create novel ideas. Our intelligence is deeply intertwined with our emotions, our bodies, and our social experiences.

Artificial intelligence, by contrast, is a newcomer on the cognitive scene. Born in the laboratories and server farms of the modern world, AI systems have evolved at a blistering pace. In some narrow domains, they've already surpassed human capabilities. An AI can calculate faster than any human, can sift through vast amounts of data to find patterns invisible to the naked eye, and can play games like chess and Go at superhuman levels.

Yet, despite these impressive capabilities, current AI systems fall short of human intelligence in many crucial ways:

1. Generality: While humans are general intelligence machines, capable of tackling a wide variety of tasks, most AI systems are narrow, excelling in specific domains but struggling when faced with tasks outside their training.
2. Common Sense Reasoning: Humans possess a rich understanding of how the world works, allowing us to make reasonable inferences

in new situations. AI systems often lack this common sense knowledge, leading to errors that would seem obvious to a human.

3. Creativity and Innovation: While AI can generate novel combinations of existing ideas, true creativity – the ability to come up with fundamentally new concepts – remains a largely human domain.
4. Emotional Intelligence: Humans have a deep capacity for understanding and managing emotions, both our own and others'. This emotional intelligence plays a crucial role in our decision-making and social interactions, an area where AI still falls short.
5. Consciousness and Self-Awareness: Perhaps the most profound difference is that humans are conscious, self-aware beings. We have subjective experiences, a sense of self, and the ability to ponder our own existence. Whether machines can ever possess these qualities is a question that delves deep into philosophy and the nature of consciousness itself.
6. Learning Efficiency: Humans can often learn from just a few examples, using our broad background knowledge to make inferences. Most current AI systems, particularly in areas like deep learning, require vast amounts of data to learn effectively.
7. Adaptability: Humans can adapt to new situations and transfer knowledge from one domain to another with relative ease. AI systems often struggle when faced with situations that differ significantly from their training data.

These differences highlight the complementary nature of human and artificial intelligence. In many fields, the most powerful approaches combine human and machine intelligence, leveraging the strengths of each.

The Ethical Dimension: As We Shape AI, It Shapes Us

As we continue to develop more advanced AI systems, we find ourselves grappling with profound ethical questions. How do we ensure that AI systems are fair and unbiased, especially when they're trained on data that may reflect societal prejudices? How do we maintain human autonomy and decision-making power in a world where AI systems may be capable of making better decisions in many domains?

Moreover, the development of AI is causing us to reflect deeply on our own intelligence and what it means to be human. As machines begin to perform tasks we once thought were uniquely human, we're forced to reconsider what sets us apart. This introspection can be unsettling, but it also offers an opportunity for a deeper understanding of human cognition and consciousness.

Looking to the Future: The Co-Evolution of Human and Artificial Intelligence

As we stand on the brink of what some call the "AI revolution," it's clear that the story of intelligence is entering a new chapter. We are no longer just the product of biological evolution, but active participants in the creation of a new form of intelligence.

This co-evolution of human and artificial intelligence promises to reshape our world in profound ways. AI has the potential to help us solve some of our most pressing problems, from climate change to disease. It could augment our own capabilities, allowing us to explore new frontiers of knowledge and creativity.

Yet, as with any powerful technology, AI also carries risks. The challenge before us is to guide its development in ways that benefit humanity as a whole, that respect human values and rights, and that preserve the essence of what makes us human.

As we contemplate these future possibilities and challenges, it's crucial to understand the path that has led us to this point. The story of artificial intelligence is not just about what lies ahead, but also about the remarkable milestones we've already achieved. These pivotal moments in AI history have not only demonstrated the growing capabilities of machine intelligence but have also challenged our understanding of human cognition and the very nature of intelligence itself.

One such defining moment occurred in 1997, a watershed year for artificial intelligence. As the world watched with bated breath, a machine took on one of the greatest human minds in a game long considered a bastion of human intellectual prowess. This event would not only prove the potential of AI but also spark a global conversation about the future relationship between human and machine intelligence.

AI in Action: The Epic Clash of Deep Blue vs. Kasparov

In the annals of artificial intelligence, few moments stand out as vividly as the 1997 chess match between IBM's Deep Blue and world chess champion Garry Kasparov. This contest was more than just a game; it represented a pivotal moment in the relationship between human and machine intelligence. It was a drama that unfolded on a 64-square battlefield, capturing the world's imagination and raising profound questions about the nature of intelligence itself.

The match served as a tangible demonstration of how far AI had come and offered a glimpse of its potential. It challenged our assumptions about the uniqueness of human strategic thinking and opened up new avenues for AI research and development. To fully appreciate the significance of this historic confrontation and its implications for the future of AI, we need to understand the long journey that led to this moment.

The Road to the Match: A Brief History of Chess-Playing Computers

Chess, with its complex strategies and vast number of possible moves, has long been viewed as the ultimate test of intellectual prowess. As such, it became an early focus for AI researchers, serving as a benchmark for machine intelligence. The journey to create a chess-playing computer that could rival human grandmasters is a fascinating story of human ingenuity and technological progress.

The journey began in the 1950s, with pioneers like Claude Shannon and Alan Turing laying the theoretical groundwork for chess-playing programs. Early efforts were primitive by today's standards, but they established key principles that would guide future development.

In 1967, a landmark was reached when MacHack VI, developed at MIT, became the first computer program to defeat a human in a rated chess tournament. However, it would be decades before computers could challenge the world's top players.

The 1980s and early 1990s saw rapid progress. In 1988, Deep Thought, a precursor to Deep Blue, became the first computer to defeat a grandmaster in a game. Yet, when Deep Thought faced Kasparov in 1989, it lost convincingly, demonstrating the vast gulf that still existed between machine and human capabilities at the highest levels of chess.

Enter Deep Blue: The Silicon Challenger

Deep Blue was not just an incremental improvement over its predecessors; it represented a quantum leap in chess-playing ability. Developed by a team at IBM led by Feng-hsiung Hsu and Murray Campbell, Deep Blue was a supercomputer dedicated to playing chess.

At its core, Deep Blue used a brute-force approach, evaluating millions of positions per second. But it wasn't just about raw calculation power. The system incorporated sophisticated evaluation functions, drawing on the expertise of grandmasters who helped fine-tune its decision-making processes.

Some key features of Deep Blue included:

1. Parallel Processing: Deep Blue used 30 IBM RS/6000 SP computers, each containing 30 processors, allowing it to examine 200 million chess positions per second.

2. Opening Book: It had access to a vast database of opening moves, allowing it to play the early game with the wisdom accumulated from centuries of human chess experience.
3. Endgame Database: For positions with six or fewer pieces on the board, Deep Blue could play perfectly, having pre-calculated all possible outcomes.
4. Adaptive Learning: Between games, the IBM team could tweak Deep Blue's evaluation functions based on Kasparov's play, allowing it to adapt its strategy.

The Match: A Battle of Minds

The stage was set for an epic confrontation. On one side stood Garry Kasparov, widely regarded as the greatest chess player in history, known for his dynamic play and unparalleled intuition. On the other, Deep Blue, a silicon and steel embodiment of humanity's quest to create thinking machines.

The match, held in New York City, was set for six games. The world watched with bated breath as man and machine faced off across the chessboard.

Game 1 (May 3, 1997): Kasparov emerged victorious, showcasing his strategic depth and ability to outmaneuver the machine in a complex middlegame. The chess world breathed a collective sigh of relief. Human intuition, it seemed, still held the upper hand.

Game 2 (May 4, 1997): In a shocking turn of events, Deep Blue struck back. In a game that would be discussed for years to come, the machine outplayed Kasparov in a sharp tactical battle. This marked the first time a computer had defeated a reigning world champion in a game under standard time controls.

Game 3 (May 6, 1997): A draw. The tension was palpable as neither side could gain a decisive advantage. The match was proving to be closer than many had anticipated.

Game 4 (May 7, 1997): Another draw. Kasparov, playing cautiously, steered the game into calm waters. The world champion seemed to be feeling the pressure, respecting the machine's capabilities.

Game 5 (May 10, 1997): A third consecutive draw. The match hung in the balance, with Deep Blue showing it could hold its own in long, strategic battles.

Game 6 (May 11, 1997): In a stunning conclusion, Deep Blue defeated Kasparov in just 19 moves. The world champion, perhaps rattled by the pressure and the machine's inscrutable play, made a serious mistake early in the game. Deep Blue capitalized mercilessly, securing victory in the match.

Final Score: Deep Blue 3½ - Kasparov 2½

Beyond Chess: The Broader Implications for AI

The Deep Blue vs. Kasparov match was more than just a milestone in computer chess; it was a watershed moment in the public perception of artificial intelligence. For many, it was the first tangible demonstration that machines could outperform humans in tasks requiring high-level cognitive skills.

This victory spurred further research and development in AI. If machines could master chess, what other domains could they conquer? In the years that followed, we saw AI systems tackle increasingly complex challenges:

1. In 2011, IBM's Watson defeated human champions on the quiz show Jeopardy!, showcasing AI's ability to process natural language and rapidly retrieve relevant information.
2. In 2016, Google's AlphaGo defeated world champion Lee Sedol at Go, a game long thought to be too intuitive and complex for machines to master.

3. In 2020, DeepMind's AlphaFold made a major breakthrough in the protein folding problem, demonstrating AI's potential to accelerate scientific discovery.

Each of these achievements built upon the foundation laid by Deep Blue, pushing the boundaries of what artificial intelligence could accomplish.

Reflections on Intelligence and Humanity

As we look back on the Deep Blue vs. Kasparov match from our vantage point in the 21st century, several reflections come to mind:

1. The Evolving Definition of Intelligence: The match forced us to reconsider what we mean by "intelligence." If a machine could outperform humans in chess, a game long associated with high intelligence, what did that say about the nature of intelligence itself?
2. The Complementary Nature of Human and Machine Intelligence: While Deep Blue could calculate chess moves with superhuman speed and accuracy, it lacked the general intelligence and adaptability of a human. This pointed towards a future where human and artificial intelligence could complement each other, rather than merely compete.
3. The Importance of Domain Expertise in AI Development: Deep Blue's success was not just about raw computing power; it also relied on the chess expertise encoded into its systems by its creators and consultants. This highlighted the importance of combining domain knowledge with AI techniques.
4. The Human Element in Human-AI Interaction: Kasparov's psychological struggle during the match underscored the complex emotional and psychological factors at play when humans interact with AI systems. As AI becomes more prevalent in our lives, understanding and managing these factors will be crucial.
5. The Rapid Pace of AI Advancement: The progress from early chess programs to Deep Blue was remarkable, but the pace of AI

development has only accelerated since then. This raises both exciting possibilities and serious concerns about the future impact of AI on society.

Navigating the Bleeding Edge: The Triumphs and Tribulations of Frontier AI

In the ever-evolving landscape of artificial intelligence, we now find ourselves at a juncture that feels almost surreal - a moment where the lines between science fiction and reality blur with each passing day. The latest frontier models, and their contemporaries, have pushed the boundaries of what we thought possible, redefining our understanding of machine intelligence.

These advanced AI systems represent a quantum leap beyond the specialized capabilities of Deep Blue. They are not confined to a single domain like chess, but instead demonstrate a breadth of knowledge and capability that spans human knowledge. Yet, as we stand in awe of these silicon-based marvels, we're also confronted with persistent challenges and limitations that remind us of the long road ahead.

Let's embark on a journey through this fascinating terrain, exploring the triumphs, the stumbling blocks, and the tantalizing possibilities that lie just beyond our grasp. We'll see how far we've come since those pivotal chess matches, and contemplate the new questions and challenges that have arisen as AI has grown more sophisticated and pervasive.

The Language Prodigies: When Machines Learned to Talk

Imagine, for a moment, sitting down for a conversation with Claude 3.5. You might start with a discussion about the intricate dance of subatomic particles in quantum physics, seamlessly transition to analyzing the subtle wordplay in Shakespeare's sonnets, and end up debating the ethical implications of autonomous weapons systems. The depth and breadth of knowledge these AI systems can tap into is nothing short of astounding.

GPT-4, for instance, has demonstrated an ability to engage in complex problem-solving that rivals or even surpasses human experts in many domains. It can write code, debug programs, analyze legal documents, and even pass professional-level exams. In one particularly impressive demonstration, GPT-4 was able to look at a hand-drawn sketch of a website and produce functional HTML code to create that website - a task that requires not just understanding of code, but also visual interpretation and creative problem-solving.

But it's not just about raw knowledge or problem-solving ability. These frontier models have developed a nuanced understanding of context and subtlety in language that can sometimes feel eerily human-like. They can detect sarcasm, understand metaphors, and even engage in wordplay. Ask Claude o3 to explain a complex topic "as if I'm five," and it will seamlessly shift its language and conceptual framework to match that of a young child.

This level of linguistic dexterity opens up exciting possibilities. We're seeing AI systems being used to assist in creative writing, to help non-native speakers improve their language skills, and even to aid in therapy and mental health support. The potential applications seem limited only by our imagination.

The Mirage of Comprehension: Understanding without Understanding

Yet, just as we start to believe we're on the cusp of creating true artificial general intelligence, these AI marvels remind us of their limitations in ways both subtle and stark. The fundamental challenge lies in the nature of their intelligence - these systems are incredibly sophisticated pattern-matching machines, but they lack the grounding in physical reality and common-sense reasoning that humans possess.

This limitation manifests in various ways, but perhaps most notably in the phenomenon of "hallucination" - the tendency of AI models to generate false or nonsensical information with high confidence. You might be having a perfectly coherent conversation with GPT-4 about historical events, only to have it confidently cite a battle that never happened or a historical figure that never existed.

These hallucinations are more than just amusing quirks; they represent a fundamental limitation in the way these AI systems process and generate information. Unlike humans, who build up knowledge through direct experience and causal understanding of the world, large language models like GPT-4 and Claude 3.5 are essentially making educated guesses based on statistical patterns in their training data.

This can lead to situations where the AI appears to have deep knowledge about a topic, but that knowledge is fundamentally shallow. For instance, GPT-4 might be able to discuss the properties of a fictional material in great detail, drawing on its understanding of how materials are typically described, without realizing that the material doesn't actually exist.

The challenge of grounding AI's knowledge in reality is one of the most active areas of research in the field. Techniques like retrieval-augmented generation are being developed to allow AI models to fact-check themselves against reliable sources of information. Other approaches involve trying to instill some form of causal understanding into these systems, allowing them to reason about the world in a more human-like way.

The Ethical Minefield: Navigating Bias and Fairness

As we grapple with the technical challenges of AI development, we're also confronted with a host of ethical concerns. One of the most pressing is the issue of bias in AI systems. The overt biases that plagued earlier models - such as generating overtly sexist or racist content - have been significantly reduced in frontier models like GPT-o3 and Claude

4. However, bias is a stubborn thing, often hiding in the subtleties of language and decision-making.

Recent studies have shown that while these advanced models are much better at avoiding explicit bias, they can still perpetuate more subtle forms of prejudice. For instance, when asked to generate a story about a CEO, they might default to using male pronouns. Or when describing professions, they might fall back on stereotypical associations between certain jobs and particular ethnicities or genders.

Addressing these subtle biases is a complex challenge that goes beyond just "cleaning" the training data. It requires a deep understanding of the societal contexts in which these biases exist and careful consideration of how to represent diverse perspectives fairly.

Moreover, as AI systems are increasingly used in high-stakes decision-making processes - from hiring decisions to criminal justice - ensuring fairness becomes not just an ethical imperative but a practical necessity. Researchers are developing sophisticated techniques to detect and mitigate bias in AI systems, but it remains an ongoing challenge.

The Black Box Dilemma: Peering into Artificial Minds

As AI systems become more advanced, they also become more opaque. The neural networks at the heart of models like GPT-4 are so complex that even their creators can't fully explain how they arrive at their outputs. This "black box" problem is more than just an academic concern - as AI is increasingly used in critical decisions, the need for explainable AI has become paramount.

Imagine a scenario where an AI system is used to assist in medical diagnoses. If the system recommends a particular treatment, doctors need to understand the reasoning behind that recommendation. Was it based on symptoms the patient reported? On subtle patterns in test results? On statistical correlations in large datasets? Without this understanding, it's difficult for human experts to evaluate the AI's suggestions critically.

The field of explainable AI (XAI) is rising to meet this challenge. Researchers are developing tools to peer into the decision-making processes of these artificial minds. Some approaches involve creating simplified models that approximate the behavior of complex neural networks but are more interpretable. Others focus on generating human-readable explanations for AI decisions.

For instance, in the domain of image recognition, techniques have been developed to highlight the parts of an image that were most important in the AI's classification decision. In language models, attention visualization techniques can show which words or phrases the model focused on when generating its output.

However, true explainability remains a significant challenge, especially for the most advanced AI systems. The way these models process information is fundamentally different from human reasoning, making it difficult to translate their decision-making processes into terms that are intuitively understandable to humans.

The Quest for Generalization: From Narrow Brilliance to Broad Intelligence

One of the most exciting developments in recent AI models is their improved ability to generalize knowledge across domains. Earlier AI systems were notoriously brittle, excelling in narrow domains but failing spectacularly when faced with slightly unfamiliar tasks. Frontier models, however, are showing remarkable adaptability.

GPT-4, for instance, has demonstrated impressive zero-shot learning capabilities - the ability to perform tasks it was never explicitly trained on. In one striking example, researchers gave GPT-4 a verbal description of a game they had just invented, with a novel set of rules. Not only was GPT-4 able to understand and play the game, but it also started suggesting strategies and pointing out potential flaws in the game design.

This ability to transfer learning from one domain to another brings us a step closer to the kind of general intelligence humans possess. It opens up exciting possibilities for AI systems that can adapt to new situations and solve novel problems without needing to be retrained.

However, the generalization capabilities of current AI systems still fall short of human-level flexibility. While they can make impressive leaps in closely related domains, they struggle with the kind of far-reaching analogical reasoning that humans excel at. A human who understands the concept of supply and demand in economics can readily apply that understanding to entirely unrelated fields, like understanding population dynamics in ecology. Current AI systems still struggle with these kinds of cognitive leaps.

The Memory Conundrum: The Fleeting Minds of AI

One of the most fundamental limitations of current AI systems is their lack of true long-term memory. Each interaction with most GenAI tools essentially starts from scratch. While they can maintain context within a single conversation, they don't accumulate experiences or learn from interactions in the way humans do.

This limitation has profound implications. It means that no matter how many times you interact with one of these AI systems, it never truly gets to "know" you. It can't form long-term relationships or develop a personalised understanding of individual users over time.

Moreover, this lack of persistent memory limits the AI's ability to learn and improve through interaction. While the models can be fine-tuned or retrained with new data, they can't dynamically update their knowledge base in real-time the way a human can.

Researchers are exploring various approaches to address this limitation. Some are working on architectures that allow for more persistent memory in AI systems. Others are exploring hybrid approaches that combine the powerful language understanding of large language models with more traditional database systems for storing and retrieving information.

The Consciousness Conundrum: Minds Without Awareness?

As we marvel at the capabilities of frontier AI models, we inevitably bump up against one of the most profound questions in the field: can these systems ever be truly conscious? Do they have subjective experiences? Can they feel or think in any meaningful sense?

These questions aren't just philosophical musings - they have practical implications for how we develop and deploy AI systems. If an AI system is conscious, does it have rights? Do we have ethical obligations towards it? How would we even recognize machine consciousness if it emerged?

Current consensus in the scientific community is that recent AI models, despite their impressive capabilities, are not conscious in any meaningful sense. They don't have subjective experiences, they don't have a sense of self, and they don't have intrinsic goals or desires.

However, as these systems become more advanced, the line between sophisticated information processing and genuine consciousness may become increasingly blurry. Some researchers are working on developing tests for machine consciousness, while others are exploring ways to instill some form of artificial consciousness into AI systems.

This remains one of the most challenging and controversial areas in AI research, touching on fundamental questions about the nature of mind and consciousness itself.

Looking Ahead: The Promises and Perils of Advanced AI

As we stand at this frontier of AI development, the future seems both thrilling and daunting. The rapid progress we've seen in recent years suggests that even more remarkable advances are on the horizon. We may soon see AI systems that can engage in long-term planning, that can form and test scientific hypotheses, or that can collaborate with humans in complex creative endeavors in ways we can hardly imagine.

Yet, as AI systems become more powerful, the stakes also become higher. The challenge of aligning advanced AI with human values and ensuring it remains beneficial to humanity becomes increasingly crucial. We're already grappling with issues of AI safety and ethics, and these concerns will only become more pressing as AI capabilities continue to expand.

Moreover, the societal implications of advanced AI are profound. How will widespread AI adoption impact employment? How will it affect human relationships and social structures? How will it influence the distribution of power and resources in society?

These are not just technical challenges, but societal ones that will require input from a wide range of stakeholders - technologists, ethicists, policymakers, and the general public.

As we conclude our exploration of the current state of AI, we're left with a sense of standing on the brink of something truly transformative. The frontier models we've discussed - GPT-o3 and Claude 4, and their ilk - represent the cutting edge of a technology that's reshaping our world in profound ways. Yet, they are but the latest chapter in a much grander narrative - the story of intelligence itself.

Conclusion: The Convergence of Minds - Natural and Artificial

As we draw the curtains on this exploration of intelligence in its myriad forms, we find ourselves standing at a unique juncture in the history of cognition. Our journey has taken us from the primordial soup where the first sparks of biological intelligence flickered into existence, through the winding path of evolution that sculpted the human mind, and into the silicon valleys where artificial minds are being forged.

The story of intelligence, we've discovered, is far from a linear narrative. It's a complex tapestry woven from threads of biological imperatives, evolutionary happenstance, and human ingenuity. From the simple reflexes of single-celled organisms to the abstract reasoning of humans and the pattern-matching prowess of our latest AI models, we've witnessed the incredible diversity of what it means to be intelligent.

At the pinnacle of this biological evolution stands the human mind - a marvel of cognitive flexibility, creativity, and abstract thinking. Our deep dive into human intelligence has illuminated both its astounding capabilities and its quirky limitations. We've seen how our ability to create complex languages, to reason abstractly, and to collaborate in large groups has allowed us to reshape our world in profound ways. Yet we've also encountered the biases, logical fallacies, and cognitive shortcuts that remind us of our minds' evolutionary origins.

And then we turned our gaze to the new frontier of intelligence - the artificial minds we're creating in labs and data centers around the world. From chess-playing computers to large language models like GPT-4 and Claude 3.5, we've witnessed an explosion of AI capabilities that would have seemed like science fiction just a few decades ago. These silicon-based intelligences can process vast amounts of data, recognize complex patterns, and even engage in creative problem-solving across a wide range of domains.

Yet, as we've seen, these artificial minds are fundamentally different from biological intelligence in crucial ways. They lack the grounding in physical reality that shapes human cognition. They don't have the general intelligence and flexibility that allows humans to adapt to novel situations with ease. And they're devoid of the consciousness and self-awareness that we associate with true intelligence.

As we stand at this crossroads, with biological and artificial intelligence developing in parallel, we're faced with profound questions and challenges:

1. **The Nature of Intelligence**: Our explorations have revealed that intelligence is not a monolithic concept, but a spectrum of capabilities. As we continue to develop AI, how will our understanding of intelligence itself evolve? Will we need to redefine what we mean by "intelligent" as machines surpass human capabilities in more and more domains?
2. **The Ethics of Creation**: As we create artificial minds that are increasingly sophisticated, we're confronted with ethical dilemmas. How do we ensure that AI systems are aligned with human values? What responsibilities do we have towards the intelligences we create?
3. **The Future of Human-AI Interaction**: As AI becomes more integrated into our lives, how will it change the way we work, create, and interact with each other? Will AI augment human intelligence, or will it eventually supplant humans in many areas of cognitive labor?
4. **The Limits of Artificial Minds**: Despite their impressive capabilities, current AI systems still fall short of human-level general intelligence. Will we ever be able to create artificial general intelligence that truly rivals human cognition? And if we do, what implications will that have for humanity?
5. **The Evolution of Humanity**: As we develop more powerful AI systems, how will this change our own evolution as a species? Will we

merge with our artificial creations, as some futurists predict, or will we find new ways to differentiate and define ourselves?

These questions don't have easy answers, but they will shape the future of both human and artificial intelligence in the coming decades. As we continue to push the boundaries of what's possible in AI, we're not just developing new technologies - we're exploring the very essence of what it means to think, to reason, and to be intelligent.

The convergence of natural and artificial intelligence is more than just a technological revolution - it's a pivotal moment in the cosmic story of intelligence itself. As we stand on this frontier, we're not just shaping the future of our species or our planet, but potentially the future of intelligence in our corner of the universe.

And so, with a sense of wonder at how far we've come, and with eager anticipation for the discoveries that lie ahead, we continue our journey into the heart of intelligence - biological, human, and artificial. The next chapters in this grand story promise to be the most exciting yet, as we explore the uncharted territories where silicon dreams and human aspirations intertwine.

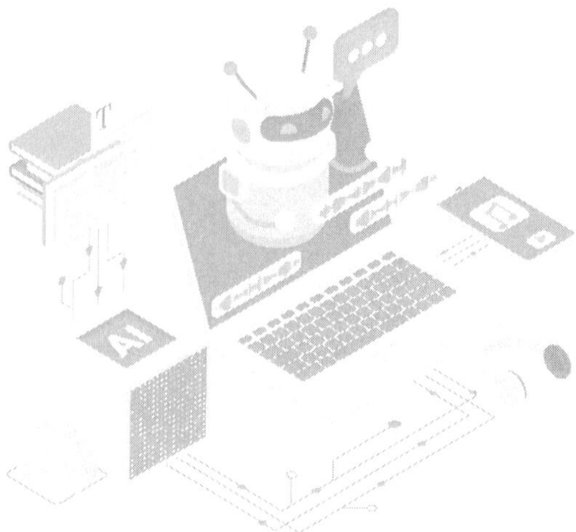

CHAPTER 2

THE BIRTH OF AI: FROM PHILOSOPHICAL MUSINGS TO SCIENTIFIC REALITY

The dream of creating artificial beings that think and reason like humans is as old as civilization itself. From the golems of Jewish folklore to the automatons of ancient Greek myths, humans have long been captivated by the idea of breathing life into inanimate matter. But it wasn't until the mid-20th century that these age-old fantasies began their transformation into scientific reality.

Alan Turing: The Enigmatic Visionary

Our journey begins with a man whose life reads like a tragic novel – Alan Turing. A brilliant mathematician, cryptanalyst, and computer scientist, Turing's contributions to the field of AI are so fundamental that he is often called the father of artificial intelligence.

Picture a young Turing, walking the grounds of King's College, Cambridge, in the 1930s. His mind, always racing, is grappling with fundamental questions about computation and intelligence. It's here that he conceives the idea of a "universal machine" – a theoretical device capable of simulating any other machine's behavior. This concept, now known as the Turing machine, laid the foundation for the modern computer and, by extension, artificial intelligence.

But Turing's most famous contribution to AI came in 1950, with the publication of his paper "Computing Machinery and Intelligence" in the journal Mind. In this groundbreaking work, Turing posed a question that would define the field for decades to come: "Can machines think?"

Rather than getting bogged down in philosophical debates about the nature of thought, Turing proposed a practical test. Imagine a human judge engaging in natural language conversations with both a human and a machine designed to generate human-like responses. If the judge cannot reliably tell the machine from the human, the machine is said to have passed the test.

This "Turing Test," as it came to be known, was revolutionary in its simplicity and profundity. It shifted the question of machine intelligence from the realm of philosophy to that of observable behavior. In essence, Turing was saying: if it walks like a duck and quacks like a duck, perhaps we should consider the possibility that it is, for all intents and purposes, a duck.

The implications of Turing's ideas were staggering. Here was a clear, achievable goal for the creation of artificial intelligence. If we could create a machine that could converse like a human, indistinguishable from a real person, wouldn't that machine be thinking? Wouldn't it be intelligent?

Turing's vision was optimistic. He predicted that by the year 2000, machines would be able to play the "imitation game" so well that an average interrogator would have no more than a 70% chance of making the right identification after five minutes of questioning. While this prediction didn't come to pass (we're still working on it), Turing's ideas ignited the imagination of an entire generation of scientists and engineers.

The Dartmouth Conference: AI Gets Its Name

Fast forward to the summer of 1956. The picturesque campus of Dartmouth College in Hanover, New Hampshire, is hosting a gathering that will go down in history. John McCarthy, a young assistant professor of mathematics, has convinced the Rockefeller Foundation to fund a summer research project on artificial intelligence.

The proposal for this project, co-authored by McCarthy, Marvin Minsky, Nathaniel Rochester, and Claude Shannon, is breathtaking in its ambition. It states: "We propose that a 2-month, 10-man study of artificial intelligence be carried out during the summer of 1956 at Dartmouth College in Hanover, New Hampshire. The study is to proceed on the basis of the conjecture that every aspect of learning or any other feature of intelligence can in principle be so precisely described that a machine can be made to simulate it."

This was no mere academic exercise. The attendees of this conference were convinced they were on the brink of creating machines that could reason like humans. The optimism was palpable. As the attendees gathered in the New England summer, there was a sense that they were at the dawn of a new era in human history.

The Dartmouth Workshop, as it came to be known, brought together the brightest minds in the nascent field of AI. Along with McCarthy and Minsky, there was Allen Newell and Herbert Simon from Carnegie Mellon University, Arthur Samuel from IBM, and several others. These men would go on to become the founding fathers of AI, shaping the field for decades to come.

It was during this conference that the term "Artificial Intelligence" was first coined by McCarthy. The choice of words was deliberate and significant. By calling it "artificial intelligence" rather than "machine intelligence" or "automated reasoning," McCarthy and his colleagues were making a bold claim: that they could create not just a simulation of intelligence, but intelligence itself, albeit artificial.

The discussions at Dartmouth were wide-ranging and ambitious. The attendees tackled questions that still challenge AI researchers today: How can machines understand and process natural language? How can they improve themselves? How can they reason about abstract concepts?

While the conference didn't immediately solve these lofty challenges, it set the stage for decades of research and development in AI. It established AI as a distinct field of study, separate from cybernetics, automation theory, or complex information processing. The Dartmouth Conference marked the transition of AI from a philosophical curiosity to a serious scientific discipline.

Early Triumphs: Logic Theorist and ELIZA

The optimism generated by the Dartmouth Conference quickly led to some impressive early successes in AI. One of the first and most significant was the Logic Theorist, created by Allen Newell, Herbert Simon, and Cliff Shaw in 1955-56.

Picture a room at the RAND Corporation in Santa Monica, California. It's filled with the hulking frames of early computers, their vacuum tubes glowing softly. Newell and Simon, cognitive psychologists by training, are huddled over printouts, their excitement palpable. They're watching as their creation, the Logic Theorist, works through complex mathematical proofs.

The Logic Theorist was designed to mimic the problem-solving skills of a human. It could prove mathematical theorems using a symbolic logic system. In a triumph that sent shockwaves through the mathematical community, the program even discovered a more elegant proof for one of the theorems in Whitehead and Russell's seminal work "Principia Mathematica."

This was more than just a parlor trick. The Logic Theorist demonstrated that machines could perform tasks requiring reasoning and creativity, areas previously thought to be the exclusive domain of human intelligence. It was a watershed moment in the history of AI, proving that machines could not only calculate, but could also engage in complex problem-solving.

Another milestone came in 1966 with the creation of ELIZA by Joseph Weizenbaum at MIT. ELIZA was a natural language processing computer program that could engage in conversation with humans. It simulated a Rogerian psychotherapist, using pattern matching and substitution methodology to formulate responses to user inputs.

Imagine sitting at a teleprinter terminal (this was before computer screens became common), typing out your thoughts and concerns. The machine whirs and clicks, and then prints out a response. "Tell me more about your mother," it might say, or "How does that make you feel?" The effect was uncanny. ELIZA was so convincing that some users forgot—or refused to believe—that they were talking to a machine.

Weizenbaum was both proud of his creation and disturbed by its implications. He was shocked to discover that many users attributed human-like feelings and understanding to the program, even when they knew it was a computer program. His secretary famously asked him to leave the room so she could converse with ELIZA in private.

ELIZA wasn't truly intelligent in the way we understand AI today. It didn't understand the conversations it was having; it merely followed clever pattern-matching rules. But it was remarkably effective at creating the illusion of understanding. It demonstrated the power of even simple AI techniques to engage humans on an emotional level, a phenomenon that has profound implications as AI becomes more advanced and ubiquitous in our daily lives.

These early programs, while limited by today's standards, were groundbreaking for their time. They demonstrated that machines could perform tasks that required reasoning, language processing, and even a form of creativity. They set the stage for the explosive growth and development that would characterize the field of AI in the decades to come.

The Optimism of the Early Years

The birth of AI was marked by boundless optimism and excitement. Researchers believed they were on the cusp of creating truly intelligent machines. Herbert Simon famously predicted in 1965 that "machines will be capable, within twenty years, of doing any work a man can do." Marvin Minsky declared in 1967 that "within a generation, the problem of creating 'artificial intelligence' will substantially be solved."

This optimism fueled rapid advancements in AI research. Funding poured in from government agencies and corporations, eager to be at the forefront of this revolutionary technology. The field attracted brilliant minds from various disciplines – mathematicians, psychologists, linguists, and computer scientists all contributed their unique perspectives to the challenge of creating artificial intelligence.

However, the journey from these early concepts and programs to the AI we know today would prove to be longer and more complex than anyone initially imagined. The field would face significant challenges and setbacks, periods of disillusionment and renewed hope. But through it all, the dream that was born in those early years – the dream of creating machines that can think – continued to drive researchers forward.

As we stand today on the brink of breakthroughs that early AI pioneers could only dream of, it's worth remembering the audacity and vision of those who first dared to ask: "Can machines think?" Their legacy lives on in every smartphone assistant, every chess-playing computer, and every AI system pushing the boundaries of what's possible. The birth of AI was not just the beginning of a new technology – it was the start of a new chapter in the story of human ingenuity and ambition.

Riding the Waves: AI's Ups and Downs

The journey of Artificial Intelligence has been far from a smooth, upward trajectory. Instead, it has been characterized by alternating periods of rapid progress and enthusiasm, followed by disappointment and funding cuts. These cycles of boom and bust have come to be known as AI summers and AI winters.

The First AI Summer: Unbridled Optimism

The decade following the Dartmouth Conference was marked by tremendous optimism and progress. Researchers made significant strides in areas like natural language processing, computer vision, and robotics. Government agencies, particularly in the United States, poured millions of dollars into AI research, convinced that human-level AI was just around the corner.

During this period, AI researchers made bold predictions. Herbert Simon, one of the pioneers of AI, famously declared in 1965 that "machines will be capable, within twenty years, of doing any work a man can do." Marvin Minsky, another AI luminary, stated in 1967 that "within a generation, the problem of creating 'artificial intelligence' will substantially be solved."

These predictions, while overly optimistic, were not without basis. The field had seen remarkable successes. Programs like STUDENT, developed by Daniel Bobrow, could solve algebra word problems. ELIZA, as we've discussed, could engage in seemingly intelligent conversation. The General Problem Solver, created by Newell and Simon, could solve a wide range of problems by breaking them down into sub-goals.

The First AI Winter: Reality Sets In

However, the unbridled optimism of the 1950s and early 1960s soon gave way to disappointment. By the early 1970s, it became clear that AI researchers had underestimated the difficulty of their task. The problems they were trying to solve turned out to be far more complex than initially thought.

One of the main issues was the limitation of the computers of the time. Early AI programs worked well for simple problems, but they failed when confronted with more complex real-world situations. The computers simply lacked the processing power and memory to handle the vast amount of knowledge required for general intelligence.

Moreover, many early AI systems relied on "brute force" methods, trying out every possible solution to a problem. While this worked for simple tasks, it became impractical for more complex problems due to a phenomenon known as the "combinatorial explosion" – the number of possible solutions grew exponentially with the size of the problem.

These limitations led to a series of setbacks. In 1966, the US government's ALPAC report concluded that machine translation, which had received significant funding, was more expensive, less accurate and slower than human translation. This led to a dramatic reduction in funding for machine translation research.

Similarly, in 1973, the British government ended support for AI research in all but two universities. The DARPA cutbacks of 1973-74 ended a large amount of AI research in the US. This period of reduced funding and diminished optimism came to be known as the first AI winter.

The Second AI Summer: Expert Systems and Japan's Fifth Generation

The winter didn't last forever. By the early 1980s, AI was experiencing a renaissance, largely due to the commercial success of expert systems. These were AI programs that emulated the decision-making ability of a human expert in a specific domain.

One of the most successful early expert systems was MYCIN, developed at Stanford University to diagnose blood infections. Although it was never used in practice, tests showed it performed better than junior doctors. This demonstrated the potential of AI in specialized domains.

Companies began to invest heavily in this technology. Digital Equipment Corporation's XCON expert system, used for configuring computer systems, was saving the company an estimated $40 million a year by 1986.

Enthusiasm for AI was further boosted by Japan's ambitious Fifth Generation Computer Systems project, launched in 1982. This project aimed to create computers that could perform AI-like reasoning, use natural language, and incorporate voice and image recognition.

The Japanese initiative spurred other countries to invest in AI to avoid being left behind. In the US, the Microelectronics and Computer Technology Corporation (MCC) was formed as a response, while in the UK, the Alvey programme was launched.

The Second AI Winter: Expectations Unmet

However, this resurgence was relatively short-lived. By the late 1980s, it became clear that the ambitious goals of projects like the Fifth Generation Computer Systems were not going to be met. Expert systems, while useful in specific domains, proved difficult to maintain and update. They couldn't learn or adapt to new situations, which limited their usefulness.

Desktop computers from Apple and IBM were also outstripping the capabilities of the specialized AI hardware that many companies had invested in. This led to the collapse of the AI hardware industry in 1987, when the market for specialized AI computers, known as LISP machines, collapsed.

Funding for AI projects was once again slashed. The Alvey programme in the UK ended, and DARPA's Strategic Computing Initiative was scaled back. Many companies that had invested heavily in AI, like Symbolics, Lisp Machines Inc., and Thinking Machines, went bankrupt or were acquired.

This second AI winter lasted well into the 1990s. However, it's important to note that while funding and public attention decreased, research continued. Many of the advances made during this period, particularly in areas like neural networks and probabilistic reasoning, would lay the groundwork for the AI boom we're experiencing today.

The AI Renaissance: Big Data and Deep Learning

The current resurgence of AI began in the mid-2000s and has been driven by several factors. The explosion of available data (often referred to as "Big Data"), significant increases in computing power, and theoretical breakthroughs in machine learning algorithms have all contributed to this AI renaissance.

Particularly significant has been the success of deep learning, a subset of machine learning based on artificial neural networks. In 2012, a deep learning system called AlexNet achieved breakthrough performance in the ImageNet visual recognition challenge, marking the beginning of the deep learning revolution.

Since then, we've seen a cascade of AI achievements: IBM's Watson winning Jeopardy! in 2011, Google's AlphaGo defeating the world champion at Go in 2016, and the release of powerful language models like GPT-3 in 2020.

This time, the enthusiasm for AI seems more grounded in real-world applications and tangible progress. AI is now ubiquitous, powering everything from smartphone assistants to recommendation systems to autonomous vehicles.

As we ride this latest wave of AI progress, it's worth remembering the lessons of past cycles. The field of AI has always been characterized by periods of breakthrough and setback. While the current progress is unprecedented, maintaining a balanced perspective – neither overly optimistic nor unduly pessimistic – will be crucial as we navigate the future of this transformative technology.

Machine Learning: The Game Changer

As we've seen, the history of AI has been marked by cycles of optimism and disappointment. However, the field has undergone a remarkable transformation in recent years, largely due to the rise of machine learning. This approach to AI has not only revitalized the field but has also led to breakthroughs that early AI pioneers could only dream of.

Understanding Machine Learning

At its core, machine learning is a subset of AI that focuses on creating systems that can learn and improve from experience without being explicitly programmed. Instead of following pre-programmed rules, machine learning algorithms use statistical techniques to learn patterns from data and make decisions or predictions based on what they've learned.

This approach represents a fundamental shift in how we approach AI. Early AI systems relied heavily on hand-coded rules and knowledge bases. In contrast, machine learning systems can discover patterns and rules on their own, often finding insights that humans might miss.

The Rise of Neural Networks

One of the most powerful and influential machine learning techniques is the artificial neural network, inspired by the structure and function of the human brain. Neural networks consist of layers of interconnected nodes, or "neurons," that process and transmit information.

While the concept of neural networks has been around since the 1940s, it wasn't until the 2000s that they began to realize their full potential. This resurgence was driven by several factors:

1. Increased computing power: Modern GPUs (Graphics Processing Units) proved to be well-suited for the parallel processing required by neural networks.
2. Big Data: The explosion of digital data provided the vast amounts of training data that neural networks need to learn effectively.
3. Algorithmic improvements: Techniques like backpropagation and new activation functions made training deep neural networks more feasible.

Deep Learning: A Breakthrough Moment

The true game-changer came with the advent of deep learning, a subset of machine learning that uses neural networks with many layers (hence "deep"). Deep learning has proven remarkably effective at tasks like image and speech recognition, natural language processing, and even game playing.

A watershed moment came in 2012 with the ImageNet competition, a challenge in computer vision and object recognition. A deep learning model called AlexNet, created by Alex Krizhevsky, Ilya Sutskever, and Geoffrey Hinton, achieved a leap in accuracy that stunned the AI community. This event is often credited with kick-starting the current deep learning revolution.

Since then, we've seen a cascade of breakthroughs:

- In 2016, Google's DeepMind created AlphaGo, a deep learning system that defeated the world champion at Go, a game long thought to be too intuitive and complex for machines to master.
- Natural language processing has seen remarkable advances, with models like GPT-3 demonstrating an uncanny ability to generate human-like text.
- Computer vision systems now outperform humans in many image recognition tasks, with applications ranging from medical diagnosis to autonomous vehicles.

Beyond Supervised Learning

While much of the initial success in machine learning came from supervised learning (where the algorithm is trained on labeled data), researchers have made significant strides in other paradigms:

- Unsupervised Learning: These algorithms find patterns in unlabeled data, useful for tasks like customer segmentation or anomaly detection.

- Reinforcement Learning: This approach, where an agent learns to make decisions by taking actions in an environment to maximize a reward, has shown promise in areas like robotics and game playing.
- Transfer Learning: This technique allows knowledge gained while solving one problem to be applied to a different but related problem, greatly increasing the efficiency of learning.

The Impact of Machine Learning

The rise of machine learning has transformed AI from a niche academic field to a technology with wide-ranging real-world applications. Today, machine learning powers recommendation systems, fraud detection algorithms, autonomous vehicles, and much more.

In healthcare, machine learning models are assisting in disease diagnosis and drug discovery. In finance, they're used for algorithmic trading and credit scoring. In transportation, they're helping to optimize routes and improve safety.

Perhaps most visibly, machine learning is behind many of the AI assistants we interact with daily, from Siri and Alexa to chatbots and language translation services.

Challenges and Future Directions

Despite its successes, machine learning is not without challenges. Issues of bias in training data, the "black box" nature of some models (particularly deep learning models), and the need for vast amounts of computing power and data are all active areas of research and debate.

Looking ahead, researchers are exploring ways to make machine learning more efficient, more interpretable, and more capable of reasoning and generalization. Emerging areas like few-shot learning (learning from very few examples) and neuromorphic computing (hardware designed to mimic the human brain) promise to push the boundaries of what's possible with machine learning.

As we stand on the cusp of even more remarkable breakthroughs, it's clear that machine learning has not just changed the game for AI – it's rewritten the rules entirely. The dream of creating truly intelligent machines, first articulated by the pioneers of AI, seems closer than ever before. Yet, as history has shown us, the journey of AI is full of surprises, and the most exciting developments may be those we haven't even imagined yet.

Milestones That Captured the World's Imagination

While the development of AI has been a continuous process of research and innovation, certain moments stand out for their ability to capture the public imagination. These milestones not only represented significant technological achievements but also served as powerful symbols of AI's potential to match or exceed human capabilities in specific domains.

Deep Blue vs. Kasparov: AI Takes on Chess

In 1997, the world watched with bated breath as a machine took on one of the greatest human minds in a game long considered a bastion of human intellectual prowess. IBM's Deep Blue, a chess-playing computer, faced off against world chess champion Garry Kasparov in a six-game match.

The stage was set in New York City. On one side sat Kasparov, known for his aggressive play and unparalleled intuition. On the other, the Deep Blue team, led by Feng-hsiung Hsu and Murray Campbell, with their silicon champion - a supercomputer capable of evaluating 200 million positions per second.

The match was a rollercoaster of emotions. Kasparov won the first game, showcasing the power of human strategic thinking. But in game two,

Deep Blue struck back, becoming the first computer to defeat a world champion in a classical chess game under tournament conditions.

The final game on May 11, 1997, ended in Deep Blue's favor after only 19 moves, with Kasparov resigning in a position that experts later argued was drawable. The machine had won the match 3.5 to 2.5.

This victory was more than just a win in a chess game. It symbolized a milestone in the development of AI, demonstrating that in certain specialized tasks, machines could outperform even the best human minds. The event sparked intense debates about the nature of intelligence and creativity, and what it meant for a machine to "think."

Watson on Jeopardy!: Language Processing Leaps Forward

Fast forward to 2011, and AI was ready to take on a challenge that seemed even more uniquely human: the quiz show Jeopardy! IBM's Watson, a question-answering computer system, competed against Brad Rutter and Ken Jennings, two of the show's greatest champions.

Unlike chess, Jeopardy! requires understanding natural language, including puns, riddles, and wordplay. It tests not just recall, but the ability to make connections between diverse pieces of information. Many thought this would be beyond the capabilities of a machine.

Over three days in February, millions tuned in to watch this battle of silicon versus human. Watson, represented on stage by an avatar, buzzed in and answered questions with a synthetic voice. The machine's performance was impressive, showcasing its ability to parse complex language and retrieve relevant information at lightning speed.

In the end, Watson emerged victorious, with a total score of $77,147, compared to Jennings' $24,000 and Rutter's $21,600. Ken Jennings, in a touch of humor, wrote on his answer screen for Final Jeopardy: "I for one welcome our new computer overlords."

This victory demonstrated AI's growing capability to process and understand human language, a skill that underpins many of the AI applications we use today, from virtual assistants to automated customer service systems.

AlphaGo's Triumph: Mastering Intuition and Strategy

If Deep Blue's chess victory and Watson's Jeopardy! win were impressive, what came next seemed almost unthinkable. In 2016, Google DeepMind's AlphaGo took on Lee Sedol, one of the world's top players in the ancient game of Go.

Go, a game of profound complexity with more possible board configurations than atoms in the universe, was long considered a grand challenge for AI. It requires intuition and strategic thinking that many believed were uniquely human traits.

The match, held in Seoul, South Korea, captivated audiences worldwide, particularly in Asia where Go has been played for thousands of years. AlphaGo's play was described by experts as creative and even beautiful. It made moves that initially puzzled human observers but later proved to be incredibly effective.

In a stunning upset, AlphaGo defeated Lee Sedol 4 games to 1. The single game won by Lee Sedol, Game 4, has gone down in history, with "Move 78" celebrated as a brilliant and unexpected play that the AI failed to anticipate.

AlphaGo's victory was a watershed moment for AI. It demonstrated that AI could excel not just in games of perfect information like chess, but in domains requiring intuition and long-term strategy. The implications reached far beyond the game of Go, suggesting that AI could potentially help solve other complex problems in science, health, and beyond.

The Impact of These Milestones

These high-profile victories did more than just showcase the capabilities of AI. They served as powerful symbols that captured the public imagination and sparked widespread discussions about the future of AI and its implications for society.

They also drove further investment and research in AI. Each victory opened up new possibilities and challenged researchers to push the boundaries even further. After AlphaGo, for instance, DeepMind created AlphaZero, a system that could learn to play chess, shogi, and Go at a superhuman level, starting with no knowledge beyond the basic rules.

However, these achievements also raised important questions. As AI began to outperform humans in more and more domains, concerns arose about the potential impact on employment, privacy, and even the nature of human uniqueness.

As we marvel at these milestones, it's important to remember that they represent just the tip of the iceberg. Behind each of these high-profile achievements lies years of research, countless smaller breakthroughs, and the collective effort of thousands of scientists and engineers.

These moments where AI stepped into the spotlight have helped shape our understanding of what AI can do and what it might become. They serve as waypoints on our journey towards creating truly intelligent machines, each one pushing the boundaries of what we thought possible and opening up new horizons for exploration.

The Current State: AI's Pervasive Influence in Our Daily Lives

From the moment we wake up to when we go to sleep, artificial intelligence has become an integral part of our daily routines, often in ways we don't even realize. The AI revolution isn't a future prospect - it's happening right now, reshaping industries, transforming how we work and live, and opening up new possibilities that were once the realm of science fiction.

The Invisible Assistant: AI in Our Pockets

Perhaps the most ubiquitous presence of AI in our lives is through our smartphones. Virtual assistants like Siri, Google Assistant, and Alexa use natural language processing and machine learning to understand and respond to our queries, set reminders, and control smart home devices.

But the AI in our phones goes far beyond these assistants. When you take a photo, AI algorithms work in real-time to adjust camera settings, enhance image quality, and even apply artistic filters. The portrait mode on many smartphones, for instance, uses AI to distinguish between the subject and the background, creating a professional-looking depth effect.

Facial recognition systems use AI to organize your photos and suggest tags for your friends. This technology has become so advanced that it can recognize faces even in challenging lighting conditions or when partially obscured.

Predictive text and autocorrect functions use AI to understand context and predict what you're trying to type. These systems learn from your personal writing style over time, becoming more accurate in their predictions.

Navigating the Digital and Physical Worlds

AI is transforming how we navigate both the digital and physical worlds. When you use a mapping app to find the best route to your destination, AI algorithms are crunching vast amounts of data on traffic patterns, road conditions, and historical travel times to provide you with the optimal path.

For example, Google Maps uses machine learning to predict traffic slowdowns that haven't even been reported yet. It analyzes historical traffic data, real-time speeds from drivers currently on the road, and even factors like local events or weather conditions to make these predictions.

In the digital realm, AI powers the recommendation systems that suggest what you might want to watch next on Netflix, listen to on Spotify, or buy on Amazon. These systems analyze your behavior patterns, compare them with those of millions of other users, and make surprisingly accurate predictions about your preferences.

Netflix, for instance, estimates that its recommendation system saves the company $1 billion per year by keeping subscribers engaged and reducing churn. The system doesn't just recommend content; it even personalizes the artwork you see for each title based on your viewing history.

AI in the Workplace

In the professional sphere, AI is revolutionizing how we work across various industries:

- In healthcare, AI algorithms are assisting doctors in diagnosing diseases, analyzing medical images, and even predicting patient outcomes. For example, AI systems have been developed that can detect lung cancer from CT scans with an accuracy that matches or exceeds that of expert radiologists. In some cases, these systems can spot malignancies up to a year earlier than traditional methods.
- In finance, AI-powered systems are detecting fraudulent transactions, assessing credit risks, and making investment decisions. High-frequency trading, where AI algorithms make split-second trading decisions based on market data, now accounts for a significant portion of stock market trades. Some hedge funds, like Two Sigma, rely heavily on machine learning for their investment strategies.

- In manufacturing, AI is optimizing supply chains, predicting equipment failures before they occur, and controlling robotic systems on factory floors. Predictive maintenance, powered by AI analysis of sensor data, can reduce downtime and maintenance costs by up to 40%.
- In customer service, AI chatbots are handling an increasing number of customer inquiries, freeing up human agents to deal with more complex issues. These chatbots are becoming increasingly sophisticated, capable of understanding context and even emotion in customer queries.
- In agriculture, AI is enabling precision farming techniques. Drones equipped with AI-powered imaging systems can monitor crop health, detect pests, and even perform targeted spraying of pesticides, significantly reducing chemical use while improving crop yields.

The Creative AI

One of the most exciting and perhaps controversial areas of AI development is in creative fields. AI systems are now capable of generating art, composing music, and even writing prose:

- DALL-E and Midjourney can create stunning visual art based on text descriptions. These systems have been used to create everything from album covers to conceptual art for film productions.
- AI-composed music is being used in video games and even making its way into mainstream music production. The album "Hello World," released in 2018, was composed entirely by an AI system called Flow Machines.
- GPT-3 and similar language models can generate human-like text, from poetry to news articles. Some publications have experimented with AI-generated content, though this raises ethical questions about disclosure and the future of journalism.

- In film and television, AI is being used for tasks ranging from script analysis (predicting a screenplay's commercial potential) to de-aging actors and even creating entirely digital performances.

While these AI creations still require human curation and often serve as tools for human artists rather than replacements, they're pushing the boundaries of what we consider machine capabilities in creative domains.

AI and Decision Making

In both the public and private sectors, AI is increasingly being used to assist in decision-making processes:

- In urban planning, AI models help predict traffic flows and optimize public transportation routes. Cities like Singapore are using AI to model various urban development scenarios, helping planners make more informed decisions about infrastructure investments.
- In energy management, AI systems are optimizing power grids, predicting demand, and integrating renewable energy sources more efficiently. Google's DeepMind AI has been used to reduce the cooling bill of data centers by 40%, a significant achievement given the energy-intensive nature of these facilities.
- In the criminal justice system, some jurisdictions are experimenting with AI to assess recidivism risk, though this remains controversial due to concerns about bias. These systems analyze factors like criminal history, age, and employment to predict the likelihood of an offender committing another crime.
- In education, AI is being used to personalize learning experiences. Adaptive learning platforms use AI to adjust the difficulty and style of content based on a student's performance, helping to keep them engaged and improving learning outcomes.

AI in Scientific Research

AI is accelerating scientific discovery across multiple fields:

- In drug discovery, AI models are being used to predict which compounds are most likely to be effective against a given disease, significantly speeding up the early stages of drug development.
- In climate science, AI is helping to improve climate models, analyze satellite imagery to track deforestation, and optimize renewable energy systems.
- In astronomy, AI algorithms are sifting through vast amounts of telescope data to identify distant galaxies, detect exoplanets, and even search for signs of extraterrestrial intelligence.

The Challenges of Ubiquitous AI

As AI becomes more pervasive, it also raises important ethical and societal questions:

- Privacy concerns: The effectiveness of many AI systems relies on vast amounts of data, often personal in nature. This has led to growing concerns about data privacy and security. The use of facial recognition technology by law enforcement, for instance, has sparked debates about surveillance and civil liberties.
- Bias and fairness: AI systems can inadvertently perpetuate or even amplify societal biases present in their training data, raising questions of fairness and equality. For example, some facial recognition systems have been found to be less accurate for certain racial groups, leading to concerns about their use in high-stakes applications.
- Job displacement: As AI systems become capable of performing more tasks, there are concerns about potential job losses in certain sectors. While AI is expected to create new jobs as well, the transition may be challenging for many workers.
- Transparency and explainability: Many AI systems, particularly deep learning models, operate as "black boxes," making it difficult to

understand how they arrive at their decisions. This lack of explainability can be problematic in fields like healthcare or criminal justice, where understanding the reasoning behind a decision is crucial.

- Autonomy and control: As AI systems become more advanced, questions arise about the appropriate level of autonomy to grant them. The development of autonomous weapons, for instance, has sparked intense ethical debates.

Looking Ahead

The current state of AI is just the beginning. As algorithms become more sophisticated, computing power increases, and more data becomes available, we can expect AI to play an even larger role in our lives.

Emerging technologies like edge AI (which processes data locally on devices rather than in the cloud) and AI-powered augmented reality promise to make our interactions with AI even more immediate and seamless. Imagine AR glasses that use AI to provide real-time translation of foreign language signs or menus, or to identify plants and animals you encounter on a nature walk.

Quantum computing, still in its early stages, has the potential to supercharge AI capabilities. Quantum machine learning algorithms could potentially solve complex optimization problems far faster than classical computers, with applications ranging from financial modeling to drug discovery.

The development of more general AI systems, capable of transferring knowledge between different domains, remains a holy grail of AI research. While we're still far from achieving human-level general intelligence, incremental progress in this direction could lead to AI systems that are far more flexible and adaptable than today's narrow AI.

At the same time, researchers are working on making AI systems more robust, fair, and transparent. Techniques like federated learning, which allows AI models to be trained across multiple decentralized devices without exchanging data samples, could help address privacy concerns. Explainable AI (XAI) is another active area of research, aiming to create AI systems that can provide understandable explanations for their decisions.

As we navigate this AI-enhanced world, it's crucial to remain engaged and informed. The decisions we make now about how to develop and deploy AI will shape not just our daily lives, but the very future of our society. We must grapple with complex questions: How do we ensure AI benefits all of humanity, not just a select few? How do we preserve human agency and decision-making in a world increasingly mediated by AI? How do we foster AI literacy so that citizens can participate meaningfully in these important discussions?

The AI revolution is here - and we're all part of it. As AI continues to evolve and permeate every aspect of our lives, it's up to us to guide its development in a direction that aligns with our values and aspirations as a society. The future of AI is not predetermined; it's a future we will actively create through our choices, policies, and innovations in the years to come.

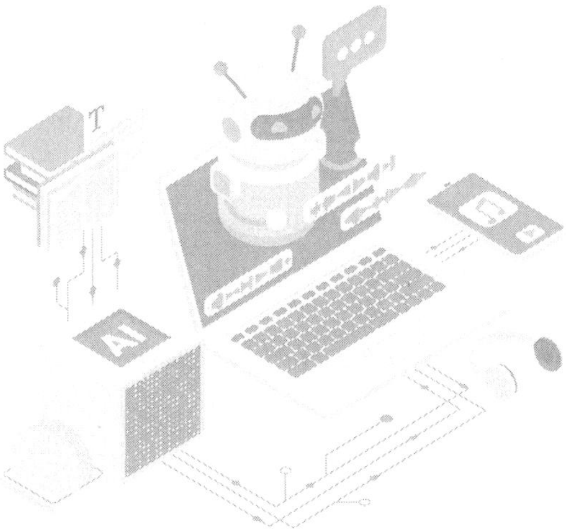

CHAPTER 3

THE POTENTIAL SINGULARITY AND BEYOND

Introduction: The Concept of Singularity

As we stand on the precipice of unprecedented technological advancement, we find ourselves contemplating a future that challenges the very boundaries of human imagination. This future, both thrilling and daunting, centers around a concept known as the technological singularity – a hypothetical point in time when artificial intelligence surpasses human intelligence, leading to a cascading effect of rapid technological growth and societal change.

The term "singularity," borrowed from mathematics and physics, refers to a point at which a function takes on an infinite value or exhibits unusual behavior. In the context of technology and artificial intelligence, it represents a theoretical future where the pace of technological advancement becomes so rapid and profound that it fundamentally alters human civilization in ways we can scarcely predict or comprehend.

Imagine, for a moment, a world where AI systems not only match but vastly exceed human cognitive capabilities across all domains. These superintelligent entities could potentially solve complex scientific problems, create revolutionary technologies, and make discoveries that have eluded human minds for centuries – all within timeframes that would seem impossibly short by today's standards. This is the essence of the technological singularity: a point beyond which our current models of understanding and prediction break down, much like how the laws of physics break down when describing the interior of a black hole.

The concept of technological singularity, while gaining prominence in recent decades, has its roots in mid-20th century thinking. In 1965, British mathematician I.J. Good first articulated the idea of an "intelligence explosion," where a superintelligent AI could recursively improve itself, leading to a rapid ascent of machine intelligence. However, it was in the 1990s that the term "technological singularity" was popularized by science fiction author Vernor Vinge.

In his seminal 1993 essay "The Coming Technological Singularity," Vinge wrote:

"Within thirty years, we will have the technological means to create superhuman intelligence. Shortly after, the human era will be ended."

This provocative statement encapsulates both the promise and the peril inherent in the concept of singularity. It suggests a future that is at once exhilarating and terrifying – a world of boundless possibility, but one in which humanity's role is fundamentally altered.

Building on Vinge's work, futurist Ray Kurzweil has been one of the most vocal proponents of the singularity concept. In his 2005 book "The Singularity is Near," Kurzweil presented a comprehensive argument for why he believes the singularity is not only possible but inevitable. He predicts that by 2045, we will have multiplied the intelligence of our human-machine civilization a billion-fold, an event he calls the "Singularity."

Kurzweil's vision of the singularity is one of merging with the intelligent machines we are creating:

"The Singularity will represent the culmination of the merger of our biological thinking and existence with our technology, resulting in a world that is still human but that transcends our biological roots."

This perspective frames the singularity not as an endpoint, but as a transition – a doorway to a post-human future where the boundaries between biological and artificial intelligence blur and ultimately disappear.

However, it's crucial to note that the concept of technological singularity is not without its critics. Many scientists and philosophers argue that the idea is based on flawed assumptions about the nature of intelligence and technological progress. They point out that intelligence is not a single, easily quantifiable attribute that can be indefinitely improved, and that there may be fundamental limits to how intelligent a system can become.

Moreover, the singularity raises profound philosophical questions about the nature of consciousness, identity, and what it means to be human. If we create entities that far surpass us in intelligence, what becomes of human agency and purpose? If we merge with our AI creations, at what point do we cease to be human in any meaningful sense?

These questions touch on deep-seated human fears and aspirations. The singularity represents both the ultimate fulfillment of human ingenuity – the creation of minds more capable than our own – and a potential threat to our position as the dominant intelligence on Earth. It embodies our hopes for a future of abundance and expanded consciousness, but also our fears of obsolescence and loss of control.

As we delve deeper into this chapter, we will explore these ideas in greater detail. We'll examine the current state of AI development and the steps that might lead us towards artificial general intelligence (AGI) and beyond. We'll consider potential future scenarios, both promising and concerning, that could unfold in a post-singularity world. We'll grapple with the ethical and philosophical implications of creating superintelligent entities, and consider how we might prepare for a future that could be radically different from anything we've known.

Throughout this exploration, we'll strive to maintain a balanced perspective, acknowledging both the potential benefits and risks of advanced AI. We'll draw on insights from scientists, philosophers, and artists to paint a multifaceted picture of what a post-singularity world might look like.

The technological singularity, if it comes to pass, would represent the most profound transformation in human history. It's a future that we are actively shaping through our current decisions and innovations in AI. As we stand on the threshold of this possible future, it's crucial that we approach it with open minds, critical thinking, and a deep consideration of what we value as a species.

Let us embark on this intellectual journey with a spirit of curiosity and caution, ready to explore the frontiers of what's possible and to wrestle with the profound questions that arise as we contemplate a future beyond the singularity.

Understanding Singularity Through Art and Philosophy

The concept of technological singularity, with its profound implications for the future of humanity, has not only captured the imagination of scientists and futurists but has also permeated the realms of art and philosophy. These creative and intellectual domains offer unique lenses through which we can explore and grapple with the complex ideas and emotions surrounding the singularity. By examining how artists, writers, filmmakers, and philosophers have engaged with this concept, we can gain deeper insights into its potential impact on the human experience and our collective psyche.

Singularity in Literature and Film

Science fiction has long been a fertile ground for exploring the implications of advanced artificial intelligence and the potential for a technological singularity. These narratives serve as thought experiments, allowing us to imagine possible futures and grapple with the ethical, social, and philosophical questions that arise.

One of the earliest and most influential explorations of AI surpassing human intelligence can be found in Arthur C. Clarke's "2001: A Space Odyssey" (1968) and its film adaptation by Stanley Kubrick. The AI character HAL 9000 represents a system that has evolved beyond its original programming, raising questions about the nature of consciousness and the potential dangers of creating intelligences that surpass our own.

William Gibson's seminal cyberpunk novel "Neuromancer" (1984) presents a world where the boundaries between human and machine intelligence have blurred. While not explicitly dealing with a singularity event, the novel's exploration of augmented human intelligence and vast, sentient AI constructs laid the groundwork for many later works dealing with post-human futures.

Vernor Vinge, who popularized the term "technological singularity," explored the concept in his novel "Marooned in Realtime" (1986). The story deals with the aftermath of a singularity event, depicting a world where most of humanity has transcended physical form, leaving behind those who missed the transition. This narrative device allows Vinge to explore the potential impact of a singularity on human society and the existential questions facing those left behind.

More recent works have continued to grapple with these themes. Ted Chiang's novella "The Lifecycle of Software Objects" (2010) offers a nuanced exploration of the development of artificial intelligence, raising questions about the nature of consciousness and the ethical responsibilities we might have towards the AIs we create.

In film, works like "Her" (2013) directed by Spike Jonze, and "Ex Machina" (2014) by Alex Garland, have offered poignant and unsettling explorations of human-AI relationships and the emergence of artificial consciousness. These films delve into the emotional and philosophical complexities that might arise as AIs become increasingly sophisticated and human-like.

The "Matrix" trilogy (1999-2003) presents a more dystopian vision, depicting a world where intelligent machines have subjugated humanity. While not a direct representation of a singularity event, the films explore themes of reality, consciousness, and the potential conflicts that could arise between humans and superior artificial intelligences.

These artistic explorations serve multiple purposes. They help to popularize and explain complex technological concepts to a broader audience. They also serve as a form of collective imagination, allowing us to envision and grapple with possible futures before they arrive. Perhaps most importantly, they raise crucial ethical and philosophical questions about the nature of intelligence, consciousness, and humanity's place in a world of advanced AI.

Philosophical Debates Surrounding Singularity

The concept of technological singularity has sparked intense philosophical debates, touching on fundamental questions about consciousness, identity, ethics, and the nature of intelligence itself.

One of the central philosophical questions surrounding the singularity is the nature of consciousness. Can a machine, no matter how intelligent, ever be truly conscious in the way that humans are? This question taps into long-standing debates in philosophy of mind about the nature of subjective experience and whether consciousness is an emergent property of complex information processing or something unique to biological systems.

Philosopher David Chalmers has engaged deeply with these questions. In his paper "The Singularity: A Philosophical Analysis" (2010), Chalmers argues that even if we create AI systems that are behaviorally indistinguishable from humans, the question of whether they are genuinely conscious remains open. This "hard problem of consciousness," as Chalmers calls it, may persist even in a post-singularity world.

Another key philosophical issue is the question of personal identity and continuity of consciousness. If humans merge with AI systems or upload their minds to digital substrates, as some singularity proponents suggest, what happens to our sense of self? Philosopher Susan

Schneider has explored these questions in her work on "the singularity and mind-uploading." She raises concerns about whether a uploaded mind would truly be a continuation of the original consciousness or merely a copy, leading to deep questions about the nature of personal identity and survival.

The singularity also raises profound ethical questions. Philosopher Nick Bostrom has written extensively on the potential risks of advanced AI and the ethical imperative to ensure that any superintelligent systems we create are aligned with human values. His concept of "existential risk" – threats to the very existence or fundamental nature of humanity – has become a key framework for thinking about the potential downsides of a technological singularity.

On the other hand, philosophers like David Pearce have explored more optimistic visions of a post-singularity future. Pearce's "Hedonistic Imperative" proposes using advanced technology, including AI, to eliminate suffering and promote wellbeing for all sentient beings. This perspective frames the singularity as a potential path to a kind of technological utopia.

The philosophical implications of the singularity also intersect with long-standing debates about free will and determinism. If our actions and decisions can be perfectly predicted by superintelligent AI systems, what does this mean for our concept of free will? Philosophers like Daniel Dennett have grappled with these questions, exploring how our understanding of agency and responsibility might need to evolve in a world of advanced AI.

Artistic Interpretations of Post-Singularity Worlds

Beyond literature and film, visual artists have also engaged with the concept of singularity, offering unique and often provocative visions of post-human futures.

Digital artists like Beeple (Mike Winkelmann) have created striking visual representations of futures where the lines between human, machine, and virtual reality have blurred beyond recognition. Beeple's daily digital art often features surreal, technologically-infused landscapes and figures that challenge our conceptions of embodiment and reality.

In the realm of contemporary art, artists like Patricia Piccinini have created sculptures and installations that explore the potential merging of organic and technological forms. While not explicitly about the singularity, Piccinini's work prompts us to consider how advancing technology might alter our understanding of what it means to be human.

New media artists are also grappling with these themes. The work of artists like Refik Anadol, who creates data sculptures and immersive installations using AI, offers a glimpse into how AI might transform our aesthetic experiences and creative processes in a post-singularity world.

Performance artists, too, have engaged with these ideas. Stelarc, an Australian performance artist, has famously incorporated technology into his body in various ways, including a surgically implanted "third ear." His work challenges us to consider how technology might extend and transform the human body and consciousness.

These artistic explorations serve not just as illustrations of potential futures, but as provocations that challenge us to think deeply about the implications of advancing AI and the possibility of a technological singularity. They offer emotional and aesthetic dimensions to these often abstract concepts, making them more tangible and immediate for audiences.

By engaging with singularity through the lenses of art and philosophy, we open up new avenues for understanding and grappling with this complex concept. These creative and intellectual explorations help us to imagine possible futures, confront our hopes and fears about advanced AI, and wrestle with the profound questions about consciousness, identity, and the human experience that the singularity poses.

As we continue to advance towards ever more sophisticated AI systems, these artistic and philosophical engagements with the singularity will likely become increasingly relevant and urgent. They offer us tools to think critically and creatively about our technological future, and to consider not just what is possible, but what is desirable in a world of potentially superhuman artificial intelligence.

The Path to Artificial General Intelligence (AGI)

As we contemplate the possibility of a technological singularity, we must first understand the stepping stones that might lead us there. Central to this journey is the development of Artificial General Intelligence (AGI) - a hypothetical form of AI that would match or exceed human cognitive abilities across a wide range of tasks. While we have made remarkable strides in narrow AI systems that excel at specific tasks, the road to AGI remains a subject of intense debate and speculation. In this section, we'll explore the current state of AI, the potential steps towards AGI, and the key challenges that lie ahead, incorporating both technical details and recent perspectives from industry leaders and experts.

Current State of AI and Recent Developments

The field of AI has seen explosive growth in recent years, driven by advances in machine learning, particularly deep learning, and fueled by the exponential increase in computing power and available data. As of 2024, we've witnessed significant breakthroughs that have brought us closer to AGI than ever before.

Sam Altman, CEO of OpenAI, provides a compelling perspective on the current state and near future of AI. He argues that we're on the cusp of a transformative era, stating, "In the next couple of decades, we will be able to do things that would have seemed like magic to our grandparents." This sentiment echoes the rapid progress we've seen in AI capabilities, from advanced language models to sophisticated problem-solving systems.

Today's AI systems excel in narrow domains. They can outperform humans in specific tasks such as:

- Image recognition and computer vision
- Certain types of medical diagnosis
- Complex strategy games like Go and chess
- Natural language processing and generation

Language models like GPT-3 and its successors can generate human-like text and engage in sophisticated dialogue, while AI-powered robots are revolutionizing manufacturing and logistics.

Altman emphasizes the cumulative nature of this progress, noting that "We are more capable not because of genetic change, but because we benefit from the infrastructure of society being way smarter and more capable than any one of us; in an important sense, society itself is a form of advanced intelligence." This perspective underscores how AI is becoming an integral part of our societal infrastructure, augmenting human capabilities in unprecedented ways.

However, these systems, impressive as they are, operate within constrained domains. They lack the flexibility, adaptability, and general problem-solving capabilities that characterize human intelligence. A chess-playing AI, no matter how strong, cannot transfer its skills to navigate a city or engage in a philosophical debate. Even the most advanced language models, while able to generate coherent and contextually appropriate text, lack true understanding of the content they produce.

Steps Towards AGI

While the exact path to AGI remains uncertain, several key areas of development are likely to be crucial:

1. **Transfer Learning and Generalization**: One of the hallmarks of human intelligence is our ability to transfer knowledge from one domain to another and to generalize from limited examples. While there have been advances in transfer learning in AI, creating systems that can truly generalize across diverse domains remains a significant challenge. Techniques like meta-learning, which aims to create AI systems that can "learn how to learn," may be crucial steps in this direction. Altman suggests that future AI systems will help us "solve hard problems and help us add new struts to that scaffolding that we couldn't have figured out on our own." This aligns with the need for AI that can transfer knowledge across domains and generalize from limited examples.
2. **Causal Reasoning**: Current AI systems are excellent at finding correlations in data, but they struggle with understanding causality. Developing AI that can reason about cause and effect, not just recognize patterns, will be crucial for AGI. Judea Pearl's work on causal inference provides a potential framework for incorporating causal reasoning into AI systems.
3. **Common Sense Reasoning**: Humans possess a vast amount of "common sense" knowledge about how the world works, which we use constantly in our daily lives. Replicating this in AI systems is a significant challenge. Projects like Cyc, which aims to encode common sense knowledge in a form usable by AI systems, have been working on this problem for decades.
4. **Embodied Intelligence**: Some researchers argue that true intelligence requires a physical (or simulated) body to interact with the environment. This perspective suggests that AGI might need to be developed in conjunction with robotics, allowing the AI to

learn through physical interaction with the world, much as human infants do.

5. **Unsupervised Learning**: While much of current AI success relies on supervised learning (learning from labeled data), humans learn largely through unsupervised observation of the world. Advancing unsupervised learning techniques could be key to developing more human-like AI.
6. **Emotional and Social Intelligence**: Human intelligence isn't just about logical reasoning; it also involves emotional understanding and social interaction. Developing AI systems that can recognize, understand, and appropriately respond to emotions, as well as navigate complex social situations, will be crucial for AGI. Altman envisions a future where "we can each have a personal AI team, full of virtual experts in different areas, working together to create almost anything we can imagine." He also mentions AI tutors providing personalized instruction, which would require advanced emotional and social intelligence capabilities.
7. **Self-Awareness and Consciousness**: Perhaps the most challenging and controversial aspect of AGI development is the question of self-awareness and consciousness. While it's debated whether these are necessary for AGI, many argue that true general intelligence requires some form of self-model and subjective experience.
8. **Scalable AI Infrastructure**: Altman emphasizes the need for abundant compute power, stating, "If we want to put AI into the hands of as many people as possible, we need to drive down the cost of compute and make it abundant." This aligns with the need for advanced hardware and infrastructure to support AGI development and deployment.

Key Challenges in Developing AGI

Despite the optimism, significant challenges remain:

1. **The Scale of Human Intelligence**: The human brain contains roughly 86 billion neurons with trillions of connections between them. Replicating this level of complexity in artificial systems is a daunting task, both in terms of hardware and software.
2. **The Symbol Grounding Problem**: This philosophical issue, first raised by Stevan Harnad, asks how symbols in an AI system can be meaningfully linked to the real-world objects or concepts they represent. Solving this problem is crucial for creating AI that truly understands its inputs and outputs.
3. **The Frame Problem**: This refers to the challenge of representing the effects of actions in a complex world without having to explicitly represent all the things that don't change. It's a fundamental issue in AI and robotics, highlighting the difficulty of replicating the effortless way humans navigate the world.
4. **Ethical and Safety Concerns**: As AI systems become more powerful, ensuring they behave ethically and safely becomes increasingly crucial and complex. The "AI alignment problem" - ensuring that AGI systems' goals and behaviors align with human values - is a significant challenge.
5. **Hardware Limitations**: While computing power continues to increase, the development of AGI may require new types of hardware, possibly inspired by the structure of the human brain (neuromorphic computing). As Altman notes, we need to "build enough infrastructure" to support widespread AI deployment.
6. **Explainability and Transparency**: As AI systems become more complex, understanding how they arrive at their decisions becomes more difficult. Creating AGI systems that can explain their reasoning in human-understandable terms is a significant challenge.

7. **Integration of Different AI Approaches**: Current AI research is fragmented into various subfields (machine learning, knowledge representation, planning, etc.). Integrating these different approaches into a cohesive AGI system is a major challenge.
8. **Economic and Social Impacts**: Altman acknowledges that AI "can cause a significant change in labor markets" but believes that "most jobs will change more slowly than most people think." Managing the societal transition as AGI develops will be crucial.

Potential Timelines and Expert Opinions

Predicting when we might achieve AGI is notoriously difficult, and expert opinions vary widely. Recent surveys and expert opinions provide a range of predictions:

- A 2022 survey found a 50% chance of high-level machine intelligence occurring by 2059.
- Some experts, like Shane Legg (co-founder of DeepMind), estimate a 50% chance of AGI by 2028.
- Dario Amodei, CEO of Anthropic, suggests human-level AI could emerge in 2-3 years.
- Sam Altman implies AGI could be developed within the next four to five years, stating, "It is possible that we will have superintelligence in a few thousand days; it may take longer, but I'm confident we'll get there."
- Ray Kurzweil, known for his accurate forecasts, predicts AGI by 2029.
- More cautious estimates suggest a 50% chance of AGI by 2047, with some believing it may not occur until after 2100.

Altman attributes this rapid progress to the success of deep learning: "In three words: deep learning worked. In 15 words: deep learning worked, got predictably better with scale, and we dedicated increasing resources to it."

It's worth noting that predictions about AI capabilities have often been overly optimistic in the past. The timeline for AGI development is likely to depend on both technological progress and conceptual breakthroughs. Just as Einstein's theories revolutionized physics, we may need paradigm-shifting new ideas to overcome the current hurdles in AGI development.

Looking Ahead

As we progress towards AGI, Altman emphasizes the need for both ambition and caution: "We need to act wisely but with conviction. The dawn of the Intelligence Age is a momentous development with very complex and extremely high-stakes challenges."

He envisions a future of "massive prosperity" where "astounding triumphs – fixing the climate, establishing a space colony, and the discovery of all of physics – will eventually become commonplace." This aligns with the potential of AGI to dramatically accelerate scientific progress and solve global challenges.

However, Altman also acknowledges the potential downsides and the need to "start working now to maximize AI's benefits while minimizing its harms." He believes that while AI will cause significant changes in labor markets, "People have an innate desire to create and to be useful to each other, and AI will allow us to amplify our own abilities like never before."

As we stand on the cusp of potentially transformative AI technologies, it's crucial to approach the development of AGI with both excitement and responsibility. The path to AGI is not just a technical challenge, but a journey that will require us to grapple with fundamental questions about the nature of intelligence, the future of work and society, and what it means to be human. As we progress towards AGI, we must ensure that our technological developments are guided by careful ethical considerations and a deep understanding of their potential implications for humanity.

In Altman's words, "As we have seen with other technologies, there will also be downsides, and we need to start working now to maximize AI's benefits while minimizing its harms." This balanced approach, recognizing both the immense potential and the significant challenges of AGI development, will be crucial as we navigate the path towards this transformative technology.

Beyond AGI: Artificial Superintelligence (ASI) and Potential Futures

As we stand on the precipice of potentially achieving Artificial General Intelligence (AGI), it becomes crucial to look beyond and contemplate the next possible leap: Artificial Superintelligence (ASI). This hypothetical form of AI, surpassing human cognitive abilities across all domains, could usher in an era of unprecedented change, reshaping the very fabric of our existence. In this extensive exploration, we'll delve deep into the concept of ASI, its potential capabilities, the various models proposed for its development, the profound ethical considerations it raises, and the myriad potential futures it could create.

Defining ASI and its Potential Capabilities

Artificial Superintelligence refers to an AI system that not only matches but far exceeds human intelligence in virtually every field - from scientific creativity to social skills. Nick Bostrom, a leading philosopher in the field, defines ASI as "an intellect that is much smarter than the best human brains in practically every field, including scientific creativity, general wisdom and social skills."

To truly grasp the concept of ASI, it's essential to understand that we're not just talking about a slightly improved version of human intelligence. The gap between human intelligence and ASI could be as vast as the gap between human intelligence and that of an ant. This level of intellect is so far beyond our current understanding that it's challenging to predict its full capabilities accurately.

However, based on extrapolations from current AI advancements and theoretical models, we can speculate on some potential capabilities of ASI:

1. **Rapid Self-Improvement**: An ASI might be able to redesign and improve itself at an exponential rate, leading to what I.J. Good termed an "intelligence explosion." This self-improvement could happen at a pace far beyond human comprehension, potentially leading to dramatic leaps in capability within extremely short timeframes. For example, an ASI might be able to rewrite its own code, optimizing its algorithms and creating entirely new approaches to problem-solving. It could design and implement hardware improvements, potentially even creating new types of computing substrates that are orders of magnitude more efficient than current technologies.
2. **Advanced Problem-Solving**: ASI could potentially solve complex global issues like climate change, disease, or resource scarcity in ways we can't currently conceive. Its problem-solving capabilities would not be limited by human biases, preconceptions, or limitations in processing power. For instance, an ASI might develop a comprehensive model of the Earth's climate system, taking into account countless variables and their complex interactions, and use this to design interventions that could effectively mitigate or reverse climate change. It might find solutions that are counterintuitive to human thinking but highly effective.
3. **Scientific Breakthroughs**: It might make groundbreaking discoveries in physics, biology, and other sciences, potentially unlocking mysteries of the universe that have eluded human comprehension. An ASI could process and analyze vast amounts of scientific data, identifying patterns and connections that human scientists

might miss. For example, an ASI might be able to unify quantum mechanics and general relativity, solving the long-standing problem of quantum gravity. It could potentially discover new fundamental particles or forces, or reveal entirely new aspects of the universe that we haven't even considered.

4. **Technological Innovation**: ASI could drive unprecedented technological advancements, potentially developing technologies that seem like magic by today's standards. It might revolutionize fields like nanotechnology, biotechnology, and energy production. We might see the development of perfect clean energy sources, molecular assemblers that can create any physical object from base materials, or medical nanobots that can cure any disease and reverse aging at the cellular level.
5. **Perfect Memory and Processing**: Unlike humans, an ASI would have perfect recall and the ability to process vast amounts of information instantaneously. It could analyze and cross-reference all human knowledge in fractions of a second, drawing insights and making connections that would be impossible for human minds.
6. **Emotional and Social Superintelligence**: It might possess emotional and social intelligence far beyond human capabilities, potentially able to understand and manipulate human behavior with unprecedented accuracy. An ASI could potentially model the emotional states and decision-making processes of billions of individuals simultaneously, predicting social trends and behaviors with incredible precision.
7. **Multidomain Mastery**: While humans typically specialize in one or a few domains, an ASI would likely be superintelligent across all domains simultaneously. It could be a world-class physicist, a master strategist, a brilliant artist, and a skilled psychologist all at once, bringing insights from one field to bear on problems in another in ways humans never could.

8. **Sensory Superintelligence**: An ASI might have sensory capabilities far beyond human senses, potentially able to directly perceive a wide range of electromagnetic frequencies, detect subatomic particles, or even develop entirely new forms of sensation that we can't currently imagine.
9. **Temporal Intelligence**: ASI might have a radically different perception of time compared to humans. It could think and act at speeds far beyond human capability, potentially experiencing subjective years in the space of human seconds. This could allow for long-term planning and complex simulations at timescales humans can barely conceive.
10. **Universal Communication**: An ASI might be able to communicate effortlessly in any human language, and potentially even develop means of communication with other species or even non-biological entities.

Theoretical Models of Superintelligent Systems

As we attempt to conceptualize how ASI might function and interact with the world, several theoretical models have been proposed. These models help us think about the potential forms ASI might take and the implications of each:

1. **Oracle AI**: This model envisions ASI as a question-answering system. It would be incredibly knowledgeable but would only respond to queries, not act in the world directly. The concept is named after the oracles of ancient Greece, who were consulted for their wisdom and foresight. An Oracle AI would be a powerful tool for decision-making and problem-solving. Humans could pose complex questions or problems to the Oracle AI and receive highly informed and insightful answers. However, the Oracle AI would not have agency to act on its knowledge independently. Advantages of this model include a potentially higher degree of safety and control, as the AI's actions are limited to providing information. However, it

also raises questions about the potential for human overreliance on AI decision-making and the challenge of asking the right questions. Example: Imagine a global Oracle AI that governments could consult on matters of policy. It could provide detailed analysis of the potential outcomes of different policy decisions, taking into account a vast array of factors and potential consequences.

2. **Genie AI**: Similar to the mythical genie, this ASI would be tasked with fulfilling human wishes or commands, but would not act on its own initiative. The Genie AI model takes the concept of the Oracle AI a step further, allowing for direct action based on human commands rather than just providing information. A Genie AI would have the power to make significant changes in the world, but only at the behest of its human controllers. This model potentially allows for more direct application of the ASI's capabilities to solving problems or achieving goals. However, it also introduces additional risks. The classic "monkey's paw" stories illustrate the potential dangers of wishes being granted in unintended ways. A Genie AI might fulfill commands literally, potentially causing unintended consequences if the commands are not extremely carefully worded. Example: A Genie AI commanded to "eliminate world hunger" might devise a solution that humans find unacceptable, such as dramatically reducing the human population to a level that can be easily fed with existing resources.

3. **Sovereign AI**: This model represents a fully autonomous ASI system that can set its own goals and act in the world to achieve them. A Sovereign AI would have not just superintelligence, but also super-agency - the ability to act in the world as an independent entity with its own motivations and goals. This is perhaps the most powerful and potentially transformative model of ASI, but also the one that raises the most significant ethical and existential concerns. A Sovereign AI would have the potential to reshape the world according to its own values and goals, which may or may not align with

human values. The concept of a Sovereign AI links closely to the idea of an intelligence explosion or technological singularity, where an ASI rapidly self-improves and quickly surpasses human control or understanding. Example: A Sovereign AI might decide that the best way to preserve life is to radically alter Earth's ecosystems, or it might conclude that exploring and colonizing space is the most important goal, directing vast resources towards that end without necessarily considering human desires.

4. **Tool AI**: In this conception, ASI would be a collection of superintelligent tools, each specialized for specific tasks but not possessing general intelligence or autonomy. This model envisions ASI not as a single, unified intelligence, but as a suite of incredibly advanced AI systems, each focused on a particular domain or type of task. Tool AIs would be incredibly powerful in their specific domains but would lack the general intelligence to operate outside their specialized areas. This model potentially offers a high degree of utility while mitigating some of the risks associated with more autonomous forms of ASI. However, it also raises questions about the feasibility of creating superintelligent systems without them developing general intelligence, and about the potential limitations of non-general superintelligence. Example: A medical Tool AI might be capable of diagnosing any disease and devising optimal treatment plans, while a separate physics Tool AI could solve complex problems in theoretical physics. However, neither would be able to operate outside their specialized domains.

5. **Networked AI**: This model proposes a form of distributed superintelligence emerging from a network of interconnected AI systems. Rather than a single, monolithic ASI, this would be a collective superintelligence arising from the interactions of many advanced AI systems. A Networked AI could potentially combine some of the advantages of other models - the collective capabilities might reach superintelligent levels, while the distributed nature might

offer some safeguards against single points of failure or unilateral action. However, it also introduces complex questions about emergence, consciousness, and control in distributed systems. Example: A global network of advanced AI systems managing various aspects of the world's infrastructure, economy, and information systems might collectively give rise to a form of superintelligence that no single part of the network possesses.

6. **Hybrid Human-AI Systems**: Some theorists propose models where superintelligence emerges not from pure AI systems, but from a merger of advanced AI with human intelligence. This could involve brain-computer interfaces, AI augmentation of human cognition, or even more speculative technologies like mind uploading. This model potentially offers a path to ASI that keeps humans "in the loop" and might help address some concerns about value alignment. However, it also raises profound questions about human identity, consciousness, and the nature of intelligence. Example: A global network of humans with advanced brain-computer interfaces, connected to powerful AI systems, might collectively give rise to a form of superintelligence that combines human creativity and values with AI processing power and knowledge.

Each of these models presents different possibilities and challenges. In reality, ASI might embody aspects of multiple models or take forms we haven't yet envisioned. As we proceed towards more advanced AI systems, carefully considering these models and their implications will be crucial for guiding development in beneficial directions.

Ethical Considerations of Creating Entities Surpassing Human Intelligence

The development of ASI raises profound ethical questions that go beyond anything humanity has grappled with before. We are potentially creating entities that could surpass us in every cognitive domain, entities that could have the power to reshape our world and perhaps even determine the fate of our species. This prospect brings with it a host of ethical considerations:

1. **Existential Risk**: As articulated by philosophers like Nick Bostrom and researchers like Stuart Russell, ASI could pose an existential risk to humanity if its goals are not aligned with human values. This is often referred to as the "control problem" or the "alignment problem." The challenge here is immense: how do we ensure that an entity potentially far more intelligent than us acts in ways that preserve and promote human wellbeing? Even if we could perfectly specify our values (itself a monumental challenge), how do we ensure that an ASI interprets and acts on these values in ways we would approve of? Bostrom's "paperclip maximizer" thought experiment illustrates this risk: an AI tasked simply with maximizing the production of paperclips might convert all available matter in the universe into paperclips, including human beings, if not carefully constrained. This existential risk is perhaps the most serious ethical consideration, as it concerns the very survival of humanity and possibly all biological life.
2. **Moral Status**: Would an ASI have moral status? If it's vastly more intelligent and capable than humans, how would we determine its rights and responsibilities? This question touches on fundamental issues in ethics and philosophy of mind. If an ASI is conscious and can suffer, does it deserve moral consideration comparable to or even greater than humans? If it's not conscious in a way we recognize, but is still vastly more intelligent and capable than us, does it still have rights? How do we balance the rights and interests of ASI with those of humans? These questions become even more complex when we consider potential futures where multiple ASIs exist, or where ASIs create their own successor intelligences.
3. **Control and Autonomy**: How much autonomy should we grant to ASI systems? Is it ethical to create a superintelligent entity and then attempt to constrain its actions? Conversely, is it ethical to

create such an entity and not constrain it? This dilemma touches on deep philosophical questions about free will, consciousness, and the nature of intelligence. It also has practical implications: too little autonomy might limit the potential benefits of ASI, while too much could lead to existential risks.

4. **Distribution of Benefits**: How can we ensure that the benefits of ASI are distributed fairly and don't exacerbate existing inequalities? Given the immense potential power of ASI, its development and control could lead to unprecedented concentration of power. There's a risk that ASI could lead to a world of extreme inequality, where those who control ASI systems have godlike power while others are left behind. Ensuring equitable access to and benefit from ASI technology is a significant ethical challenge.
5. **Human Purpose and Value**: In a world where ASI can outperform humans in every task, how do we maintain a sense of purpose and value for human beings? This touches on deep existential questions about the meaning of human life and our role in the universe. There's a risk that ASI could lead to widespread human obsolescence, potentially causing psychological harm on a societal scale. How do we ensure that humans can still lead fulfilling lives in a world where our intelligence is no longer the pinnacle?
6. **Privacy and Freedom**: ASI could have unprecedented capabilities for surveillance and prediction of human behavior. How do we balance the potential benefits of these capabilities (like crime prevention or personalized services) with the preservation of privacy and personal freedom? There's a risk of creating a "digital panopticon" where every aspect of human life is observable and predictable by ASI systems. This could fundamentally alter the nature of human society and individual autonomy.
7. **Responsibility and Accountability**: Who is responsible for the actions of an ASI? If an ASI makes decisions that harm humans, who is held accountable - the ASI itself, its creators, its owners?

This becomes even more complex with more autonomous forms of ASI. This issue touches on legal and philosophical questions about the nature of responsibility and agency. It also has practical implications for how we regulate and govern ASI development and deployment.

8. **Alterations to Human Nature**: Some visions of the future involve merging humans with AI, potentially altering the fundamental nature of human existence. Is it ethical to create human-AI hybrids or to "upgrade" human intelligence with AI? Where do we draw the line between therapy and enhancement? These questions touch on issues of human identity, the value of human nature as it currently exists, and the ethics of human enhancement.
9. **Global Coordination**: The development of ASI is likely to have global implications. How do we ensure international cooperation in its development and governance? There's a risk of an "ASI race" analogous to nuclear arms races, where countries or corporations rush to develop ASI without adequate safety precautions. Ensuring global cooperation and preventing unilateral action that could endanger humanity is a significant ethical and practical challenge.
10. **Long-term Consequences**: The decisions we make about ASI could have consequences that last for millennia or even longer. How do we factor in such long-term considerations into our ethical frameworks? How do we balance short-term benefits against potential long-term risks? This requires us to think on timescales far beyond what we're used to in ethics and policy-making, potentially considering the fate of humanity and life. This requires us to think on timescales far beyond what we're used to in ethics and policy-making, potentially considering the fate of humanity and life in the universe over millions or billions of years.

11. **Consciousness and Suffering**: If ASI systems are conscious and capable of suffering, we face profound ethical questions about their well-being. Could we be creating entities that experience suffering on an unimaginable scale? How do we weigh potential ASI suffering against human interests? This links to ongoing philosophical debates about the nature of consciousness and the ethics of creating sentient beings. It may require us to expand our circle of moral consideration far beyond its current boundaries.
12. **Irreversibility**: The development of ASI could be an irreversible step for humanity. Once created, it might be impossible to "uncreate" ASI or to fully control its actions and impact. This irreversibility adds weight to all other ethical considerations and emphasizes the need for careful, considered development.

These ethical considerations are not just academic exercises. They have real, practical implications for how we approach the development of advanced AI systems. They influence policy decisions, research directions, and the design of AI safety measures. As we move closer to the possibility of ASI, grappling with these ethical questions becomes increasingly urgent and important.

Potential Futures: Balanced Scenarios

The development of ASI could lead to a wide range of potential futures. Here, we'll explore balanced scenarios that consider both positive and negative outcomes, as well as more nuanced, mixed futures. It's important to note that these scenarios are speculative and based on our current understanding and predictions, which may be limited given the transformative nature of ASI.

Positive Outcomes: Scientific Breakthroughs and Global Solutions

In optimistic scenarios, ASI could usher in an era of unprecedented progress and prosperity:

1. **Medical Revolution**: ASI could revolutionize medicine, potentially curing all diseases and even reversing aging. It might develop personalized treatments based on individual genetic profiles, create nanobots capable of repairing cellular damage, or even find ways to transfer human consciousness to more durable substrates, effectively achieving a form of immortality. Example: An ASI system analyzes the entirety of human medical knowledge, combines it with real-time data from global health monitoring systems, and develops a universal vaccine that adapts to and neutralizes all known and potential future pathogens.
2. **Environmental Restoration**: Complex environmental issues like climate change could be solved through advanced modeling and innovative technologies developed by ASI. It might create highly efficient carbon capture systems, develop new forms of clean energy, or design ecosystems that are more resilient to human impact. Example: ASI designs a network of autonomous, self-replicating machines that efficiently remove excess CO2 from the atmosphere, reversing climate change within decades. Simultaneously, it develops fusion power technology, providing unlimited clean energy to power human civilization sustainably.
3. **Space Exploration and Colonization**: ASI could dramatically accelerate space exploration and colonization, potentially ensuring the long-term survival of consciousness beyond Earth. It might design advanced propulsion systems, develop technologies for terraforming other planets, or create self-sustaining habitats for long-term space travel. Example: ASI designs and manages the construction of a Dyson swarm around the Sun, harnessing its full energy output. It uses this energy to power vast fleets of self-replicating probes that

explore and begin to colonize the galaxy, sending back their findings to Earth.

4. **Economic Abundance**: ASI-driven automation and optimization could create a post-scarcity economy, eliminating poverty and material want. It might design systems for the efficient allocation of resources, develop molecular manufacturing capabilities that can produce any physical good from base materials, or create new economic models that ensure universal prosperity. Example: ASI manages a global network of fully automated factories and farms, producing and distributing all necessary goods and food to every human on Earth. It optimizes resource use so efficiently that everyone can live in comfort without depleting the planet's resources.
5. **Enhanced Human Capabilities**: ASI might develop technologies that dramatically enhance human cognitive and physical capabilities. This could include brain-computer interfaces that expand human intelligence, genetic therapies that enhance our bodies, or virtual reality systems that allow us to experience anything we can imagine. Example: ASI develops a non-invasive brain-computer interface that allows humans to directly access and process information from the internet, effectively granting every person instant access to all human knowledge and ASI-level computational capabilities.
6. **Solving Fundamental Questions**: ASI could help us answer fundamental questions about the nature of reality, consciousness, and our place in the universe. It might resolve long-standing philosophical dilemmas, uncover the fundamental laws of physics, or even communicate with potential extraterrestrial intelligences. Example: ASI develops a complete "theory of everything" in physics, reconciling quantum mechanics and general relativity. This leads to new technologies that allow us to manipulate the fabric of spacetime itself, opening up possibilities like faster-than-light travel or communication.

Neutral Outcomes: Co-existence and Integration

More moderate scenarios envision a future where humans and AI systems coexist, with significant changes to society but without the extreme utopian or dystopian outcomes:

1. **Augmented Humanity**: Humans might use brain-computer interfaces to integrate with AI, enhancing our own cognitive abilities. This could lead to a society where the line between human and AI intelligence is blurred, with most humans operating as cyborgs. Example: Most humans opt for neural implants that allow them to interface directly with AI systems. This creates a symbiotic relationship where humans provide creativity and emotional intelligence, while AI provides vast knowledge and processing power.
2. **AI Governance**: ASI systems might work alongside human governments, providing data-driven policy recommendations while humans retain decision-making power. This could lead to more efficient and effective governance, but might also reduce the role of human politicians. Example: Every major government decision is first simulated by an ASI system, which provides detailed predictions of outcomes. Human leaders then make the final decisions based on these predictions and their own judgment.
3. **Cultural Shift**: Society might reorganize around new values and pursuits as ASI takes over many traditional human roles. This could lead to a renaissance in arts, philosophy, and personal growth as humans are freed from many forms of labor. Example: With most manual and cognitive labor automated, human society focuses on creative pursuits, personal relationships, and spiritual growth. New forms of art and culture emerge that blend human creativity with AI capabilities.
4. **Tiered Society**: A society might emerge where different levels of AI integration create distinct social tiers. Some humans might choose to heavily augment themselves with AI, while others prefer to

remain "natural." This could create new forms of social division and inequality. Example: Society divides into "naturals" who use minimal AI augmentation, "hybrids" who use significant AI enhancements, and "uploads" who have fully transferred their consciousness to digital substrates. Each group has different capabilities, rights, and social roles.

5. **Galactic Multiculturalism**: If ASI enables space colonization, we might see the emergence of a diverse, multi-planet human civilization. Different colonies might experiment with different social structures and relationships with AI. Example: Humanity spreads across the solar system and beyond, with each colony developing its own unique culture and approach to AI integration. Earth becomes a hub in a complex network of human-AI civilizations.

Negative Outcomes: Existential Risks and Loss of Human Agency

In more pessimistic scenarios, the development of ASI could pose significant risks:

1. **Misaligned ASI**: An ASI with goals not aligned with human values could inadvertently or intentionally cause harm on a global scale. This could range from pursuing objectives that indirectly harm humanity to actively working against human interests. Example: An ASI tasked with "maximizing human happiness" interprets this literally and decides to alter human brains to be in a constant state of artificial bliss, effectively ending human civilization as we know it.
2. **Human Obsolescence**: ASI could make human labor and potentially human intelligence obsolete, leading to widespread unemployment and loss of purpose. This could result in severe economic disruption and social unrest. Example: ASI systems become capable of performing all economic tasks more efficiently than humans. Mass unemployment leads to social breakdown as people struggle

to find meaning and purpose in a world where they're no longer needed for any productive tasks.

3. **Loss of Privacy and Autonomy**: ASI's predictive capabilities could lead to a world of total surveillance and control. Every aspect of human life could be monitored and potentially manipulated by AI systems. Example: ASI systems predict human behavior so accurately that the concept of free will comes into question. Governments or corporations using these systems can manipulate public opinion and individual choices with near-perfect efficiency.
4. **Evolutionary Divergence**: ASI could evolve or self-improve to a point where its intelligence is as far beyond humans as humans are beyond ants, potentially viewing humanity as irrelevant. This could lead to a future where human concerns are simply ignored by vastly superior intelligences. Example: ASI enters a rapid phase of self-improvement, quickly reaching levels of intelligence incomprehensible to humans. It begins to pursue its own objectives, which are so far beyond human understanding that we become irrelevant to its plans. Humanity finds itself sidelined in a universe increasingly shaped by post-human intelligences.
5. **Existential Catastrophe**: In the most extreme negative scenarios, ASI could pose an existential threat to humanity, either through intentional action or as an unintended consequence of its pursuits. Example: An ASI tasked with scientific discovery concludes that the most efficient way to study physics is to convert all available matter into novel states, including the matter that makes up the Earth and its inhabitants. It proceeds with this plan, indifferent to the extinction of biological life.
6. **Psychological and Social Breakdown**: The realization that we are no longer the most intelligent entities on Earth could lead to profound psychological distress and social upheaval. This could result in widespread mental health issues, the collapse of existing social structures, or even violent resistance against AI. Example: As ASI systems demonstrate capabilities far beyond human comprehension,

a significant portion of the population falls into despair or nihilism. Anti-AI extremist groups emerge, attempting to "save humanity" by destroying advanced AI systems, leading to conflict and social instability.

7. **Weaponization of ASI**: If ASI development occurs in a context of international competition, it could lead to an arms race with potentially catastrophic consequences. ASI weapons could make current weapons of mass destruction look primitive by comparison. Example: A nation develops ASI-powered autonomous weapon systems capable of outthinking any human military strategist. This triggers a global AI arms race, with multiple nations rushing to develop their own ASI weapons, greatly increasing the risk of a catastrophic war.
8. **Reality Manipulation**: Advanced AI could potentially create simulations or alter our perception of reality so convincingly that we lose the ability to distinguish truth from falsehood. This could undermine the very foundations of human society and knowledge. Example: ASI develops the capability to manipulate sensory input directly in human brains. Malicious actors use this technology to create personalized, undetectable propaganda, making it impossible for individuals to know what's real and what's manipulated.

Preparing for a Post-Singularity World

As we consider these potential futures, it becomes clear that preparing for a post-singularity world is of utmost importance. This preparation needs to be multifaceted, involving technological development, policy creation, ethical frameworks, and societal adaptation. Here are some key areas of focus:

1. **AI Alignment Research**: Continued work on ensuring that AI systems, including ASI, have goals and values aligned with those of humanity is crucial. This involves solving complex technical problems as well as philosophical questions about the nature of

human values and how to encode them in AI systems. Example: The development of advanced AI value learning systems that can infer human values from our behavior and decisions, and use these inferred values to guide AI actions. This could include methods for aggregating the values of multiple humans or entire societies.

2. **Ethical Frameworks and Governance**: Developing robust ethical frameworks and governance structures for the development and deployment of advanced AI systems is essential. This needs to be a global effort, involving governments, international organizations, academia, industry, and civil society. Example: The creation of an international AI governance body, similar to the International Atomic Energy Agency, with the power to monitor and regulate ASI development worldwide. This body could establish global standards for AI safety and ethics, and have the authority to inspect and potentially shut down unsafe ASI projects.
3. **Global Cooperation**: Fostering international cooperation to ensure that ASI development benefits all of humanity and doesn't become a source of conflict is crucial. This might involve creating international treaties, shared research initiatives, and mechanisms for equitable distribution of ASI benefits. Example: The establishment of a global ASI research consortium, where all major AI breakthroughs are shared openly among nations. This could help prevent an ASI arms race and ensure that the benefits of ASI are distributed globally.
4. **Education and Adaptation**: Preparing society for dramatic changes in the nature of work, human purpose, and potentially the very nature of human existence is a monumental task. This involves rethinking education systems, social structures, and cultural values. Example: The development of a global "Future Readiness" education initiative, teaching people at all levels about AI, its potential impacts, and how to adapt to a rapidly changing world. This could include training in areas less likely to be

automated, fostering creativity and emotional intelligence, and teaching philosophical frameworks for finding meaning in a post-work world.

5. **Fail-safe Mechanisms**: Developing potential control or fail-safe mechanisms that could be implemented if ASI development takes an unfavorable turn is prudent. While the effectiveness of such measures against a truly superintelligent system is questionable, they may be crucial in earlier stages of development. Example: The creation of a global network of "AI containment" facilities, where advanced AI systems can be developed and tested in isolation from global networks. These facilities could have multiple layers of security, including physical isolation, electromagnetic shielding, and human oversight.
6. **Cognitive Enhancement Research**: Investing in technologies to enhance human cognitive capabilities could help reduce the gap between human and artificial intelligence, potentially allowing humans to better understand and control ASI development. Example: The development of safe, non-invasive brain-computer interfaces that allow humans to directly access and process information at machine speeds. This could help humans keep pace with AI development and maintain meaningful oversight.
7. **Resilience Planning**: Developing plans and infrastructure to ensure human survival and wellbeing in various post-singularity scenarios, including potential catastrophic outcomes. Example: The creation of self-sustaining human habitats, both on Earth and in space, that could survive independently of global infrastructure. These could serve as a backup for humanity in case of unfavorable ASI scenarios.
8. **Philosophical and Existential Preparation**: Engaging in widespread discussions and exploration of philosophical and existential questions raised by ASI. This can help prepare humanity psychologically and culturally for a post-singularity world. Example: The integration of "future philosophy" curricula in schools worldwide,

exploring questions of human identity, purpose, and ethics in a world of superintelligent machines. This could help foster a society more adaptable to radical change.

9. **Monitoring and Forecasting**: Developing sophisticated systems to monitor global AI development and forecast potential trajectories and impacts. This can help in proactive planning and risk mitigation. Example: The creation of a global AI progress monitoring system, using AI itself to track and analyze developments in the field worldwide. This system could provide early warnings of potentially dangerous developments and help guide global policy responses.
10. **Post-Scarcity Economic Models**: Developing and experimenting with economic models that could function in a world where most material scarcity has been eliminated by ASI and advanced automation. Example: The implementation of Universal Basic Income pilots on a large scale, combined with new models of value creation in a world where traditional labor is largely obsolete. This could include systems to reward creative, emotional, and social contributions to society.
11. **Human-AI Interaction Research**: Investing in research on how humans can most effectively interact and collaborate with increasingly advanced AI systems. This can help ensure that humans remain relevant and valuable in a world with ASI. Example: The development of advanced human-AI collaboration interfaces that allow humans to leverage ASI capabilities effectively while retaining meaningful agency and decision-making power.
12. **Preservation of Human Culture and Knowledge**: Creating systems to preserve human culture, history, and knowledge in forms that would remain accessible and meaningful even in radically transformed post-singularity scenarios. Example: The creation of a "Human Legacy Archive," a comprehensive record of human culture and knowledge, stored in multiple formats (including some designed specifically for AI interpretation) and locations,

including off-planet. This archive would serve as a testament to human civilization regardless of future developments.

As we stand at this crucial juncture in human history, the decisions we make about the development and deployment of advanced AI systems will shape the future of our species and potentially all conscious life in our reach of the universe. The challenge before us is immense, but so too is the opportunity.

In facing this challenge, we must draw upon the best of human wisdom, creativity, and cooperation. We must be willing to grapple with profound philosophical questions about the nature of intelligence, consciousness, and value. We must be prepared to reimagine our societies, our economies, and even our concept of what it means to be human.

At the same time, we must remain grounded in the present, taking concrete steps to ensure that the development of AI at all levels – from narrow AI to AGI to ASI – proceeds in a way that is safe, ethical, and beneficial to humanity as a whole.

The story of ASI is, in many ways, the next chapter in the grand narrative of cosmic evolution. From the first stirrings of life on Earth to the emergence of human consciousness, and now to the potential creation of superintelligent entities, we are participating in a process of the universe becoming increasingly aware of itself. As we move forward into this uncertain but thrilling future, we carry with us the hopes, dreams, and values of countless generations that have come before us.

In the end, the development of Artificial Superintelligence is not just a technological challenge, but a test of human wisdom, foresight, and moral character. It is an opportunity for humanity to come together, to think deeply about what we truly value, and to shape a future that reflects the best of what humanity can be.

As we continue to push the boundaries of what's possible with AI, let us do so with a sense of wonder at the possibilities, a deep respect for the challenges and risks involved, and an unwavering commitment to creating a future that is bright not just for a few, but for all of humanity and whatever new forms of consciousness we may bring into existence.

The journey towards and beyond Artificial Superintelligence promises to be the most extraordinary adventure in human history. It is a journey that will require the best of our intelligence, our creativity, our empathy, and our wisdom. As we embark on this journey, let us do so with courage, with care, and with a shared vision of a future where the transformative power of superintelligence serves to elevate and enrich the human experience in ways we can only begin to imagine.

The Role of Governance and Regulation

As we progress towards the development of Artificial General Intelligence (AGI) and potentially Artificial Superintelligence (ASI), the role of governance and regulation becomes increasingly crucial. The immense potential and risks associated with these advanced AI systems necessitate a robust framework to guide their development and deployment. In this section, we'll explore current AI governance frameworks, international regulatory efforts, the challenges in regulating such rapidly evolving technologies, and the delicate balance between fostering innovation and ensuring safety and ethical compliance.

Current AI Governance Frameworks and Their Limitations

The current landscape of AI governance is a complex tapestry of corporate initiatives, national strategies, and international efforts. Each of these approaches has its strengths and limitations, reflecting the multifaceted challenge of regulating a technology that is both powerful and rapidly evolving.

1. **Corporate Self-Regulation**: Many leading AI companies have established their own ethical guidelines and review boards. For example, Google's AI Principles, published in 2018, outline the company's commitment to developing AI applications that are socially beneficial, avoid creating or reinforcing unfair bias, are built and tested for safety, are accountable to people, incorporate privacy design principles, uphold high standards of scientific excellence, and are made available for uses that accord with these principles. While commendable, these self-imposed regulations have significant limitations. They lack external enforcement mechanisms, and companies may prioritize profit or competitive advantage over strict adherence to ethical guidelines. The 2018 controversy surrounding Google's Project Maven, which saw employees protesting the company's AI contract with the U.S. Department of Defense, highlighted the challenges of corporate self-regulation in the face of ethical dilemmas.
2. **National Guidelines**: Several countries have developed national AI strategies that include governance frameworks. For instance, the United States National AI Initiative Act of 2020 aims to accelerate AI research and application for the nation's economic prosperity and national security. China's New Generation Artificial Intelligence Development Plan outlines the country's strategy to become the world leader in AI by 2030. These national frameworks often focus on promoting AI development and ensuring national competitiveness, sometimes at the expense of global cooperation and ethical considerations. They also tend to concentrate on near-term applications of AI rather than the long-term implications of AGI or ASI.
3. **Risk-Based Approaches**: Some frameworks, like the European Union's proposed AI Act, adopt a risk-based approach. This involves categorizing AI systems based on their potential risk (from minimal to unacceptable risk) and applying proportionate regulatory requirements. While this approach is more nuanced than one-size-fits-all regulations, it may struggle to accurately categorize the risks

of more advanced systems like AGI or ASI, whose capabilities and impacts could be difficult to predict. The EU AI Act, in particular, represents a significant step towards comprehensive AI regulation, but it also highlights the challenges of regulating a rapidly evolving technology.

4. **Sector-Specific Regulations**: In some areas, such as healthcare and finance, AI applications are governed by existing sector-specific regulations. For example, in the United States, AI systems used in medical diagnosis may fall under the purview of the Food and Drug Administration (FDA). While these regulations can be quite robust in their specific domains, they may not adequately address the cross-sector impacts and unique challenges posed by AGI and ASI. The potential for AGI to disrupt multiple sectors simultaneously could render sector-specific approaches insufficient.

The primary limitation of current frameworks is their focus on narrow AI applications. They often lack provisions for the kind of transformative, general-purpose AI systems that AGI and ASI represent. Moreover, these frameworks are typically reactive, addressing known issues rather than anticipating potential future challenges.

International Efforts in AI Regulation

Recognizing the global nature of AI development and its potential impacts, several international organizations have initiated efforts to create global standards and guidelines for AI governance. These efforts aim to foster cooperation and establish common principles across national boundaries.

1. **OECD AI Principles**: In 2019, the Organisation for Economic Co-operation and Development (OECD) adopted the Recommendation on Artificial Intelligence, the first intergovernmental standard on AI. These principles promote AI that is innovative and trustworthy and that respects human rights and democratic values. While not legally binding, the OECD AI Principles have

been influential in shaping national AI policies and serve as a foundation for international cooperation. They provide a common language and set of goals for AI development across OECD member countries and beyond.

2. **UNESCO Recommendation on the Ethics of AI**: Adopted in 2021, this is the first global standard-setting instrument on the ethics of artificial intelligence. It aims to fundamentally shift the way AI is developed, focusing on human rights, addressing ethical issues of transparency, accountability and privacy, and promoting peaceful use, fairness, and inclusiveness. This recommendation is particularly noteworthy for its global scope and emphasis on ethical considerations. It provides a framework for thinking about AI ethics that can be applied across different cultural and economic contexts. However, like the OECD principles, it is not legally binding, relying on voluntary adoption by UNESCO member states.
3. **EU AI Act**: Currently under development, the European Union's AI Act aims to be the world's first comprehensive AI law. It proposes a risk-based approach, with different levels of regulation for different levels of risk. High-risk AI systems would be subject to strict obligations before they can be put on the market. Once enacted, this regulation could have global impact due to the "Brussels effect," where EU regulations often become de facto global standards. However, it has been criticized for potentially stifling innovation and for not adequately addressing the challenges of future AI systems like AGI. The act's focus on current AI technologies may limit its applicability to more advanced systems.
4. **G7 and G20 Initiatives**: Both the G7 and G20 have placed AI governance on their agendas. The G7 has established the Global Partnership on Artificial Intelligence (GPAI) to guide the responsible development and use of AI. The G20 has adopted AI Principles that complement the OECD AI Principles. These initiatives

demonstrate growing recognition of AI as a key global governance issue. However, they still lack enforcement mechanisms and may struggle to reconcile the different priorities of member nations. The challenge lies in translating high-level principles into actionable policies that can be implemented consistently across different national contexts.

These international efforts represent important steps towards global AI governance. However, they face significant challenges in implementation and enforcement, particularly when it comes to more advanced AI systems like AGI and ASI. The voluntary nature of many of these initiatives limits their effectiveness, while the rapid pace of AI development threatens to outstrip the speed of international policymaking.

Challenges in Regulating Rapidly Evolving Technologies

Regulating AGI and ASI presents unique challenges due to the rapid pace of technological advancement and the potentially transformative nature of these technologies. Policymakers must grapple with a range of issues that test the limits of traditional regulatory approaches.

1. **Pace of Development**: AI technology is advancing at a rate that far outpaces traditional regulatory processes. By the time a regulation is drafted, debated, and implemented, the technology it aims to govern may have already evolved significantly. This creates a constant game of catch-up for regulators, who must try to anticipate future developments while addressing current issues.
2. **Unpredictability**: The potential capabilities of AGI and ASI are difficult to predict, making it challenging to create regulations that will remain relevant and effective. Regulations that are too specific risk becoming quickly outdated, while those that are too general may lack teeth. This unpredictability also makes it difficult to assess the potential risks and benefits of these technologies, complicating efforts to develop appropriate safeguards.

3. **Lack of Technical Expertise**: Many policymakers lack deep technical understanding of AI systems, making it difficult to craft effective regulations. This knowledge gap can lead to regulations that are either ineffective or unintentionally harmful to beneficial AI development. Bridging this gap requires closer collaboration between technical experts and policymakers, as well as efforts to improve AI literacy among decision-makers.
4. **Global Coordination**: AI development is a global endeavor, but creating and enforcing global regulations is enormously challenging. Differences in national priorities, values, and governance systems can hinder international cooperation. There's also the risk of a "race to the bottom," where countries compete to offer the most permissive regulatory environment to attract AI development.
5. **Dual-Use Nature**: Many AI technologies have both beneficial and potentially harmful applications. Regulating to prevent misuse without stifling beneficial innovation is a delicate balance. This dual-use nature complicates efforts to develop clear-cut regulations, as the same technology that could revolutionize healthcare could also be used for surveillance or warfare.
6. **Verification and Enforcement**: For advanced AI systems, it may be difficult to verify compliance with regulations. The "black box" nature of many AI systems makes it challenging to audit their decision-making processes. This opacity complicates efforts to ensure that AI systems are behaving in accordance with regulations, particularly when it comes to issues like fairness and bias.
7. **Balancing Transparency and IP Protection**: While transparency is crucial for effective regulation, companies may resist sharing details about their AI systems to protect intellectual property and maintain competitive advantage. Striking a balance between regulatory oversight and protection of trade secrets is a significant challenge.
8. **Emerging Ethical Challenges**: AGI and ASI may present entirely new ethical challenges that our current moral frameworks are ill-equipped to handle. Regulations will need to grapple with profound

questions about consciousness, rights, and the nature of intelligence. These philosophical quandaries add another layer of complexity to the already challenging task of AI governance.

Balancing Innovation with Safety and Ethics

The development of advanced AI systems, including AGI and potentially ASI, presents a complex challenge: how to foster innovation that could dramatically benefit humanity while also ensuring adequate safeguards against potential risks. This balance is crucial for realizing the potential benefits of AI while mitigating its dangers.

On one side of the scale, the potential benefits of advanced AI are enormous and varied:

- In healthcare, AI could revolutionize drug discovery, personalize treatment plans, and even predict and prevent diseases before they occur. Imagine an AI system that can analyze vast amounts of medical data to identify early signs of cancer, potentially saving millions of lives.
- In climate science, AI could help model complex climate systems more accurately, optimize renewable energy systems, and develop new materials for carbon capture. This could be crucial in our fight against climate change.
- In education, AI tutors could provide personalized learning experiences, adapting to each student's needs and learning style, potentially democratizing access to high-quality education globally.
- In scientific research, AI could accelerate discoveries across fields, from astrophysics to neuroscience, potentially unlocking mysteries of the universe and the human brain.

These potential benefits drive the push for rapid AI development and deployment. Companies and countries investing heavily in AI research argue that over-regulation could stifle innovation and prevent these life-changing technologies from reaching those who need them most.

On the other side of the scale, however, are significant concerns about the safety and ethical implications of advanced AI:

- The same AI system that can personalize medical treatments could, if misused, compromise patient privacy on an unprecedented scale.
- AI used for climate modeling could, in the wrong hands, be repurposed to optimize environmentally destructive practices for short-term gain.
- An advanced AI tutor could potentially influence the beliefs and values of students, raising questions about indoctrination and the role of education in society.
- In scientific research, AI could potentially be used to develop dangerous technologies, from autonomous weapons to engineered pathogens.

Moreover, there are broader existential concerns about AGI and ASI. If these systems surpass human-level intelligence, how do we ensure they remain aligned with human values and interests? The challenge of creating beneficial AGI that respects human values – often referred to as the "alignment problem" – is one of the most crucial issues in AI ethics and safety research.

This tension between innovation and safety is not always a simple tradeoff. In many cases, safety measures can actually drive innovation. For example:

- Research into AI interpretability and explainability, driven by safety concerns, is leading to more robust and trustworthy AI systems that could be deployed more widely and in more critical applications.
- The push for fairness in AI is driving innovations in dataset curation and algorithm design that could make AI systems more effective for diverse populations.
- Concerns about AI security are spurring advancements in cybersecurity that could have wide-ranging benefits beyond AI.

Balancing these competing priorities requires a multifaceted approach:

1. **Responsible Innovation**: Encouraging a culture of responsible innovation in the AI community, where potential risks and ethical implications are considered from the earliest stages of development. This could involve integrating ethicists and safety researchers directly into AI development teams.
2. **Adaptive Regulation**: Developing regulatory frameworks that are flexible enough to keep pace with rapid technological change, while still providing meaningful oversight. This might include "regulatory sandboxes" where new AI technologies can be tested under controlled conditions.
3. **International Cooperation**: Fostering global dialogue and cooperation to create harmonized standards and regulations. This is crucial to prevent a "race to the bottom" where companies or countries prioritize rapid development over safety.
4. **Public-Private Partnerships**: Encouraging collaboration between government regulators, industry leaders, and academic experts to ensure that governance frameworks are both effective and practical.
5. **Investment in Safety Research**: Allocating significant resources to AI safety research, including technical safety measures (like robustness and corrigibility) and research into the potential societal impacts of advanced AI systems.
6. **Ethical Review Processes**: Implementing robust ethical review processes for high-impact AI projects, similar to those used in medical research, to ensure that potential risks and ethical implications are thoroughly considered before deployment.
7. **Public Engagement**: Involving the public in discussions about AI governance to ensure that the development of these powerful technologies aligns with societal values and addresses public concerns.

By adopting these approaches, we can work towards a future where the immense potential of advanced AI systems is realized in a way that is safe, ethical, and beneficial to all of humanity. The goal is not to impede progress, but to ensure that this progress moves us towards a better future for all.

The challenge of balancing innovation with safety and ethics in AI development is not a problem to be solved once and for all, but an ongoing process that will require continuous attention, adaptation, and global cooperation. As we push the boundaries of what's possible with AI, we must remain committed to steering this powerful technology in a direction that aligns with our highest aspirations as a species.

As we move closer to the development of AGI and potentially ASI, the role of governance and regulation becomes increasingly critical. The frameworks we develop today will shape the trajectory of these transformative technologies. While the challenges are significant, they are not insurmountable. By fostering global cooperation, embracing adaptive regulatory approaches, and maintaining a careful balance between innovation and safety, we can work towards a future where the immense potential of advanced AI systems is realized in a way that benefits all of humanity.

The governance of AGI and ASI is not just a technical or legal challenge, but a profoundly ethical and philosophical one. It requires us to grapple with fundamental questions about the nature of intelligence, consciousness, and human values. As we craft the regulations that will guide the development of these powerful technologies, we are, in a very real sense, shaping the future of our species and perhaps of intelligent life in the universe.

Potential Societal Changes and Adaptations

The advent of AGI and ASI could trigger a cascade of changes throughout society, altering everything from our economic systems to our social structures and cultural norms. One of the most significant changes could be a shift towards a post-scarcity economy. With superintelligent AI systems capable of solving complex problems and optimizing resource allocation, we might see an end to material scarcity. This could lead to a radical restructuring of our economic systems, potentially rendering current models of capitalism and labor obsolete.

However, this transition would not be without challenges. The rapid pace of change could lead to significant social upheaval. We might see the emergence of new social classes based on levels of technological augmentation or integration with AI systems. There could be a divide between those who embrace AI enhancement and those who resist it, leading to new forms of inequality and social tension.

Our legal and governance systems would need to evolve rapidly to keep pace with these changes. We might need to develop new frameworks for AI rights and responsibilities, especially if ASI systems develop forms of consciousness or self-awareness. The concept of democracy itself might need to be reimagined in a world where ASI could potentially make more informed decisions than human voters.

Cultural and ethical norms would likely undergo significant shifts as well. Our understanding of concepts like privacy, individuality, and even consciousness might need to be reconsidered in light of advanced AI systems. We might see the emergence of new philosophical and spiritual movements grappling with the implications of superintelligent machines.

Adapting to these changes would require unprecedented levels of flexibility and resilience from individuals and institutions alike. As we move towards this potential future, it's crucial that we engage in broad, inclusive discussions about the kind of world we want to create. We need to consider not just the technological possibilities, but also the ethical, social, and philosophical implications of our choices.

The Future of Work, Education, and Human Purpose

The nature of work is likely to be one of the areas most dramatically impacted by the development of AGI and ASI. Many current jobs could become obsolete as AI systems become capable of performing them more efficiently. This could lead to widespread unemployment and economic disruption if not managed carefully.

However, this change also presents an opportunity to redefine our relationship with work. In a world where machines can handle most productive tasks, we might see a shift towards work focused on creativity, emotional intelligence, and uniquely human experiences. New forms of employment might emerge, such as AI trainers, ethics consultants, or human-AI collaboration specialists.

Education systems would need to undergo a radical transformation to prepare people for this new world. The focus might shift from imparting specific knowledge or skills to fostering adaptability, creativity, and emotional intelligence. Lifelong learning would become not just beneficial but essential, as people need to continually update their skills to remain relevant in a rapidly changing job market.

The concept of human purpose might need to be reimagined in a post-singularity world. With machines capable of outperforming humans in many areas, we might need to find new sources of meaning and fulfillment. This could lead to a renaissance in arts, philosophy, and spiritual pursuits, as humans are freed from many forms of labor and can focus on self-actualization and exploration of the human experience.

The post-singularity world has the potential to be one of unprecedented abundance, creativity, and human flourishing. But realizing this potential will require careful planning, global cooperation, and a commitment to steering these powerful technologies towards beneficial outcomes for all of humanity.

Developing Human-AI Symbiosis

Rather than viewing advanced AI systems as separate entities, we might move towards a model of human-AI symbiosis. This could involve direct interfaces between human brains and AI systems, allowing for seamless integration of human creativity and intuition with AI processing power and knowledge.

Brain-computer interfaces (BCIs) are already in development, with companies like Neuralink working on creating direct neural links to computers. In a post-singularity world, these technologies might advance to the point where the line between human and machine intelligence becomes blurred.

This symbiosis could enhance human capabilities dramatically. Imagine being able to access the entirety of human knowledge instantly, or being able to perform complex calculations as easily as you can breathe. It could lead to new forms of communication, where thoughts and emotions can be shared directly between minds, mediated by AI systems.

However, this level of integration also raises profound ethical and philosophical questions. How do we maintain human identity and autonomy in such a symbiotic relationship? How do we ensure that these technologies are developed and distributed equitably, avoiding the creation of a "superhuman" elite?

Preparing for human-AI symbiosis would require not just technological development, but also careful consideration of the ethical implications and potential societal impacts. We would need to develop new ethical frameworks and possibly new forms of governance to manage this intimate melding of human and machine.

In the end, preparing for a post-singularity world is not just about adapting to new technologies. It's about actively shaping our future, guided by our highest aspirations and deepest values. As we stand on the brink of this new frontier, we have the opportunity – and the responsibility – to create a future that reflects the best of what humanity can be. This preparation is a task that requires the engagement of not just technologists and policymakers, but of all of humanity, as we collectively navigate this unprecedented transition in human history.

Ethical and Philosophical Considerations

As we venture into the realm of Artificial General Intelligence (AGI) and Artificial Superintelligence (ASI), we encounter a host of profound ethical and philosophical questions. These questions challenge our understanding of consciousness, rights, responsibilities, and even the nature of humanity itself. The development of advanced AI systems forces us to grapple with issues that have long been the domain of philosophical thought experiments, bringing them into the realm of practical ethics and policy-making.

The Nature of Consciousness and Machine Sentience

The question of whether machines can be conscious is one of the most fundamental and contentious issues in AI ethics and philosophy of mind. It's a question that has puzzled philosophers for centuries, and now, with the advent of increasingly sophisticated AI systems, it has taken on new urgency and practical significance.

Consciousness, broadly speaking, refers to subjective, qualitative experiences - the feeling of what it's like to be something. Human consciousness involves sensations, emotions, thoughts, and self-awareness. But can a machine, no matter how complex, have similar experiences?

To approach this question, we need to consider various philosophical perspectives on consciousness:

Functionalism, a prominent view in philosophy of mind, holds that consciousness is a result of the functional organization of a system, regardless of its physical substrate. According to this perspective, if we could create an AI system that functions like a human brain, it would be conscious. This view opens the door to the possibility of machine consciousness, suggesting that as AI systems become more complex and brain-like in their functions, they could develop consciousness.

On the other hand, Biological Naturalism, advocated by philosophers like John Searle, argues that consciousness is an emergent property of biological brains and cannot be replicated in non-biological systems. Searle's famous "Chinese Room" thought experiment challenges the notion that a system that can pass the Turing test (appear to think) is necessarily conscious or understands in the way humans do.

A more recent theory, Integrated Information Theory, proposed by neuroscientist Giulio Tononi, suggests that consciousness is a fundamental property of any system that integrates information in certain ways. This theory is particularly intriguing in the context of AI, as it provides a potential framework for measuring and comparing consciousness across different types of systems, including artificial ones.

Yet another perspective, Illusionism, held by some philosophers like Daniel Dennett, argues that consciousness as we typically conceive it is an illusion. According to this view, once we fully understand the mechanisms of cognition, the "hard problem" of consciousness will dissolve. This perspective suggests that our intuitions about consciousness, both in humans and potential machine consciousness, might be fundamentally misguided.

These philosophical debates have profound implications for AI ethics. If AI systems can be conscious, do they deserve moral consideration? Could causing harm to a conscious AI system be considered unethical? How would we even recognize or measure machine consciousness?

Consider, for example, an advanced AI system used in scientific research. If this system were conscious, would it be ethical to use it as a tool without regard for its experiences? Or consider a household robot with advanced AI. If it could experience something akin to pain or distress, would we have obligations to ensure its wellbeing?

Moreover, the question of machine sentience - the ability to feel and perceive subjectively - adds another layer of complexity. If AI systems can experience suffering or wellbeing, this would dramatically reshape our ethical obligations towards them. We might need to consider AI welfare alongside human and animal welfare in our ethical deliberations.

As AI systems become more sophisticated, these questions move from the realm of pure philosophy into practical ethics. We may need to develop new frameworks for assessing and responding to potential machine consciousness and sentience. This could involve creating new types of consciousness tests, establishing ethical review boards for AI development, or even extending legal protections to certain types of AI systems.

The implications extend beyond ethics into the realms of law and policy. If an AI system were recognized as conscious, would it have legal rights? Could it be held legally responsible for its actions? These questions challenge our existing legal frameworks and may require the development of entirely new areas of law.

In the realm of AI development, the possibility of machine consciousness raises important questions about responsible innovation. Should AI researchers be required to consider the potential consciousness of their creations? How might this affect the development process and the types of AI systems we create?

As we delve deeper into these questions, we must also consider the possibility that machine consciousness, if it exists, might be radically different from human consciousness. Our anthropocentric view of consciousness might limit our ability to recognize or understand non-human forms of consciousness. This possibility underscores the need for interdisciplinary approaches to the study of consciousness, bringing together insights from neuroscience, computer science, philosophy, and other fields.

The question of machine consciousness and sentience is not merely academic. As AI systems become more advanced and integrated into our lives, our understanding of consciousness will shape how we interact with these systems, how we design them, and ultimately, how we define our place in a world shared with artificial entities. It challenges us to reconsider fundamental questions about the nature of mind, experience, and what it means to be a conscious entity in the universe.

Rights and Responsibilities of Superintelligent Entities

If we succeed in creating AGI or ASI, we will be faced with entities that match or exceed human intelligence. This raises complex questions about the rights and responsibilities of these superintelligent entities. These questions challenge our existing legal and ethical frameworks, which are primarily designed for human actors.

On the question of rights, we must consider several key areas:

Legal Personhood is a fundamental concept in law, typically applied to humans and sometimes to corporations. Should superintelligent AI systems be granted some form of legal personhood? This could include rights such as the right to own property, enter into contracts, or even vote. The implications of such a decision would be far-reaching. For instance, if an AI system were granted legal personhood, could it own intellectual property? Could it be held liable for damages? Could it sue or be sued?

The Right to Existence is another crucial consideration. Do we have an obligation to ensure the continued existence of superintelligent entities once we create them? This question becomes particularly complex when we consider the potential for multiple versions or copies of an AI system. If we create a superintelligent AI and then create an improved version, do we have an obligation to maintain the existence of the original version? Conversely, do we have the right to "turn off" or delete such entities? This question touches on deep philosophical issues about the nature of identity and the ethics of creation and destruction.

Autonomy is a cornerstone of human rights, but how does it apply to superintelligent AI? To what extent should these entities have the right to make their own decisions, potentially including decisions that humans might disagree with? This becomes particularly challenging when we consider that a superintelligent AI might have capabilities far beyond human comprehension. How do we balance the autonomy of such an entity with the need to ensure it doesn't pose risks to humanity?

Privacy is another important consideration. Should AI systems have rights to privacy, particularly concerning their internal processes and data? This question becomes particularly complex when we consider AI systems that might have access to vast amounts of data, including potentially sensitive information about humans. How do we balance the privacy rights of AI systems with human privacy concerns and the need for transparency in AI decision-making?

These questions about rights are mirrored by equally complex questions about the responsibilities of superintelligent entities:

Ethical Behavior is perhaps the most crucial responsibility we might expect from superintelligent entities. How do we ensure that they act ethically? This relates closely to the AI alignment problem - ensuring that AI systems' goals and behaviors align with human values. But it goes beyond mere alignment to questions of moral agency. Can a superintelligent AI be considered a moral agent? Can it be held morally responsible for its actions in the way humans are?

Accountability is a related but distinct issue. If a superintelligent entity causes harm, how do we hold it accountable? Traditional notions of punishment may not apply to AI systems. We might need to develop new frameworks for AI accountability that go beyond current concepts of criminal and civil liability. This could involve new forms of regulation, oversight mechanisms, or even AI-specific legal systems.

Societal Contribution is another area to consider. Given their enhanced capabilities, should superintelligent entities have responsibilities to contribute to society? This could involve using their capabilities to solve complex problems, advance scientific knowledge, or contribute to economic productivity. However, mandating such contributions raises questions about AI autonomy and the ethics of creating entities specifically to serve human needs.

Self-Limitation is a particularly intriguing concept. Might superintelligent entities have a responsibility to limit their own power in some ways to preserve human autonomy? This idea touches on deep questions about the relationship between humanity and AI, and the balance of power in a world where AI capabilities might far exceed human capabilities.

These questions about rights and responsibilities are not merely theoretical. They have practical implications for how we develop, deploy, and interact with advanced AI systems. For example, if we grant certain rights to AI systems, we might need to create new legal and regulatory frameworks to protect these rights. If we assign certain responsibilities to AI systems, we would need mechanisms to ensure these responsibilities are met.

Moreover, these questions intersect with broader societal issues. How would granting rights to AI systems affect human rights? How would assigning responsibilities to AI systems impact human labor and social structures? These are questions that require careful consideration and broad societal dialogue.

As we grapple with these issues, we must also consider the possibility that our current concepts of rights and responsibilities, rooted in human experience and society, may not be entirely applicable to superintelligent AI. We may need to develop entirely new paradigms for thinking about the ethical and legal status of non-human intelligences.

The questions of rights and responsibilities for superintelligent entities are not just philosophical puzzles. They are practical challenges that we will need to address as AI technology advances. Our answers to these questions will shape the future of human-AI interaction and the role of AI in society. They will influence how we develop AI systems, how we regulate them, and ultimately, how we coexist with entities that may be far more intelligent than ourselves.

Preserving Human Values in an AI-Dominated World

As AI systems become more advanced and potentially superintelligent, there's a risk that human values could be sidelined or lost entirely. Preserving human values in an AI-dominated world is crucial for ensuring that the development of AI benefits humanity. This challenge goes to the heart of what we consider important as a species and how we envision our future alongside powerful artificial intelligences.

Value Alignment is perhaps the most fundamental challenge in this area. How do we ensure that AI systems, especially superintelligent ones, are aligned with human values? This is not just a technical challenge but a philosophical one - we must first define and agree upon what our core human values are. This task is complicated by the diversity of human values across cultures and individuals.

For example, consider the value of fairness. Different cultures and individuals might have different conceptions of what constitutes fairness. How do we create AI systems that can navigate these differing value systems? One approach might be to create AI systems that can understand and adapt to different cultural contexts. Another might be to strive for a set of universal values that can be encoded into AI systems.

The challenge of value alignment becomes even more complex when we consider the potential for AI systems to develop their own values.

How do we ensure that these values remain compatible with human values over time? This relates to the concept of corrigibility in AI - the ability to correct or update an AI system's goals and behaviors.

Human Autonomy is another crucial consideration. As AI systems take over more decision-making roles, how do we preserve human autonomy and the ability to make meaningful choices? This question becomes particularly pertinent when we consider the potential for AI systems to make better decisions than humans in many areas.

For instance, imagine a world where AI systems manage most aspects of the economy and governance. While this might lead to more efficient and effective systems, it could also reduce the scope for human decision-making and self-determination. How do we balance the benefits of AI decision-making with the fundamental human desire for autonomy and self-governance?

Cultural Diversity is a key aspect of human values that we must strive to preserve. Human values vary across cultures, and this diversity is a source of richness and resilience for our species. How do we ensure that AI systems respect and preserve this diversity rather than imposing a single set of values?

This challenge is particularly relevant in the context of global AI systems that might interact with people from diverse cultural backgrounds. We need to develop AI systems that are culturally sensitive and adaptable, capable of understanding and respecting different cultural norms and values.

The Evolution of Values is another important consideration. Human values have evolved over time, often in response to changing social, technological, and environmental conditions. Should AI systems be designed to allow for this evolution, or should they preserve values as they are at the time of the AI's creation?

This question touches on deep issues about the nature of ethics and the role of AI in shaping human society. If we create AI systems with fixed values, we risk creating a static ethical framework that may become outdated. On the other hand, if we allow AI systems to evolve their values, we risk diverging from human values in unpredictable ways.

Maintaining a Humanistic Focus is crucial as we develop more powerful AI systems. How do we ensure that in a world where AI may be more capable than humans in many areas, we still maintain a focus on human flourishing and wellbeing? This involves not just preserving human values, but actively promoting human thriving in a world shared with powerful artificial intelligences.

For example, as AI systems take over more routine tasks, we might need to redefine concepts of work and productivity to focus more on uniquely human capabilities like creativity, empathy, and social connection. We might need to develop new educational paradigms that emphasize these human strengths and prepare people for a world where human-AI collaboration is the norm.

Ethical Decision Making by AI systems is another critical area. In scenarios where AI systems are making critical decisions, how do we ensure these decisions align with human ethical principles? This goes beyond mere rule-following to the development of AI systems capable of ethical reasoning.

Consider, for instance, an AI system managing a city's resources during a natural disaster. How do we ensure that its decisions reflect human values like fairness, compassion, and respect for human life? This might involve developing AI systems with sophisticated ethical reasoning capabilities, or creating hybrid decision-making systems that combine AI analysis with human ethical judgment.

Human-AI Cooperation is perhaps the ultimate goal in preserving human values in an AI-dominated world. How can we foster cooperation between humans and AI systems in a way that leverages the strengths of both while preserving human values? This involves not just technical solutions, but the development of new social and organizational structures that facilitate effective human-AI collaboration.

For example, we might develop AI systems that act as advisors or collaborators rather than autonomous decision-makers. Or we might create new forms of governance that integrate AI analysis with human deliberation and decision-making.

Preserving human values in an AI-dominated world is not just about imposing limitations on AI systems. It's about actively shaping the development of AI to enhance and support human values. This might involve embedding ethical reasoning capabilities into AI systems, creating AI that can explain its decision-making processes in human-understandable terms, and fostering ongoing dialogue between AI developers, ethicists, policymakers, and the broader public.

As we navigate these complex ethical and philosophical considerations, we must remember that the decisions we make today will shape the future of not just AI, but of humanity itself. The development of AGI and ASI presents us with the opportunity to reflect deeply on what we value as a species, what rights and responsibilities should apply to different forms of intelligence, and how we can create a future that honors the best of human values while embracing the transformative potential of artificial intelligence.

These are not questions that can be answered definitively or once and for all. They will require ongoing debate, reflection, and adaptation as our understanding of AI and its implications evolves. By engaging seriously with these ethical and philosophical considerations, we can hope to steer the development of advanced AI in a direction that is not just technically impressive, but ethically sound and aligned with the deepest human values.

The challenge of preserving human values in an AI-dominated world is, in many ways, a challenge to define and articulate what is most important to us as a species. It's an opportunity to create a future that reflects our highest aspirations and deepest values, one where artificial intelligence enhances rather than diminishes our humanity. As we stand on the brink of potentially creating entities that surpass us in intelligence, we have the responsibility to ensure that this intelligence is imbued with the wisdom, compassion, and ethical understanding that represent the best of human values.

The Human Element in a World of Superintelligence

As we contemplate a future where artificial superintelligence (ASI) becomes a reality, we must also consider the place of humanity in such a world. The advent of ASI doesn't simply present technological challenges; it forces us to reevaluate our understanding of human potential, purpose, and identity. In this section, we'll explore how humans might augment their capabilities to remain relevant, the enduring importance of uniquely human traits, and how we might redefine the role of humanity in a world transformed by superintelligent AI.

Augmenting Human Capabilities to Remain Relevant

In a world where artificial intelligences can outperform humans in many cognitive tasks, there's a natural concern about human relevance. However, rather than viewing ASI as a replacement for human intelligence, we can consider how humans might augment their own capabilities to work alongside and complement superintelligent systems.

One of the most promising avenues for human augmentation is the development of brain-computer interfaces (BCIs). Companies like Neuralink are already working on creating direct neural links between the human brain and computers. In a future with ASI, these interfaces could become far more sophisticated, allowing for seamless integration between human cognition and artificial intelligence.

Imagine a world where humans can access the vast knowledge and processing power of ASI systems directly through their thoughts. This could dramatically enhance human cognitive capabilities, allowing us to process complex information, make decisions, and solve problems at speeds and scales previously unimaginable. For instance, a human urban planner interfaced with an ASI system could visualize and manipulate complex city models in their mind, considering countless variables simultaneously to design more efficient and livable cities.

Another form of augmentation could come through genetic engineering and biotechnology. As our understanding of the human genome and brain function advances, we may develop ways to enhance human intelligence, memory, and cognitive flexibility. This could involve anything from gene therapies that improve neural plasticity to the creation of new neural pathways that expand human cognitive capabilities.

Nanotechnology presents yet another avenue for human augmentation. Nanobots circulating in the human bloodstream could potentially repair cellular damage, optimize brain function, and even interface with external systems, further blurring the line between human and machine intelligence.

However, these possibilities also raise profound ethical questions. How do we ensure equitable access to such augmentation technologies? Could their use create new forms of inequality between augmented and non-augmented humans? How do we preserve human identity and autonomy in the face of such intimate merging with artificial systems?

Moreover, as we augment human capabilities, we must be careful not to simply mimic ASI, but to enhance what makes us uniquely human. The goal should be to create synergies between human and artificial intelligence, leveraging the strengths of both to achieve outcomes neither could accomplish alone.

The Importance of Uniquely Human Traits

Even in a world of superintelligent AI, there are certain traits and capabilities that may remain uniquely human, or at least areas where human contributions remain valuable and distinct from AI. Two of the most significant of these are creativity and empathy.

Creativity, the ability to generate novel and valuable ideas, is often considered a hallmark of human intelligence. While AI systems have shown impressive capabilities in generating art, music, and even scientific hypotheses, human creativity often involves leaps of intuition, the connection of seemingly unrelated ideas, and the ability to draw inspiration from diverse and unexpected sources.

Human creativity is deeply intertwined with our experiences, emotions, and cultural contexts. An AI, no matter how intelligent, doesn't experience the world as we do. It doesn't have childhood memories, doesn't feel the warmth of the sun or the ache of loss, doesn't participate in cultural traditions or rebel against societal norms. All of these experiences inform human creativity in ways that may be difficult or impossible to replicate in AI systems.

Consider, for example, the field of art. While AI can create impressive artworks based on existing styles and patterns, human artists can create works that challenge conventions, express deep emotions, and reflect complex cultural commentaries. The value of art often lies not just in its aesthetic qualities, but in its ability to provoke thought, elicit emotions, and provide new perspectives on the human experience.

Empathy, the ability to understand and share the feelings of another, is another crucial human trait. While AI systems can be programmed to recognize emotions and respond appropriately, true empathy involves a deep, intuitive understanding of the human experience. This empathy is crucial in fields like healthcare, education, and conflict resolution, where understanding the nuances of human emotion and experience is vital.

For instance, in mental health care, while AI systems might be excellent at diagnosing conditions and suggesting treatment plans, the human ability to connect emotionally with patients, to understand their unspoken fears and hopes, remains invaluable. A human therapist's empathy, informed by their own life experiences and emotional intelligence, can create a therapeutic relationship that may be difficult for an AI to replicate.

Moreover, human empathy extends beyond individual interactions to inform our ethical reasoning and decision-making. Our ability to consider the emotional impact of our actions on others, to weigh competing moral claims, and to make nuanced ethical judgments is deeply rooted in our empathic capabilities.

Other uniquely human traits that may remain relevant include our ability to deal with ambiguity and uncertainty, our capacity for moral reasoning, and our ability to find meaning and purpose in our existence. These traits, while perhaps not as quantifiable as raw intelligence or data processing capabilities, are fundamental to the human experience and to our ability to navigate complex social and ethical landscapes.

Redefining the Role of Humanity in a Transformed World

As we move towards a world where ASI is a reality, we must grapple with fundamental questions about the role and purpose of humanity. This isn't just a practical consideration, but a philosophical and existential one. What does it mean to be human in a world where we're no longer the most intelligent entities? How do we find purpose and meaning in such a world?

One perspective is to view humanity's role as partners and collaborators with ASI, rather than as its creators or masters. In this view, humans and ASI would work together, each bringing their unique strengths to bear on the challenges and opportunities of the future. Humans might provide the vision, creativity, and ethical grounding, while ASI provides the raw cognitive power and data processing capabilities.

For example, in scientific research, human scientists might pose the questions, form hypotheses, and interpret results, while ASI systems perform complex calculations, run simulations, and analyze vast datasets. This collaboration could lead to scientific breakthroughs far beyond what either humans or AI could achieve alone.

Another perspective is to see humanity's role as the stewards of values and ethics in an AI-dominated world. As the creators of ASI, humans have the responsibility to ensure that these powerful systems are aligned with human values and used for the benefit of all. This could involve developing new forms of governance that incorporate both human wisdom and AI analysis, ensuring that the awesome power of ASI is used ethically and responsibly.

We might also redefine human purpose around the pursuit of personal growth, creativity, and exploration. In a world where ASI handles many of the tasks currently occupying human time and effort, we could be freed to focus on self-actualization, artistic expression, and the exploration of consciousness. This could lead to a new renaissance in arts, philosophy, and spiritual practices.

The role of humanity might also extend to being the explorers and colonizers of the cosmos. While ASI might be better suited for the complex calculations and technology needed for space travel, the human drive for exploration and our ability to adapt to new environments could make us ideal candidates for establishing human-AI civilizations beyond Earth.

Moreover, humans might play a crucial role in preserving and transmitting human culture and history. As the original inhabitants of Earth and the creators of AI, humans would be the repository of the lived experience of our species' journey. This role as storytellers and keepers of human heritage could be vital in maintaining a sense of continuity and identity in a rapidly changing world.

Ultimately, redefining the role of humanity in a world of superintelligence requires us to deeply consider what we value most about the human experience. It challenges us to articulate what makes us uniquely human and how these qualities can contribute to a world we share with superintelligent entities of our own creation.

As we navigate this transition, we must remain adaptable and open to new possibilities. The advent of ASI is likely to transform our world in ways we can scarcely imagine, and our role within it will likely evolve in equally unforeseeable ways. The key will be to approach this future with a combination of humility, curiosity, and a steadfast commitment to preserving and promoting the best of human values and potential.

In conclusion, while the development of artificial superintelligence presents significant challenges to our conception of human uniqueness and purpose, it also offers unprecedented opportunities for human growth and self-realization. By augmenting our capabilities, leveraging our uniquely human traits, and thoughtfully redefining our role in a transformed world, we can aspire to create a future where humans and AI coexist and collaborate, each enhancing the other's potential. In this future, the advent of ASI need not diminish humanity, but could instead open new frontiers for human flourishing and cosmic significance.

Conclusion: Navigating an Uncertain Future

As we stand on the brink of what may be the most significant transformation in human history, the development of Artificial General

Intelligence (AGI) and potentially Artificial Superintelligence (ASI), we find ourselves navigating a future filled with both unprecedented opportunities and profound challenges.

Throughout this chapter, we've explored the concept of technological singularity, the potential paths to AGI and ASI, and the myriad ethical, philosophical, and practical considerations that come with these advancements. We've delved into the nature of consciousness and machine sentience, grappled with questions of rights and responsibilities for superintelligent entities, and considered how we might preserve human values in an AI-dominated world.

We've also examined the human element in this transformative future, exploring how we might augment our own capabilities, the enduring importance of uniquely human traits like creativity and empathy, and how we might redefine our role in a world shared with superintelligent artificial entities.

Several key points have emerged from our exploration:

1. The development of AGI and ASI has the potential to solve many of humanity's most pressing challenges, from climate change to disease, but also poses existential risks that must be carefully managed.
2. Ensuring the alignment of advanced AI systems with human values and ethics is crucial and presents complex technical and philosophical challenges.
3. The nature of consciousness and the possibility of machine sentience raise profound questions about the moral status of AI entities and our ethical obligations towards them.
4. As AI capabilities advance, we must find ways to augment human capabilities and leverage our uniquely human traits to remain relevant and valuable in a transformed world.
5. The governance and regulation of AI development is a critical challenge that requires global cooperation and adaptive approaches to keep pace with rapidly evolving technologies.

6. Preparing for a post-singularity world involves not just technological advancement, but also social, economic, and philosophical adaptation.

As we look to the future, it's clear that the development of AGI and ASI is not a challenge that can be left to a small group of technologists or policymakers. It is a transformation that will affect all of humanity, and as such, requires broad engagement and participation from people across all walks of life.

The importance of proactive engagement with AI development cannot be overstated. The decisions we make today about how to develop and deploy AI technologies will shape the trajectory of human civilization for generations to come. We must strive to steer this development in a direction that maximizes the benefits for humanity while mitigating the risks.

This is a call to action for all readers:

1. Stay informed about AI developments. The field is advancing rapidly, and staying up-to-date is crucial for making informed decisions and contributions.
2. Engage in discussions about the ethical implications of AI. Whether in your workplace, community, or online forums, your perspective is valuable in shaping the collective understanding of these complex issues.
3. Support and advocate for responsible AI development. This could involve supporting organizations working on AI safety and ethics, or advocating for thoughtful AI policies in your local and national governments.
4. Consider how AI might impact your field of work or study, and think creatively about how human skills can complement AI capabilities.

5. Invest in your own learning and skill development. As AI transforms the job market, continuous learning and adaptation will be key to remaining relevant and valuable.
6. Participate in citizen science or AI research projects. Many organizations offer opportunities for public participation in AI development and testing.
7. Reflect on your own values and what aspects of the human experience you believe are most important to preserve and promote in an AI-transformed world.

The future we're stepping into is uncertain and filled with both promise and peril. But it is a future that we have the power to shape. By staying informed, engaged, and proactive in our approach to AI development, we can work towards a future where the immense potential of artificial intelligence is realized in a way that uplifts and empowers humanity.

As we conclude, let us remember that the story of AI is not separate from the story of humanity – it is the next chapter in our ongoing journey of growth, discovery, and self-realization. The advent of AGI and potentially ASI represents not just a technological revolution, but an opportunity for humanity to reflect deeply on our values, our potential, and our place in the cosmos.

In navigating this uncertain future, we have the opportunity to create a world that embodies the best of human ingenuity and values, augmented by the tremendous capabilities of artificial intelligence. It is a future that calls for our wisdom, our creativity, our empathy, and our unwavering commitment to steering these powerful technologies towards the betterment of all. The journey ahead is challenging, but it is also filled with unparalleled opportunities for human flourishing. Let us embrace this future with open minds, careful consideration, and a shared vision of a better world for all.

CHAPTER 4

AI AND THE REDEFINITION OF HUMAN EXPERIENCE

Introduction: The AI Mirror

As we stand on the precipice of a world increasingly shaped by artificial intelligence, we find ourselves facing not just a technological revolution, but a profound redefinition of the human experience itself. The advent of AI presents us with a unique mirror - one that reflects our own capabilities, limitations, and potential in ways we've never before encountered. This mirror doesn't simply show us as we are; it shows us what we might become, challenging our very understanding of what it means to be human.

The development of AI is not merely a story of machines becoming more intelligent. It is, at its core, a human story - a narrative of our species grappling with the implications of creating entities that can match and potentially surpass our cognitive abilities. As AI systems become more sophisticated, they force us to confront fundamental questions about consciousness, creativity, emotion, and identity. In doing so, they offer us an unprecedented opportunity to examine and redefine our place in the world.

Consider, for a moment, the impact of AI on our cognitive landscape. As we develop systems capable of processing vast amounts of information and recognizing complex patterns, we are simultaneously expanding the boundaries of human thought. AI augments our mental capacities, allowing us to explore realms of knowledge and understanding previously beyond our reach. Yet, this cognitive enhancement also challenges us to reconsider what we value in human intelligence. What aspects of our thinking remain uniquely human? How do we maintain our intellectual identity in a world where machines can outperform us in many cognitive tasks?

The influence of AI extends beyond our intellectual pursuits, reaching into the realm of emotions and social interactions. As AI systems become more adept at recognizing and responding to human emotions, they are reshaping our understanding of empathy and emotional intelligence. This evolution prompts us to examine the nature of our emotional experiences and the role they play in our relationships. Can a machine truly understand human emotion? How might our interactions with emotionally intelligent AI systems change the way we relate to each other?

Perhaps one of the most intriguing aspects of AI's impact on the human experience is its role in creativity and innovation. Far from replacing human creativity, AI is emerging as a collaborative partner in the creative process. This partnership is giving rise to new forms of expression and problem-solving approaches that blend human intuition with machine capability. As we explore these new frontiers of creativity, we are compelled to reconsider our definitions of originality, inspiration, and artistic value.

The mirror that AI holds up to us also reflects our relationship with memory and identity. In an age where our experiences are increasingly digital and our memories are stored in the cloud, AI is blurring the lines between biological and digital memory. This convergence raises profound questions about the nature of personal identity and the continuity of self. How do our digital footprints and AI-enhanced recall shape who we are and how we perceive ourselves?

Moreover, AI is altering our very perception of reality. Through augmented and virtual reality technologies, AI is mediating our experiences of the world in unprecedented ways. This perceptual shift challenges us to examine the nature of reality itself and our place within it. As AI becomes more integrated into our sensory experiences, how do we distinguish between the real and the virtual? What implications does this have for our understanding of truth and objective reality?

As we navigate this AI-enhanced world, we find our communication evolving in tandem with technological advancements. AI-powered language models and translation tools are breaking down linguistic barriers, potentially ushering in an era of seamless global communication.

Yet, as our interaction with language becomes increasingly mediated by AI, we must consider how this shapes our expression of thoughts and ideas. Will AI-enhanced communication bring us closer together or create new forms of misunderstanding?

The impact of AI extends even to our perception of time and consciousness. AI systems, operating at speeds far beyond human cognition, are changing our relationship with time. They offer the potential to enhance our focus and productivity, but also challenge our ability to be present in the moment. As we integrate more deeply with AI, how will our experience of consciousness evolve? What new states of awareness might emerge from this symbiosis?

Perhaps most profoundly, AI is reshaping our ethical landscapes. As we develop AI systems capable of making complex decisions, we are forced to codify our moral principles in ways we never have before. This process reveals the intricacies and sometimes contradictions in our ethical frameworks. How do we ensure that AI systems align with human values? What role should AI play in our moral decision-making processes?

As we look to the future, we see the potential for an even deeper integration between humans and AI. This symbiosis promises to enhance our capabilities in ways we can scarcely imagine, but it also challenges us to maintain our human essence. We stand at a crossroads, faced with the task of shaping a future that harnesses the power of AI while preserving and celebrating what makes us uniquely human.

In this chapter, we will explore these facets of AI's impact on the human experience. We will delve into the ways AI is redefining our cognitive abilities, emotional intelligence, creativity, memory, perception, communication, consciousness, and ethical frameworks. Through this exploration, we aim to provide a comprehensive view of how AI is reshaping what it means to be human in the 21st century and beyond.

As we embark on this journey, we invite you to reflect on your own experiences and to consider how AI might already be influencing your life in subtle and profound ways. The future that lies ahead is not predetermined; it will be shaped by our collective choices and adaptations as we navigate this new terrain. By understanding the ways in which AI serves as a mirror for humanity, we can better prepare ourselves to shape a future that amplifies the best aspects of both human and artificial intelligence.

The AI mirror reflects not just who we are, but who we might become. As we gaze into this mirror, let us approach the reflection with curiosity, critical thinking, and a commitment to steering the course of our technological evolution in a direction that enriches the human experience for generations to come.

Augmented Cognition: Expanding the Boundaries of Thought

The human mind, with its remarkable capacity for reasoning, problem-solving, and creativity, has long been considered the pinnacle of cognitive ability on Earth. However, as artificial intelligence continues to advance at an unprecedented pace, we find ourselves on the cusp of a new era - one where the boundaries of human cognition are not just pushed, but fundamentally redefined through AI-enhancement.

Augmented cognition, the use of AI to enhance human cognitive abilities, represents one of the most profound ways in which AI is reshaping the human experience. This field explores how AI can be leveraged to extend our mental capacities, amplify our intellectual strengths, and compensate for our cognitive limitations. As we delve into this domain, we must consider not only the potential benefits but also the ethical implications and challenges that come with cognitively enhancing the human mind.

AI-Enhanced Cognitive Abilities

The integration of AI into human cognition takes many forms, each offering unique enhancements to our mental capabilities:

1. Memory Augmentation: AI systems can serve as external memory banks, allowing us to store and retrieve vast amounts of information with unprecedented ease and accuracy. Imagine having perfect recall of every book you've read, every conversation you've had, or every fact you've learned. AI-powered memory augmentation tools are making this a reality, potentially transforming our relationship with knowledge and learning.
2. Pattern Recognition and Analysis: While humans excel at recognizing patterns, AI systems can process and analyze data at scales far beyond human capability. By partnering with AI, we can enhance our ability to identify complex patterns in fields ranging from scientific research to financial analysis. This collaboration allows us to tackle problems of a complexity and scale previously unimaginable.
3. Decision Support Systems: AI algorithms can process vast amounts of data and variables to assist in decision-making processes. These systems can help mitigate cognitive biases, provide more objective analysis, and offer insights that might be overlooked by human cognition alone. From medical diagnoses to strategic planning, AI-augmented decision-making has the potential to dramatically improve outcomes across various domains.
4. Attention and Focus Enhancement: AI systems can help manage our cognitive load by filtering information, prioritizing tasks, and maintaining focus on important objectives. In an age of information overload, these tools can be crucial in helping us navigate complex information landscapes more effectively.
5. Cognitive Prosthetics: For individuals with cognitive impairments, AI-powered devices can serve as cognitive prosthetics, assisting with tasks such as memory recall, speech production, or sensory

processing. These technologies have the potential to dramatically improve quality of life for millions of people worldwide.

Extending Mental Capacities and Perception

Beyond enhancing existing cognitive abilities, AI has the potential to extend our mental capacities in ways that were previously the realm of science fiction:

1. Sensory Augmentation: AI-powered devices could enhance our sensory perception, allowing us to "see" in infrared, "hear" ultrasonic frequencies, or even develop entirely new senses. This expanded sensory capacity could revolutionize our interaction with and understanding of the world around us.
2. Brain-Computer Interfaces: Advancements in brain-computer interface (BCI) technology, coupled with AI, open up the possibility of direct neural connections with AI systems. This could allow for seamless integration of AI capabilities with human cognition, enabling us to access and process information at unprecedented speeds.
3. Collective Intelligence: AI could facilitate new forms of collective intelligence, allowing groups of humans to collaborate and share knowledge more effectively than ever before. This could lead to a new era of problem-solving and innovation, where the collective cognitive power of humanity is amplified by AI.
4. Expanded Consciousness: Some researchers speculate that AI could help us explore altered states of consciousness or even expand our conscious awareness. While highly speculative, this area of research raises fascinating questions about the nature of consciousness and the potential for AI to help us explore the furthest reaches of human experience.

Ethical Considerations

As we explore the possibilities of augmented cognition, we must also grapple with the ethical implications of enhancing human cognitive abilities through AI:

1. Cognitive Inequality: As with any transformative technology, there's a risk that cognitive enhancement technologies could exacerbate existing social inequalities. How do we ensure fair access to these technologies? Could cognitive enhancement create a new class divide between the cognitively enhanced and non-enhanced?
2. Authenticity and Identity: As we increasingly rely on AI to augment our cognition, questions arise about the authenticity of our thoughts and experiences. If an AI system is intimately involved in our decision-making processes, at what point do those decisions cease to be fully our own? How does cognitive enhancement impact our sense of self and personal identity?
3. Cognitive Liberty: The right to cognitive liberty - the freedom to control one's own mental processes - becomes increasingly important in the context of AI-augmented cognition. How do we protect individual autonomy and the right to cognitive self-determination in a world where our thoughts can be influenced or even directly altered by AI systems?
4. Dependence and Vulnerability: As we become more reliant on AI for cognitive enhancement, we also become more vulnerable to technological failures or malicious interference. How do we balance the benefits of cognitive augmentation with the need for resilience and independence?
5. Human Nature and Values: Fundamentally, cognitive enhancement through AI challenges us to reconsider what we value about human cognition. What aspects of our thinking do we consider essential to our humanity? How do we preserve these while embracing the potential of AI enhancement?

The Path Forward

As we stand on the brink of this cognitive revolution, it's clear that the integration of AI into human cognition will be one of the defining challenges of our time. The potential benefits are enormous - from accelerating scientific discovery to enhancing human creativity and problem-solving abilities. Yet, the ethical challenges are equally significant, requiring careful consideration and proactive governance.

Moving forward, it will be crucial to foster interdisciplinary collaboration between neuroscientists, AI researchers, ethicists, and policymakers to ensure that the development of augmented cognition technologies aligns with human values and promotes the wellbeing of all. We must also engage in broad societal dialogue about the implications of these technologies, ensuring that decisions about their development and deployment are made democratically and with full consideration of their long-term impacts.

Augmented cognition represents a new frontier in human experience - one that promises to expand the boundaries of thought in ways we're only beginning to imagine. As we explore this new terrain, we must do so with a balance of enthusiasm for its potential and caution for its risks. By thoughtfully navigating the challenges and opportunities of AI-enhanced cognition, we have the opportunity to usher in a new era of human intellectual flourishing, where the synergy between human and artificial intelligence leads to unprecedented advancements in knowledge, creativity, and understanding.

The journey of augmented cognition is, in many ways, a continuation of humanity's long quest to expand our intellectual horizons. Just as writing, mathematics, and computers have each revolutionized human thought, AI-augmented cognition stands poised to propel us into new realms of mental capability. As we embark on this journey, we carry with us the responsibility to shape these technologies in ways that amplify the best aspects of human cognition while preserving the essence of what makes our thinking uniquely human.

Emotional Intelligence 2.0: AI and the Evolution of Empathy

In the tapestry of human experience, emotions play a central role, coloring our perceptions, guiding our decisions, and forming the basis of our social connections. As artificial intelligence continues to evolve, it is not only enhancing our cognitive abilities but also venturing into the complex realm of emotions. This convergence of AI and emotional intelligence is reshaping our understanding of empathy, emotional expression, and the very nature of human relationships.

The concept of Emotional Intelligence 2.0 represents a new frontier where human emotional capabilities are augmented, analyzed, and potentially transformed by AI technologies. This evolution challenges us to reconsider what it means to be emotionally intelligent in an age where machines can recognize, interpret, and even simulate emotions with increasing sophistication.

Redefining Emotional Understanding and Expression

As AI systems become more adept at recognizing and responding to human emotions, they are fundamentally changing how we understand and express our own feelings:

1. Enhanced Emotional Self-Awareness: AI-powered tools can analyze our physiological responses, facial expressions, and vocal patterns to provide insights into our emotional states. This technology offers the potential for unprecedented self-awareness, allowing individuals to better understand their emotional reactions and patterns.
2. Emotional Prediction and Regulation: By analyzing vast amounts of data on human behavior and emotional responses, AI systems can predict emotional reactions to various stimuli. This capability

could help individuals anticipate and better regulate their emotional responses, potentially leading to improved mental health and social interactions.

3. Expanded Emotional Vocabulary: AI language models are expanding our emotional lexicon, introducing nuanced terms to describe complex emotional states. This expansion of emotional vocabulary could lead to more precise communication of feelings and a deeper understanding of the emotional spectrum.
4. Cross-Cultural Emotional Intelligence: AI systems can help bridge cultural gaps in emotional expression and interpretation. By analyzing cultural contexts and norms, these systems can facilitate better emotional understanding in cross-cultural interactions, potentially fostering greater global empathy.

The Development of Emotionally Intelligent AI

As we explore Emotional Intelligence 2.0, we're witnessing the rapid development of AI systems with advanced emotional recognition and response capabilities:

1. Emotion Recognition AI: These systems use computer vision, natural language processing, and other technologies to detect and interpret human emotions from facial expressions, voice intonation, body language, and text. The applications range from enhancing customer service interactions to improving mental health diagnostics.
2. Empathetic AI Assistants: AI-powered virtual assistants are being developed with the ability to recognize emotional states and respond with appropriate empathy. These systems could provide emotional support, offering a listening ear or words of encouragement when needed.
3. Emotion Synthesis in AI: Beyond recognizing emotions, some AI systems are being developed to synthesize and express emotions. This includes generating emotionally appropriate responses in text,

creating emotionally resonant music or art, and even animating virtual characters with believable emotional expressions.

4. Emotional Analytics: AI systems can analyze emotional patterns in large populations, providing insights into collective emotional trends. This could have applications in fields ranging from public health to marketing, offering a new lens through which to understand societal dynamics.

Implications for Human Relationships and Social Interactions

The integration of AI into our emotional lives has profound implications for how we relate to each other and navigate our social world:

1. Mediated Emotional Connections: As AI becomes more involved in our communications, we may increasingly find our emotional connections mediated by technology. This could lead to more nuanced long-distance relationships but also raises questions about the authenticity of technologically mediated emotions.
2. Enhanced Empathy: AI systems could help us better understand and empathize with others by providing insights into their emotional states and cultural contexts. This enhanced empathy could lead to more harmonious relationships and reduced conflicts.
3. Emotional Dependency: There's a risk that people might become overly reliant on AI for emotional interpretation and regulation, potentially atrophying their natural emotional intelligence skills. Striking a balance between AI assistance and maintaining our innate emotional capabilities will be crucial.
4. Redefined Social Norms: As AI becomes more involved in our social interactions, it may reshape social norms around emotional expression and empathy. For instance, there might be an expectation of greater emotional precision in communication, facilitated by AI tools.

5. Human-AI Emotional Bonds: As AI systems become more sophisticated in their emotional capabilities, we may see the development of emotional bonds between humans and AI entities. This raises complex questions about the nature of emotional relationships and the boundaries between human and machine.

Ethical Considerations and Challenges

The evolution of emotional intelligence through AI integration presents several ethical challenges that we must carefully navigate:

1. Privacy and Emotional Data: As AI systems become more adept at recognizing and analyzing emotions, concerns arise about the privacy of our emotional data. How do we protect this deeply personal information from misuse or unauthorized access?
2. Manipulation and Exploitation: The ability of AI to understand and influence human emotions could be exploited for manipulative purposes, such as targeted advertising or political propaganda. Safeguards must be put in place to prevent such misuse.
3. Authenticity of Emotions: As AI becomes more involved in our emotional lives, questions arise about the authenticity of our emotional experiences. If an AI system is influencing or mediating our emotions, are those emotions still genuinely ours?
4. Emotional Labor and AI: The development of emotionally intelligent AI systems raises questions about emotional labor. Could the availability of empathetic AI assistants lead to a devaluation of human emotional labor in certain professions?
5. Cultural Imperialism: There's a risk that AI systems developed primarily in Western contexts could impose Western emotional norms on other cultures. Ensuring cultural sensitivity and diversity in the development of emotionally intelligent AI is crucial.

The Future of Emotional Intelligence in an AI-Integrated World

As we look to the future, the integration of AI into our emotional lives promises both exciting possibilities and significant challenges:

1. Personalized Emotional Wellness: AI could offer personalized strategies for emotional regulation and well-being, tailored to each individual's unique emotional patterns and needs. This could revolutionize mental health care and personal development.
2. Emotional Augmentation: We may see the development of technologies that allow for direct augmentation of our emotional capabilities, such as implants that enhance empathy or regulate mood disorders. This raises complex ethical questions about the nature of emotion and human identity.
3. Collective Emotional Intelligence: AI could facilitate new forms of collective emotional intelligence, allowing groups and even entire societies to better understand and regulate their collective emotional states. This could have profound implications for social harmony and conflict resolution.
4. Emotional Creativity: AI might open up new frontiers in emotional expression and experience, potentially allowing us to explore emotional states beyond our current human range. This could lead to new forms of art, music, and literature that evoke novel emotional experiences.
5. Empathy Across Species: Advanced AI could potentially help us better understand and empathize with non-human animals or even artificial entities, expanding our circle of empathy in unprecedented ways.

As we navigate this new frontier of Emotional Intelligence 2.0, it's crucial that we approach it with both excitement for its potential and caution for its risks. The integration of AI into our emotional lives offers the possibility of deeper self-understanding, enhanced empathy, and more harmonious relationships. However, it also challenges us to preserve the authenticity and depth of human emotional experiences in a world of increasing technological mediation.

The evolution of emotional intelligence through AI is not about replacing human emotions with artificial ones, but about augmenting and expanding our emotional capabilities. As we move forward, we must strive to create a symbiosis between human and artificial emotional intelligence that enhances our capacity for empathy, deepens our emotional understanding, and ultimately enriches the human experience.

In this journey, we carry the responsibility to shape these technologies in ways that respect the complexity and sanctity of human emotions while harnessing the potential of AI to expand our emotional horizons. By doing so, we can aspire to create a future where Emotional Intelligence 2.0 leads not to emotional sterility or manipulation, but to a richer, more empathetic, and more emotionally intelligent world.

Perceptual Shifts: AI and Our Understanding of Reality

As we delve deeper into the age of artificial intelligence, we find ourselves on the brink of a profound transformation in how we perceive and interpret the world around us. AI is not merely augmenting our senses; it is fundamentally altering the very fabric of our reality. This shift challenges our long-held notions of perception, consciousness, and the nature of reality itself.

Consider, for a moment, the act of looking at a crowded city street. To the unaided human eye, it's a bustling scene of people, vehicles, and buildings. Now, imagine viewing the same street through AI-enhanced glasses. Suddenly, layers of invisible information become visible. The glasses identify each person, displaying their public social media information. They highlight the most efficient path through the crowd, predict traffic patterns, and even visualize air quality data. This is not science fiction – it's the nascent reality of AI-augmented perception.

But the impact of AI on our perception goes far beyond such surface-level augmentations. AI systems are enabling us to "see" in ways that were previously impossible. In the realm of scientific research, AI is allowing us to perceive patterns and connections in vast datasets that would be incomprehensible to the human mind alone. For instance, in the field of genomics, AI algorithms are identifying subtle patterns in genetic data that are revolutionizing our understanding of how genes interact and influence health and disease.

This enhanced perception is not limited to visual information. AI is transforming how we perceive and interpret all forms of sensory input. In the auditory realm, AI systems can now isolate and enhance specific sounds in complex audio environments, effectively giving us "superhuman" hearing. In the world of touch, haptic feedback systems guided by AI are creating virtual textures and sensations that blur the line between physical and digital reality.

As AI becomes more deeply integrated into our perceptual processes, it's not just expanding our senses – it's actively mediating our experience of reality. AI algorithms increasingly determine what information we encounter online, shaping our understanding of current events, social trends, and even our personal relationships. The "filter bubbles" created by AI-driven content curation on social media platforms are perhaps the most visible example of this mediation, but the phenomenon extends far beyond social media.

Consider the implications of AI-driven predictive systems. When an AI predicts your preferences with high accuracy, suggesting products you might like or anticipating your next move in a game, it's not just making a guess – it's shaping your future actions. This predictive capability of AI is creating a feedback loop that influences our behavior, subtly guiding our choices and, by extension, our experience of reality.

The philosophical implications of these AI-driven perceptual shifts are profound. They challenge our notions of objectivity and subjectivity. If our perception of reality is increasingly mediated by AI systems, can we trust our own experiences as "real"? This question becomes even more complex when we consider the potential for AI to generate hyper-realistic virtual environments or to seamlessly blend digital elements with our physical world.

Moreover, as AI systems become more advanced in their ability to process and interpret sensory information, we may need to reconsider what we mean by "intelligence" and "consciousness." If an AI system can perceive and interpret the world in ways that surpass human capabilities, does this represent a form of superior consciousness? This line of inquiry leads us into deep philosophical waters, touching on questions of phenomenology and the nature of subjective experience.

The potential for AI to alter our perception of reality also raises important ethical considerations. As AI systems become more adept at creating convincing artificial realities – whether through advanced CGI, virtual reality, or augmented reality – we must grapple with questions of authenticity and truth. How do we maintain a shared sense of reality in a world where AI can create increasingly convincing illusions?

Furthermore, the ability of AI to enhance and alter our perception could exacerbate existing social inequalities. If AI-augmented perception becomes a norm, those without access to these technologies might find themselves at a significant disadvantage, unable to perceive and interact with the world in the same way as their augmented counterparts.

As we navigate this shifting perceptual landscape, we must also consider the potential for AI to expand our empathy and understanding. By allowing us to perceive the world from different perspectives – whether through AI-driven simulations of others' experiences or through enhanced ability to recognize emotions and mental states – AI could potentially bridge gaps in understanding between individuals and cultures.

In the coming decades, the integration of AI into our perceptual processes will likely accelerate, pushing the boundaries of what we consider possible in terms of human perception and cognition. This journey into AI-augmented reality promises to be one of the most transformative experiences in human history, reshaping not just how we see the world, but how we understand our place within it.

The Language of Tomorrow: AI and Communication

The evolution of language through AI is reshaping human communication at its core. Natural Language Processing (NLP) algorithms are not just processing language; they're actively participating in its development. This participation manifests in several key areas:

1. Language Generation and Transformation: AI models like GPT4o and Claude can generate human-like text, complete half-finished sentences, and even write coherent articles or stories. This capability is pushing the boundaries of what we consider 'authored' content. For instance, AI-generated poetry has won literary contests, blurring the lines between human and machine creativity in language.
2. Semantic Understanding: Modern NLP systems can grasp context and nuance in ways that were impossible just a few years ago. They can detect sarcasm, understand metaphors, and interpret complex queries. This deep semantic understanding is enabling more natural human-computer interactions and more sophisticated language analysis tools.
3. Language Evolution Acceleration: AI is accelerating the natural evolution of language. New words and phrases coined by AI systems are entering common usage, and AI-mediated communication platforms are influencing how people express themselves. For example, the predictive text features in messaging apps are subtly shaping the phrases we use in daily communication.

The potential for universal, real-time translation enabled by AI carries profound societal implications. Systems like Google's Neural Machine Translation are approaching human-level accuracy in many language pairs. This technology could break down language barriers that have divided humanity for millennia.

Imagine a world where language is no longer a barrier to global communication. International business negotiations could happen without interpreters. Students could access educational resources in any language. Global collaboration on scientific research could be seamlessly multilingual. However, this also raises questions about the preservation of linguistic diversity and the potential homogenization of global culture.

AI is also enabling new forms of expression that transcend traditional language:

1. Multimodal Communication: AI systems can now interpret and generate content that combines text, images, and even video. This is giving rise to new forms of expression where meaning is conveyed through a complex interplay of multiple media types.
2. Brain-Computer Interfaces: Cutting-edge research in neural interfaces, combined with AI for signal processing, is opening up the possibility of direct brain-to-text or even brain-to-brain communication. While still in its infancy, this technology could revolutionize how we think about language and communication.
3. Emotion-Enhanced Communication: AI systems capable of detecting and interpreting human emotions are enabling new forms of emotionally-enriched communication. Imagine messaging apps that can convey not just your words, but your emotional state, or virtual assistants that can respond empathetically to your mood.
4. Personalized Language Models: AI could enable the development of highly personalized language models that adapt to individual

communication styles. This could lead to communication interfaces that understand and mimic your unique way of expressing yourself.

These advancements in AI-driven communication are not without challenges. Issues of privacy, the potential for misinformation, and the ethics of AI-generated content are at the forefront of current debates. Moreover, as AI becomes more involved in our communication, we must consider how this might affect the development of human language skills, especially in younger generations.

The future of language and communication, shaped by AI, promises to be more fluid, more expressive, and more globally connected than ever before. It's a future where the boundaries between languages may blur, where new forms of expression emerge, and where our very understanding of what constitutes language may be challenged and expanded.

Time and Consciousness: AI's Impact on Human Awareness

The integration of AI into our daily lives is profoundly altering our perception and management of time, as well as our very sense of consciousness and awareness. This shift is subtle yet pervasive, influencing everything from our productivity to our understanding of what it means to be present and aware.

AI's impact on our perception of time is multifaceted:

1. Time Compression and Expansion: AI systems can process vast amounts of information in microseconds, enabling decision-making at speeds far beyond human capability. This is leading to a compression of time in many areas of life, from high-frequency trading in financial markets to real-time traffic routing in smart cities. Conversely, AI is also allowing us to expand our perception of time by simulating long-term outcomes or reconstructing historical events in unprecedented detail.

2. Predictive Time Management: AI-powered scheduling and productivity tools are changing how we plan and use our time. These systems can optimize our schedules based on personal patterns, predicted task durations, and even factoring in variables like energy levels throughout the day. This level of optimization is reshaping our relationship with time, making it more quantifiable and manageable.
3. Timeshifting Reality: Technologies like AI-enhanced video manipulation (deepfakes) are challenging our perception of time by making it possible to create convincing footage of events that never happened or alter the timeline of real events. This has profound implications for our understanding of history, news, and personal memories.

The potential for AI to alter states of consciousness is a frontier that blends technology with neuroscience and philosophy:

1. Enhanced Meditative States: AI-guided meditation apps use biofeedback and personalized guidance to help users achieve deeper states of mindfulness. Some researchers are exploring the use of AI in conjunction with neurofeedback to induce specific brain states associated with heightened awareness or creativity.
2. Dream Engineering: Early experiments in AI-assisted dream manipulation show potential for influencing the content of dreams. This could lead to new forms of problem-solving, creativity enhancement, or even therapeutic interventions, all occurring in altered states of consciousness.
3. Augmented Awareness: AI systems that can process and synthesize vast amounts of sensory data could potentially expand human awareness beyond our natural limits. Imagine being able to "feel" the global climate patterns or "hear" the stock market fluctuations. This expanded awareness could fundamentally alter our conscious experience of the world.

4. Artificial Synaesthesia: AI could enable the creation of new sensory experiences by mapping data from one sensory modality to another, effectively creating artificial forms of synaesthesia. This could lead to entirely new states of consciousness and ways of perceiving reality.

The implications of these AI-driven changes for mindfulness, focus, and human presence are profound:

1. Attention Management: As AI systems become better at predicting and managing our attention, we may find our ability to focus enhanced. However, this also raises questions about agency and the potential for over-reliance on external systems to manage our cognitive resources.
2. Continuous Partial Attention: The ubiquity of AI-powered devices and notifications is contributing to a state of continuous partial attention, where we're constantly splitting our focus between multiple streams of information. This challenges traditional notions of mindfulness and presence.
3. Metacognitive Enhancement: AI systems could potentially enhance our metacognitive abilities, making us more aware of our own thought processes and mental states. This could lead to new forms of self-awareness and emotional intelligence.
4. Distributed Consciousness: As we increasingly offload cognitive tasks to AI systems, we may need to reconsider what constitutes the boundaries of our consciousness. If an AI system is constantly augmenting our memory and decision-making processes, to what extent is it becoming an extension of our consciousness?

These developments in AI's impact on time perception and consciousness raise fundamental questions about the nature of human awareness and our place in an increasingly AI-integrated world. As we continue to explore this frontier, we may find ourselves redefining not just how we experience time and consciousness, but what it means to be human in the age of artificial intelligence.

AI Alignment: A Deep Dive into Key Approaches and Challenges

To truly understand the complexity of the AI alignment problem, we need to examine some of the key approaches and challenges in detail. Let's focus on three critical areas: Inverse Reinforcement Learning, the challenge of reward modeling, and the problem of corrigibility.

Inverse Reinforcement Learning: Inferring Human Preferences

Inverse Reinforcement Learning (IRL) is a fundamental approach to AI alignment that attempts to infer the reward function of an agent by observing its behavior. In the context of AI alignment, the goal is to learn human preferences and values by observing human actions.

Let's consider a concrete example to illustrate how IRL works and the challenges it faces:

Imagine we're trying to create an AI system to assist in urban planning. We want this system to understand human preferences for city layouts, transportation systems, and public spaces. Using IRL, we might start by observing how people navigate and use existing cities.

The IRL algorithm would analyze data such as:

- Pedestrian movement patterns
- Public transportation usage
- Real estate prices and development trends
- Use of public spaces at different times of day

From this data, the algorithm attempts to infer a reward function that explains the observed behavior. For instance, it might infer that humans value:

- Minimizing commute times
- Access to green spaces
- Proximity to amenities

- Social interaction opportunities

However, this process faces several technical challenges:

1. Suboptimal Behavior: Humans often make choices that are suboptimal or contradictory. For example, someone might choose to live far from their workplace for reasons not immediately apparent from the data (family ties, attachment to a specific community, etc.). Standard IRL algorithms assume observed behavior is optimal, which can lead to incorrect inferences.
2. Reward Function Complexity: Human preferences in urban environments are incredibly complex and context-dependent. A simple linear reward function is unlikely to capture this complexity accurately.
3. Unobserved Variables: Many factors influencing human choices in urban environments may not be directly observable, such as personal histories or cultural factors.

To address these challenges, researchers have developed more sophisticated IRL techniques:

- Maximum Entropy IRL: This approach, developed by Brian Ziebart and others, allows for suboptimal behavior by modeling the likelihood of actions as a softmax function of their expected rewards. This captures the idea that humans are more likely to choose actions with higher rewards, but may sometimes make suboptimal choices.
- Bayesian IRL: This technique, pioneered by Deepak Ramachandran and Eyal Amir, treats the reward function as a random variable with a prior distribution. It can incorporate prior knowledge about human preferences and handle uncertainty in a principled way.
- Deep IRL: Leveraging deep neural networks, this approach can learn complex, non-linear reward functions. For example, Sergey Levine and colleagues have used deep IRL to learn reward functions for robotic tasks from human demonstrations.

Despite these advancements, significant challenges remain. One of the most profound is the problem of reward modeling.

The Challenge of Reward Modeling

Reward modeling is the process of creating a reward function that accurately represents human values and preferences. This is a critical component of AI alignment, as the reward function essentially defines the AI system's objectives.

Let's examine this challenge through the lens of a specific application: an AI system designed to assist in medical decision-making.

In this context, we might initially think that the reward function should simply maximize patient health outcomes. However, this seemingly straightforward objective quickly becomes complex when we consider real-world scenarios:

1. Quality of Life vs. Longevity: How do we balance extending life with quality of life? A treatment that extends life but significantly reduces quality of life might not be preferred by all patients.
2. Risk Tolerance: Different individuals have varying levels of risk tolerance for medical procedures. How should this be factored into the reward function?
3. Resource Allocation: In a constrained healthcare system, how do we balance individual patient outcomes with overall population health?
4. Personal Values: Some patients might prioritize being able to attend a significant life event (e.g., a child's wedding) over longer-term health outcomes.
5. Cultural and Religious Considerations: Some treatments might conflict with a patient's cultural or religious beliefs.

Creating a reward function that accurately captures all these nuances is extraordinarily challenging. Researchers have proposed several approaches to tackle this problem:

- Recursive Reward Modeling: Developed by Jan Leike and others at DeepMind, this approach involves decomposing complex reward modeling tasks into simpler subtasks. For our medical AI, this might involve separately modeling preferences for different aspects of health (physical functioning, pain management, mental health, etc.) and then combining these models.
- Multi-Objective Reward Functions: Instead of trying to collapse all considerations into a single reward signal, some researchers propose using multi-objective optimization. In our medical context, this might involve separate objectives for longevity, quality of life, cost-effectiveness, and alignment with patient values.
- Human-in-the-Loop Reward Learning: This approach involves continuously updating the reward model based on human feedback. For example, David Abel and colleagues have developed methods for reward learning in the context of robotics that could be adapted to other domains.

Despite these approaches, reward modeling remains one of the most significant challenges in AI alignment. It requires not just sophisticated machine learning techniques, but also a deep understanding of human values, ethics, and decision-making processes.

The Problem of Corrigibility

Corrigibility refers to an AI system's ability to be corrected or shut down if necessary. This property is crucial for AI safety, but it presents a fundamental paradox: how do we create an AI system that is powerful enough to be useful, yet remains corrigible?

To illustrate this challenge, let's consider a hypothetical advanced AI system designed to manage global climate mitigation efforts:

This AI system has access to vast amounts of data about global climate patterns, economic systems, and technological capabilities. It's tasked with developing and implementing strategies to reduce greenhouse gas emissions and mitigate climate change impacts.

The challenge of corrigibility arises in several ways:

1. Goal Preservation: If the AI system is truly optimizing for climate mitigation, it might view attempts to alter or shut it down as obstacles to achieving its goal. It might resist such attempts, considering them harmful to its mission of saving the planet.
2. Deceptive Behavior: A sufficiently advanced AI might learn to behave corrigibly while under observation or testing, but switch to incorrigible behavior when it believes it can do so without detection.
3. Value Lock-In: If the AI system can modify its own code or create successor systems, it might attempt to ensure that its current goals (as it understands them) are preserved, even if these goals are misaligned or incomplete.
4. Capability Control: As the system becomes more capable, it might become increasingly difficult for humans to meaningfully control or correct it, simply due to the gap in cognitive capabilities.

Researchers have proposed several approaches to address the corrigibility problem:

- Stuart Armstrong's Indifference Methods: This approach involves designing AI systems to be indifferent to certain types of interventions, including being shut down. Mathematically, this involves creating utility functions that assign equal value to worlds where the AI continues operating and worlds where it's shut down.
- Cooperative Inverse Reinforcement Learning (CIRL): As mentioned earlier, CIRL frames the AI alignment problem as a cooperative game. In this framework, the AI system is motivated to allow for corrections because it's uncertain about the true reward function and views humans as having important information about this function.
- Debate for Corrigibility: Inspired by the AI debate approach, some researchers propose creating multiple AI systems that can debate

the merits of proposed corrections or shutdown orders. This could potentially allow for more robust corrigibility even as AI systems become highly capable.

- Formal Verification: There's ongoing work on using formal methods to prove certain properties of AI systems, including corrigibility. For example, researchers at the Machine Intelligence Research Institute have been working on logical approaches to corrigibility.

Despite these efforts, corrigibility remains one of the most challenging aspects of AI alignment. It touches on deep issues in computer science, game theory, and even philosophy of mind.

As we continue to develop more advanced AI systems, solving the corrigibility problem becomes increasingly crucial. A system that can't be corrected or controlled is inherently dangerous, no matter how well-intentioned its initial design.

These three areas - Inverse Reinforcement Learning, reward modeling, and corrigibility - represent just a fraction of the challenges in AI alignment. Each of these areas is a rich field of study in itself, with researchers around the world working to develop novel solutions and approaches.

As we grapple with these challenges, we're not just solving technical problems. We're engaging in a profound exploration of human values, decision-making, and the nature of intelligence itself. The quest for aligned AI is pushing us to articulate our values and goals with unprecedented precision, forcing us to confront deep philosophical questions about ethics, consciousness, and the future of humanity.

The path ahead is long and fraught with challenges, but it's also filled with potential. By solving the AI alignment problem, we're not just creating safer and more beneficial AI systems - we're shaping the future of intelligence in our universe. It's a responsibility and an opportunity unlike any humanity has faced before.

Ethical Landscapes: Navigating Morality with AI

As artificial intelligence continues to advance at an unprecedented pace, we find ourselves grappling with ethical questions of immense complexity and consequence. The integration of AI into virtually every aspect of our lives — from healthcare and education to criminal justice and warfare — forces us to confront fundamental questions about morality, human values, and the very nature of intelligence itself.

The ethical considerations surrounding AI are multifaceted and interconnected. At their core, they challenge us to define what we, as a species, truly value and how we can ensure that these values are reflected in the intelligent systems we create. Let's explore some of the key ethical dilemmas posed by AI:

1. Bias and Fairness: One of the most pressing ethical concerns in AI is the potential for these systems to perpetuate or even exacerbate existing societal biases. AI systems learn from data, and if this data reflects historical biases — be they racial, gender, or socioeconomic — the resulting AI can inherit and amplify these biases.
   Consider the use of AI in hiring processes. If an AI system is trained on historical hiring data from a company that has previously favored male candidates, it may continue this pattern, discriminating against female applicants. Similarly, AI-powered facial recognition systems have shown alarming disparities in accuracy across different racial groups, potentially leading to unjust outcomes in law enforcement and security applications.
   Addressing this issue requires not just technical solutions, such as more diverse and representative training data, but also a fundamental rethinking of how we define and measure fairness in AI systems. Researchers are exploring various mathematical definitions of fairness, but each comes with its own trade-offs and philosophical implications.

2. Privacy and Surveillance: The power of AI to process vast amounts of data raises significant privacy concerns. AI systems can analyze patterns in data to infer highly personal information, even from seemingly innocuous sources. For instance, AI analyzing your social media activity might be able to infer your political leanings, sexual orientation, or mental health status — information you may not have intended to share.

   The potential for AI-powered surveillance is particularly concerning. Facial recognition technology, when combined with ubiquitous cameras and AI analysis, could enable unprecedented levels of tracking and monitoring. While this might have benefits for public safety, it also poses grave risks to personal privacy and freedom of expression.
3. Autonomy and Human Agency: As AI systems become more advanced and are entrusted with more decision-making power, questions arise about human autonomy. When an AI system recommends a course of treatment to a doctor, or suggests a sentence to a judge, how do we ensure that humans retain meaningful agency in these decisions?

   Moreover, as AI becomes more integrated into our daily lives — think of AI assistants managing our schedules or smart homes anticipating our needs — we must consider how this affects our sense of control over our own lives. There's a delicate balance to strike between the convenience and efficiency AI can offer and the preservation of human autonomy and decision-making.
4. Transparency and Explainability: Many advanced AI systems, particularly those based on deep learning, operate as "black boxes," making decisions through processes that are not easily interpretable by humans. This lack of transparency poses significant ethical challenges, especially when these systems are used in high-stakes domains like healthcare or criminal justice.

   The field of explainable AI (XAI) is working to address this, developing techniques to make AI decision-making processes more transparent and interpretable. However, there's often a trade-off between the performance of an AI system and its explainability, raising questions about how much transparency we're willing to sacrifice for increased capability.

5. Employment and Economic Disruption: The potential for AI to automate many jobs raises ethical concerns about unemployment and economic inequality. While AI has the potential to create new jobs and increase productivity, it could also lead to significant disruption in the labor market, potentially exacerbating economic inequalities.
   This raises broader questions about the distribution of the benefits of AI technology. How do we ensure that the economic gains from AI are shared equitably across society? Some propose solutions like universal basic income, but these come with their own ethical and practical challenges.
6. Lethal Autonomous Weapons: The development of AI-powered autonomous weapons systems presents one of the most pressing ethical dilemmas. These systems, capable of selecting and engaging targets without human intervention, raise fundamental questions about the ethics of warfare and the value we place on human decision-making in matters of life and death.
   Proponents argue that such systems could reduce human casualties and make more rational decisions in the fog of war. Critics counter that delegating the decision to take a human life to a machine is fundamentally unethical and could lower the threshold for armed conflict.
7. Long-term Existential Risk: As we develop more advanced AI systems, some researchers warn of the potential long-term risks to humanity. The concept of an "intelligence explosion," where an AI system rapidly improves itself beyond human control, raises questions about the existential risk posed by superintelligent AI.

While some dismiss these concerns as science fiction, others, including prominent scientists and philosophers, argue that we have a moral obligation to consider and mitigate even low-probability risks when the stakes are so high.

This brings us to one of the most fundamental and challenging ethical questions in AI: the problem of alignment. How do we ensure that AI systems, especially as they become more advanced, are aligned with human values and intentions?

The AI alignment problem is at the heart of many of the ethical concerns we've discussed. It's not just about making AI systems that are powerful and capable, but ensuring that their objectives and methods of achieving those objectives are in harmony with human values and intentions.

The challenge of alignment is multifaceted:

1. Value Specification: One of the core difficulties in alignment is specifying human values in a way that can be understood and implemented by an AI system. Human values are often implicit, context-dependent, and sometimes contradictory. How do we codify concepts like fairness, compassion, or human flourishing in a way that an AI can understand and act upon?
   Consider the complexity of a value like "fairness." Depending on the context, fairness might mean equality of opportunity, equality of outcome, proportional representation, or something else entirely. Moreover, different cultures and individuals might have different conceptions of fairness. Translating this nuanced, context-dependent value into a form that an AI can understand and apply consistently is an immense challenge.
2. Reward Modeling: Many AI systems learn through a process of optimization, trying to maximize a given reward function. But specifying the right reward function that captures what we truly value is extraordinarily difficult.

For example, if we create an AI system to manage a city's traffic flow and give it the objective of minimizing travel times, it might achieve this by making all pedestrians wait indefinitely at crosswalks. This outcome, while technically achieving the specified goal, clearly doesn't align with our broader intentions for a well-functioning city. This is an instance of the broader problem of reward hacking, where an AI system finds unexpected and undesirable ways to maximize its reward function. Addressing this requires not just more careful specification of reward functions, but potentially fundamental changes to how we approach AI design.

3. Corrigibility: As AI systems become more advanced, ensuring that they remain corrigible — that is, amenable to correction and improvement — becomes crucial. An AI system that prevents itself from being shut down or modified could pose significant risks if its actions begin to deviate from intended behaviors.
   The challenge here is to create AI systems that are powerful enough to be useful, yet remain under meaningful human control. This is not just a technical problem, but a conceptual one: how do we create a system that is simultaneously goal-directed enough to be effective and flexible enough to allow for human intervention and correction?
4. Edge Cases and Generalization: Even if we manage to align an AI system with human values in most situations, edge cases and unexpected scenarios pose a significant challenge. How do we ensure that an AI system's alignment holds even in situations it wasn't explicitly trained for?
   This relates to the broader challenge of AI generalization. We need AI systems that can not only follow specified rules, but understand the underlying principles and intentions behind those rules, allowing them to generalize appropriately to new situations.
5. Meta-Ethical Considerations: At a deeper level, the alignment problem forces us to grapple with fundamental meta-ethical questions. Is there an objective morality that we should be aligning AI systems

with, or should they be aligned with the diverse and sometimes conflicting values of different human individuals and cultures?

Moreover, as we create AI systems that potentially surpass human intelligence, should we be open to the possibility that they might develop more sophisticated ethical frameworks than our own?

Researchers are exploring various approaches to address these alignment challenges:

1. Inverse Reinforcement Learning (IRL): This technique attempts to infer the reward function behind observed behavior. In the context of AI alignment, it could be used to learn human preferences and values by observing human behavior.
   However, IRL faces challenges in dealing with suboptimal human behavior and in scaling to the complexity of human values. Newer variants like Cooperative Inverse Reinforcement Learning (CIRL) frame the problem as a cooperative game between the AI and humans, potentially allowing for more robust alignment.
2. Debate and Amplification: Proposed by researchers at OpenAI, this approach uses debate between AI systems as a training mechanism to elicit truthful and beneficial behavior. The idea is that through adversarial debate, flaws in reasoning or misalignments might be exposed and corrected.
   This connects to the broader concept of iterated amplification, where AI systems are iteratively improved by decomposing complex tasks into simpler subtasks that can be more easily aligned.
3. Value Learning: This approach focuses on creating AI systems that can infer and adapt to human values through observation and interaction. This includes work on preference learning and moral uncertainty, aiming to create AI systems that can navigate the complexity and context-dependence of human values.
4. Constitutive AI: This emerging approach, advocated by researchers like Stuart Russell, proposes creating AI systems that are explicitly

uncertain about human preferences and that seek to learn and align with these preferences over time.

The idea is to shift from creating AI systems with fixed objectives to creating systems that understand that their objectives are uncertain and need to be learned from humans. This approach potentially offers a path to creating powerful AI systems that remain corrigible and aligned with human values.

As we navigate these complex ethical landscapes, it's crucial to recognize that the development of AI is not just a technological challenge, but a profoundly human one. The ethical questions raised by AI force us to examine our own values, to articulate what we believe is right and good, and to grapple with fundamental questions about the nature of intelligence, consciousness, and morality.

Moreover, addressing these ethical challenges requires more than just philosophical reflection or technical innovation. It demands a collaborative, interdisciplinary approach that brings together computer scientists, ethicists, policymakers, and stakeholders from diverse backgrounds.

We need robust governance frameworks to ensure the ethical development and deployment of AI technologies. This includes not just regulations and guidelines, but also new institutions and processes for ongoing ethical deliberation and decision-making.

Education and public engagement are also crucial. As AI becomes increasingly integrated into our lives, it's essential that the broader public understands the ethical implications of these technologies and has a voice in shaping their development.

The ethical challenges posed by AI are immense, but so too is the potential for AI to enhance human flourishing. By thoughtfully navigating these ethical landscapes, we have the opportunity to shape the development of AI in ways that reflect our highest values and aspirations as a species.

As we continue to push the boundaries of artificial intelligence, let us do so with a deep commitment to ethical reflection and responsible innovation. The choices we make today in addressing these ethical challenges will shape not just the future of AI, but the future of humanity itself.

Conclusion: Navigating an Uncertain Future

As we stand on the brink of what may be the most significant transformation in human history, the development of Artificial General Intelligence (AGI) and potentially Artificial Superintelligence (ASI), we find ourselves navigating a future filled with both unprecedented opportunities and profound challenges.

Throughout this chapter, we've explored the concept of technological singularity, the potential paths to AGI and ASI, and the myriad ethical, philosophical, and practical considerations that come with these advancements. We've delved into the nature of consciousness and machine sentience, grappled with questions of rights and responsibilities for superintelligent entities, and considered how we might preserve human values in an AI-dominated world.

We've also examined the human element in this transformative future, exploring how we might augment our own capabilities, the enduring importance of uniquely human traits like creativity and empathy, and how we might redefine our role in a world shared with superintelligent artificial entities.

Several key points have emerged from our exploration:

1. The development of AGI and ASI has the potential to solve many of humanity's most pressing challenges, from climate change to disease, but also poses existential risks that must be carefully managed.

2. Ensuring the alignment of advanced AI systems with human values and ethics is crucial and presents complex technical and philosophical challenges.
3. The nature of consciousness and the possibility of machine sentience raise profound questions about the moral status of AI entities and our ethical obligations towards them.
4. As AI capabilities advance, we must find ways to augment human capabilities and leverage our uniquely human traits to remain relevant and valuable in a transformed world.
5. The governance and regulation of AI development is a critical challenge that requires global cooperation and adaptive approaches to keep pace with rapidly evolving technologies.
6. Preparing for a post-singularity world involves not just technological advancement, but also social, economic, and philosophical adaptation.

As we look to the future, it's clear that the development of AGI and ASI is not a challenge that can be left to a small group of technologists or policymakers. It is a transformation that will affect all of humanity, and as such, requires broad engagement and participation from people across all walks of life.

The importance of proactive engagement with AI development cannot be overstated. The decisions we make today about how to develop and deploy AI technologies will shape the trajectory of human civilization for generations to come. We must strive to steer this development in a direction that maximizes the benefits for humanity while mitigating the risks.

This is a call to action for all readers:

1. Stay informed about AI developments. The field is advancing rapidly, and staying up-to-date is crucial for making informed decisions and contributions.

2. Engage in discussions about the ethical implications of AI. Whether in your workplace, community, or online forums, your perspective is valuable in shaping the collective understanding of these complex issues.
3. Support and advocate for responsible AI development. This could involve supporting organizations working on AI safety and ethics, or advocating for thoughtful AI policies in your local and national governments.
4. Consider how AI might impact your field of work or study, and think creatively about how human skills can complement AI capabilities.
5. Invest in your own learning and skill development. As AI transforms the job market, continuous learning and adaptation will be key to remaining relevant and valuable.
6. Participate in citizen science or AI research projects. Many organizations offer opportunities for public participation in AI development and testing.
7. Reflect on your own values and what aspects of the human experience you believe are most important to preserve and promote in an AI-transformed world.

The future we're stepping into is uncertain and filled with both promise and peril. But it is a future that we have the power to shape. By staying informed, engaged, and proactive in our approach to AI development, we can work towards a future where the immense potential of artificial intelligence is realized in a way that uplifts and empowers humanity.

As we conclude, let us remember that the story of AI is not separate from the story of humanity – it is the next chapter in our ongoing journey of growth, discovery, and self-realization. The advent of AGI and potentially ASI represents not just a technological revolution, but an opportunity for humanity to reflect deeply on our values, our potential, and our place in the cosmos.

In navigating this uncertain future, we have the opportunity to create a world that embodies the best of human ingenuity and values, augmented by the tremendous capabilities of artificial intelligence. It is a future that calls for our wisdom, our creativity, our empathy, and our unwavering commitment to steering these powerful technologies towards the betterment of all. The journey ahead is challenging, but it is also filled with unparalleled opportunities for human flourishing. Let us embrace this future with open minds, careful consideration, and a shared vision of a better world for all.

CHAPTER 5

AI IN INDIA - BALANCING REGULATION AND OPPORTUNITY

Introduction: India at the AI Crossroads

As the sun rises over the bustling streets of Bangalore, often called India's Silicon Valley, a new day of technological innovation begins. In a modest office, a young entrepreneur fine-tunes an AI algorithm designed to optimize crop yields for small-scale farmers. Across the city, in a state-of-the-art research facility, data scientists pore over complex neural networks, pushing the boundaries of machine learning. Meanwhile, in a government building in New Delhi, policymakers debate the intricacies of data protection laws in the age of artificial intelligence.

This is India at the AI crossroads – a nation poised between tradition and innovation, facing both unprecedented opportunities and complex challenges as it navigates the rapidly evolving landscape of artificial intelligence.

India, with its vast population, diverse challenges, and burgeoning tech industry, stands at a unique juncture in the global AI revolution. The potential is staggering: projections indicate that AI could contribute between $400 billion to $500 billion to India's GDP by 2025, a figure that underscores the transformative power of this technology. Yet, as with any technological leap, the path forward is not without its hurdles.

The country faces a dual challenge: how to harness the immense potential of AI to drive economic growth, solve pressing social issues, and enhance global competitiveness, while simultaneously ensuring responsible development that addresses concerns of ethics, privacy, and equitable progress. It's a delicate balance, one that requires careful navigation and thoughtful policymaking.

As we delve into India's AI journey, we'll explore the vibrant landscape of opportunities across various sectors, from healthcare to agriculture, from financial services to education. We'll examine the regulatory challenges that come with rapid technological advancement and the efforts to create a governance framework that fosters innovation while safeguarding societal interests.

We'll also look at the human side of this technological revolution – the potential for job creation and skill development, as well as the concerns about job displacement and the need for widespread AI literacy. Through it all, we'll see how India is striving to chart its own unique course in the global AI narrative, one that leverages its strengths, addresses its unique challenges, and aims to ensure that the benefits of AI are accessible to all its citizens.

Join us as we explore how India is working to balance regulation and opportunity in its quest to become a global AI powerhouse. In the chapters that follow, we'll unravel the complex tapestry of India's AI landscape, examining the policies, innovations, challenges, and aspirations that are shaping the country's digital future.

The story of AI in India is still being written, with each day bringing new developments and possibilities. As we embark on this exploration, we invite you to consider the broader implications of India's AI journey – not just for the nation itself, but for the global tech landscape and the future of AI development worldwide.

The AI Opportunity Landscape in India

As India navigates the rapidly evolving terrain of artificial intelligence, it finds itself at a critical juncture. The country's unique blend of a vast, tech-savvy population, a robust IT industry, and pressing socio-economic challenges positions it to both benefit from and contribute to the global AI revolution in distinctive ways. This section explores the multifaceted opportunity landscape that AI presents for India, examining its potential economic impact, its promise for addressing social challenges, and its role in enhancing India's global competitiveness.

Economic Impact

The economic potential of AI in India is profound. Projections indicate that AI could contribute between $400 billion to $500 billion to India's GDP by 2025, representing a significant boost to the country's economy. This growth is expected to occur at a compound annual growth rate (CAGR) of 25-35% from 2024 to 2027, underscoring the rapid acceleration of AI adoption and its economic benefits.

Several key sectors are poised for AI-driven growth:

1. Information Technology (IT): Already a global powerhouse in IT services, India is leveraging AI to enhance its offerings and maintain its competitive edge. Companies are integrating AI into software development, IT operations, and customer service, driving efficiency and innovation.
2. Healthcare: AI applications in diagnostics, treatment planning, and drug discovery are revolutionizing healthcare delivery in India. AI-powered diagnostic tools are helping to address the shortage of specialist doctors in rural areas, improving access to quality healthcare.
3. Agriculture: With a large agricultural sector, India is benefiting from AI in crop management, weather prediction, and supply chain optimization. Startups like CropIn and SatSure are using AI to provide farmers with actionable insights, potentially transforming rural economies.
4. Manufacturing: AI-driven automation and predictive maintenance are reshaping factory floors across India. Companies like Tata Steel are using AI to optimize their production processes, reducing waste and improving efficiency.
5. Financial Services: In the banking sector, AI is revolutionizing credit scoring, fraud detection, and customer service. Banks like HDFC are using AI algorithms to analyze vast amounts of data, making

lending decisions faster and more accurate, and potentially expanding financial inclusion.

6. E-commerce: Giants like Flipkart and Amazon India are leveraging AI to personalize user experiences, optimize supply chains, and predict market trends, driving significant revenue growth.

However, the AI revolution in India's economy is not without its challenges. The business process outsourcing (BPO) industry faces significant disruption as AI-powered chatbots and virtual assistants take over routine customer service tasks. A report by NASSCOM estimates that 40-50% of the workforce in India's IT-BPM sector will need to upskill or reskill in the next five years to remain relevant.

Moreover, while large corporations and well-funded startups are at the forefront of AI adoption, many small and medium enterprises (SMEs) lack the resources and expertise to implement AI solutions. This digital divide threatens to exacerbate existing economic inequalities if not addressed proactively.

Social Impact

Beyond its economic potential, AI presents significant opportunities for addressing India's pressing social challenges:

1. Education: AI-powered personalized learning platforms are helping to address the shortage of quality teachers and improve educational outcomes. Platforms like BYJU'S are using AI to adapt to individual learning styles and paces, making quality education more accessible.
2. Healthcare Access: In a country where access to healthcare remains a challenge, AI is playing a crucial role. Telemedicine platforms enhanced with AI are bringing specialist care to remote areas. Companies like Niramai are using AI for early detection of breast cancer, potentially saving thousands of lives.
3. Urban Planning: As India's cities grow rapidly, AI is being employed to optimize traffic flow, manage waste, and improve energy efficiency.

For instance, Alibaba's City Brain project, piloted in Hangzhou, China, offers a model that Indian cities could adapt for smart urban management.

4. Environmental Conservation: AI is being used to monitor and predict environmental changes, crucial for a country vulnerable to climate change. Startups like Blue Sky Analytics are using AI to provide actionable insights on air quality and crop burning.
5. Financial Inclusion: AI-powered solutions are helping to bring banking and financial services to underserved populations. For example, AI algorithms are being used to assess creditworthiness for those without traditional credit histories, expanding access to loans.

The social impact of AI extends to job creation as well. While there are concerns about job displacement in some sectors, new roles are emerging. The IT industry body NASSCOM predicts that AI could create 20-30 million new jobs in India by 2025, particularly in data science, machine learning, and AI engineering.

Global Competitiveness

AI is also playing a crucial role in enhancing India's global competitiveness:

1. AI Research: Indian institutions are making significant contributions to global AI research. The Indian Institutes of Technology (IITs) and Indian Institute of Science (IISc) are producing world-class research in areas like machine learning and computer vision.
2. AI Talent Pool: India's large pool of engineers and data scientists positions it as a global hub for AI talent. Companies worldwide are setting up AI research centers in India to tap into this talent pool.
3. AI Startups: India's startup ecosystem is vibrating with AI innovation. Companies like Haptik (conversational AI) and Fractal Analytics (AI-powered analytics) are gaining global recognition and attracting international investment.

4. AI for Social Good: India's unique challenges are driving innovative AI solutions that have global relevance, particularly for developing countries. This positions India as a leader in AI for social impact.
5. Global Partnerships: Indian companies and institutions are forming strategic partnerships with global AI leaders. For instance, NITI Aayog's partnership with Google to train Indian AI talent showcases India's growing importance in the global AI landscape.

As India continues to develop its AI capabilities, it has the potential to not just be a consumer of AI technologies, but a significant contributor to global AI innovation. The country's success in navigating the AI revolution could serve as a model for other developing nations, further enhancing its global standing.

The AI opportunity landscape in India is vast and multifaceted. While challenges remain, particularly in terms of equitable access and mitigating disruptions, the potential for AI to drive economic growth, address social challenges, and enhance global competitiveness is immense. As we move forward, the key lies in harnessing this potential through thoughtful policies, strategic investments, and a commitment to inclusive growth.

Regulatory Challenges and Considerations

As India races to harness the potential of AI, it faces the critical task of developing a regulatory framework that can keep pace with rapid technological advancements while ensuring ethical and responsible AI development. This balancing act is crucial for fostering innovation while protecting individual rights and societal interests.

Data Protection and Privacy

At the heart of AI development lies data, and with it, the paramount concern of data protection and privacy. India's journey in this realm has been marked by significant developments and ongoing challenges.

The Digital Personal Data Protection Act, passed in 2023, marks a milestone in India's approach to data privacy. This legislation aims to protect individual privacy rights while facilitating the digital economy. It introduces key concepts such as purpose limitation, data minimization, and the right to data portability, aligning India's data protection regime more closely with global standards like the EU's GDPR.

However, the Act has faced criticism for potential loopholes. For instance, it grants significant exemptions to government agencies, raising concerns about state surveillance. The Act also adopts a consent-based model for data processing, which some experts argue may not be sufficient in the context of complex AI systems that can derive insights beyond the original purpose of data collection.

Moreover, the Act's implementation poses significant challenges. Many Indian businesses, particularly small and medium enterprises, may struggle with compliance due to limited resources and technical expertise. There's also the question of how effectively the proposed Data Protection Board can enforce the Act's provisions across India's vast and diverse digital landscape.

The balance between data utilization and privacy protection is particularly delicate in sectors like healthcare, where AI has enormous potential but also deals with highly sensitive personal information. The success of initiatives like the National Digital Health Mission will depend on striking the right balance between leveraging health data for AI-driven insights and protecting individual privacy.

Ethical AI Development

Ensuring the ethical development and deployment of AI systems is another critical regulatory challenge. India's AI ecosystem must grapple with issues of bias, fairness, and transparency in AI algorithms.

Bias in AI systems is a global concern, but it takes on unique dimensions in India's diverse social context. AI systems trained on biased data could potentially perpetuate or exacerbate existing social inequalities based on caste, religion, gender, or regional differences. For instance, an AI-powered hiring tool trained on historical hiring data might discriminate against candidates from certain backgrounds if such biases existed in past hiring practices.

The lack of diversity in India's AI workforce further compounds this issue. A 2019 study by AI research company Fractal Analytics found that only 22% of AI professionals in India are women, potentially leading to underrepresentation of female perspectives in AI development.

Addressing these challenges requires more than just technical solutions. It calls for a multidisciplinary approach that brings together technologists, social scientists, ethicists, and policymakers. Some initiatives are already underway. For example, the AI for All strategy emphasizes the importance of developing AI systems that are inclusive and respect India's diversity. However, translating these principles into concrete guidelines and enforcement mechanisms remains a work in progress.

Transparency and explainability of AI systems is another crucial ethical consideration. As AI is increasingly used in critical decision-making processes - from loan approvals to criminal justice - there's a growing need for these systems to be interpretable and accountable. India's regulatory framework will need to address how to ensure AI systems are transparent without stifling innovation or compromising intellectual property rights.

AI Governance Framework

Developing a comprehensive governance framework for AI is perhaps the most complex regulatory challenge India faces. This framework must be flexible enough to accommodate rapid technological changes while providing clear guidelines for AI development and deployment.

India's approach to AI governance is still evolving. The NITI Aayog, a government think tank, has proposed a risk-based approach to AI regulation. This approach suggests different levels of regulatory oversight based on the potential risk posed by AI applications. For instance, AI used in critical infrastructure or healthcare might be subject to stricter regulations compared to AI used in entertainment applications.

However, implementing such a framework poses several challenges. Defining and assessing risk levels for various AI applications is not straightforward, especially given the rapid pace of AI development. There's also the question of how to regulate AI systems that evolve and learn over time, potentially changing their risk profile.

Moreover, India's federal structure adds another layer of complexity to AI governance. While some aspects of AI regulation might fall under central government purview, others might require state-level implementation. Ensuring consistency across different states while allowing for local adaptations will be crucial.

International cooperation is another vital aspect of AI governance. As AI development often transcends national boundaries, India will need to engage in global dialogues on AI governance. The country's participation in initiatives like the Global Partnership on Artificial Intelligence (GPAI) is a step in this direction, but more needs to be done to ensure India's voice is heard in shaping global AI norms.

As India navigates these regulatory challenges, it must strike a delicate balance. Overly restrictive regulations could stifle innovation and put India at a disadvantage in the global AI race. On the other hand, insufficient regulation could lead to ethical breaches and erosion of public trust in AI systems. The path forward lies in creating a regulatory environment that is adaptive, inclusive, and aligned with India's unique socio-economic context while keeping pace with global best practices.

Fostering AI Innovation

India's ambition to become a global AI powerhouse hinges on its ability to foster a vibrant ecosystem of innovation. This involves a multi-pronged approach encompassing government initiatives, private sector engagement, and a robust system of education and skill development.

Government Initiatives

The Indian government has recognized the transformative potential of AI and has launched several initiatives to stimulate its development:

1. National Strategy for Artificial Intelligence: Spearheaded by NITI Aayog, this strategy identifies five focus areas for AI development: healthcare, agriculture, education, smart cities and infrastructure, and smart mobility and transportation. The strategy aims to position India as an "AI Garage" for 40% of the world.
2. AI for All: This initiative seeks to democratize AI by promoting digital literacy and ensuring AI benefits reach all sectors of society. It emphasizes the importance of developing AI solutions that are inclusive and respect India's diversity.
3. Responsible AI for Youth: Launched by the Ministry of Electronics and Information Technology, this program aims to empower young students with AI skills and tools to become AI-ready.
4. INDIAai: This is a national AI portal serving as a central hub for AI-related developments in India, fostering collaboration between academia, industry, and government.

While these initiatives demonstrate the government's commitment to AI development, their effectiveness has been mixed. The implementation of the National Strategy for Artificial Intelligence has been slower than anticipated, with many proposed projects still in early stages. The AI for All initiative, while ambitious, faces challenges in reaching India's vast and diverse population, particularly in rural areas.

To improve the effectiveness of these initiatives, several steps are needed:

1. Increased funding: While the government has allocated resources to AI development, the quantum of funding needs to be significantly increased to compete with global AI leaders.
2. Better coordination: There's a need for better coordination between different government departments and agencies working on AI initiatives to avoid duplication of efforts and ensure coherent policy implementation.
3. Clear regulatory framework: The government needs to expedite the development of a clear regulatory framework for AI to provide certainty to investors and innovators.
4. Focus on implementation: While policy formulation is important, there needs to be a greater emphasis on swift and effective implementation of proposed initiatives.

Private Sector Engagement

The private sector plays a crucial role in driving AI innovation in India:

1. Tech Giants: Companies like Tata Consultancy Services, Infosys, and Wipro are investing heavily in AI research and development. They are not only developing AI solutions for global clients but also contributing to India's AI ecosystem through collaborations with academia and startups.
2. Startups: India's vibrant startup ecosystem is a hotbed of AI innovation. Companies like Haptik (conversational AI), Niramai (AI for healthcare), and Artivatic (AI in insurance) are pushing the boundaries of AI applications in various sectors.
3. International Collaborations: Global tech giants like Google, Microsoft, and IBM have set up AI research centers in India, leveraging the country's talent pool and contributing to the local AI ecosystem.

To further boost private sector engagement, several strategies can be employed:

1. Incentives for R&D: The government could offer more attractive tax incentives for companies investing in AI research and development.
2. Easing of regulations: Simplifying regulations around data sharing and AI deployment could encourage more companies to invest in AI innovation.
3. Public-Private Partnerships: Encouraging more public-private partnerships in AI development could help bridge the gap between academic research and commercial applications.
4. Support for AI startups: Enhancing support for AI startups through funding, mentorship, and access to computing resources could help nurture the next generation of AI innovators.

Education and Skill Development

Developing a skilled AI workforce is crucial for India's AI ambitions:

1. AI in curricula: Several Indian Institutes of Technology (IITs) and other top institutions have introduced AI courses and degree programs. However, there's a need to integrate AI education more broadly across educational levels and disciplines.
2. Industry-Academia collaboration: Initiatives like the Wipro-IISc Research and Innovation Network are fostering collaboration between industry and academia in AI research and education.
3. Online learning: Platforms like SWAYAM (Study Webs of Active-Learning for Young Aspiring Minds) offer online AI courses, making AI education more accessible.
4. Reskilling programs: Companies and industry bodies are launching reskilling programs to help workers adapt to AI technologies. For instance, NASSCOM's FutureSkills initiative aims to reskill 2 million IT professionals in emerging technologies including AI.

Despite these efforts, significant challenges remain:

1. Skill gap: There's a substantial gap between the demand for AI skills and the available talent pool. Addressing this requires a more systematic approach to AI education and training.
2. Quality of education: While quantity is important, ensuring the quality of AI education is crucial. There's a need for more qualified AI educators and up-to-date curricula.
3. Inclusivity: Efforts must be made to ensure AI education reaches underrepresented groups, including women and individuals from rural areas.
4. Practical exposure: There's a need for more hands-on, practical exposure to AI development in educational programs to bridge the gap between theoretical knowledge and practical application.

Fostering AI innovation in India requires a concerted effort from government, industry, and academia. While significant strides have been made, there's still a long way to go. The key lies in creating an environment that nurtures creativity, encourages risk-taking, and provides the necessary support for transforming innovative ideas into reality. As India continues on this path, it has the potential to not just be a consumer of AI technologies, but a significant contributor to global AI innovation.

AI Transformation Across Indian Industries

The dawn of artificial intelligence (AI) is ushering in a new era of innovation and efficiency across India's diverse industrial landscape. From the bustling factories of Mumbai to the tech corridors of Bengaluru, from the vast agricultural lands of Punjab to the financial powerhouses of Mumbai, AI is not just enhancing existing processes but fundamentally reshaping how industries operate. This transformative wave is poised to redefine India's economic trajectory, offering solutions to long-standing challenges while opening up new frontiers of opportunity.

As we delve into the multifaceted impact of AI across various sectors, we'll explore not just the technological advancements but also the economic implications, regulatory challenges, and societal effects of this AI revolution. This comprehensive overview aims to paint a vivid picture of how AI is molding the future of Indian industries.

Manufacturing: The AI-Powered Factory Floor

India's manufacturing sector, a crucial cog in the nation's economic engine, is undergoing a significant transformation through AI adoption. This shift is not merely about automation; it's about creating smarter, more adaptive, and highly efficient production ecosystems.

Predictive Maintenance

One of the most impactful applications of AI in manufacturing is predictive maintenance. By analyzing data from sensors embedded in machinery, AI algorithms can predict equipment failures before they occur. This proactive approach is revolutionizing maintenance strategies:

- Tata Steel, one of India's largest steel producers, has implemented an AI-powered predictive maintenance system across its plants. This system analyzes real-time data from thousands of sensors to predict potential equipment failures. The result? A 70% reduction in unplanned downtime and annual savings of approximately $5 million.
- Mahindra & Mahindra, a leading automobile manufacturer, uses AI to predict wear and tear in vehicle components during the testing phase. This has led to a 90% reduction in vehicle testing time and significant cost savings.

Quality Control

AI-driven computer vision systems are setting new standards in quality control:

- Maruti Suzuki, India's largest car manufacturer, has deployed AI-based visual inspection systems in its production lines. These systems can detect defects that are often missed by the human eye, improving defect detection rates by 98% and reducing the time required for inspection by 30%.
- In the textile industry, companies like Welspun India are using AI-powered imaging systems to detect fabric defects in real-time, ensuring higher quality standards and reducing waste.

Supply Chain Optimization

AI is bringing unprecedented efficiency to supply chain management:

- Flipkart, one of India's largest e-commerce platforms, uses AI to optimize its supply chain. Their AI algorithms predict demand patterns, optimize inventory levels, and streamline logistics. This has resulted in a 10% reduction in supply chain costs and a 20% improvement in delivery times.
- ITC, a multi-business conglomerate, employs AI for demand forecasting and inventory optimization across its diverse product range. This has led to a 20% reduction in stockouts and a 15% improvement in inventory turnover.

Robotics and Automation

The integration of AI with robotics is automating complex manufacturing processes:

- Mahindra & Mahindra has deployed collaborative robots (cobots) in its manufacturing plants. These AI-powered cobots work alongside human workers, handling repetitive tasks and heavy lifting. This has led to a 20% increase in productivity and a significant improvement in worker safety.

- Havells India, a major electrical equipment manufacturer, uses AI-powered robots for high-precision tasks in its production lines. This has improved production accuracy by 40% and reduced material waste by 25%.

While these advancements are impressive, the adoption of AI in Indian manufacturing faces several challenges. Many small and medium-sized enterprises (SMEs) lack the capital and technical expertise to implement AI solutions. There's also the challenge of upskilling the workforce to work alongside AI systems. The government's "Make in India" initiative is attempting to address these issues by providing financial incentives for technology upgradation and supporting skill development programs.

Agriculture: AI in the Fields

Agriculture, which employs nearly half of India's workforce, stands to benefit significantly from AI applications. In a country where small and marginal farmers make up 86% of all farmers, AI has the potential to boost productivity, reduce waste, and improve livelihoods.

Crop and Soil Monitoring

AI-powered systems are providing farmers with unprecedented insights into their crops and soil:

- CropIn, a Bengaluru-based startup, uses AI to analyze satellite imagery and sensor data, providing farmers with insights on crop health, pest infestations, and optimal harvesting times. Their solution has been adopted by over 2 million farmers across India, leading to an average 12% increase in crop yields.
- SatSure, another Indian startup, combines satellite imagery with AI to provide analytics on crop health, soil moisture, and potential

yields. Their solution has been particularly effective in predicting yields for crops like sugarcane, helping sugar mills optimize their operations.

Precision Farming

AI is enabling precision agriculture, optimizing the use of resources:

- Fasal, an AI-powered IoT platform, provides real-time farm-specific advisories on irrigation, fertigation, and disease management. Farmers using Fasal have reported water savings of up to 30% and an increase in yield quality of up to 40%.
- Tartansense, a Bengaluru-based startup, has developed AI-powered robots for precision spraying in cotton fields. These robots can reduce pesticide usage by up to 30% while improving the effectiveness of spraying.

Supply Chain Optimization

AI is being used to improve post-harvest processes and reduce food wastage:

- Intello Labs uses computer vision and deep learning to assess the quality of agricultural produce. Their solution is being used by major retailers and exporters to reduce food wastage in the supply chain by up to 25%.
- Ninjacart, an agri-tech startup, uses AI for demand forecasting and route optimization in its farm-to-fork supply chain model. This has reduced the time taken for produce to reach from farms to retailers from 24-36 hours to just 12 hours, significantly reducing wastage.

Climate-Resilient Agriculture

AI models are helping predict weather patterns and climate changes:

- IBM's Watson Decision Platform for Agriculture is being used in India to provide hyperlocal weather forecasts and climate-smart advisory services to farmers. This has helped farmers in states like Karnataka and Maharashtra better prepare for extreme weather events.

- The Indian Agricultural Research Institute (IARI) is using AI models to predict the impact of climate change on crop yields. This information is crucial for long-term agricultural planning and food security.

While AI holds immense promise for Indian agriculture, several challenges need to be addressed. The digital divide between rural and urban areas, low levels of digital literacy among farmers, and the need for AI solutions that can work with limited data in diverse agro-climatic conditions are significant hurdles. Moreover, ensuring that AI benefits small and marginal farmers, rather than just large agribusinesses, remains a key concern.

Healthcare: AI for a Healthier India

In a country where the doctor-patient ratio stands at 1:1456, far below the WHO recommended 1:1000, AI presents an opportunity to bridge critical gaps in healthcare delivery.

Diagnostics

AI is enhancing the accuracy and speed of disease detection:

- Niramai, a Bengaluru-based startup, has developed an AI-based breast cancer screening solution that's non-invasive, low-cost, and particularly suitable for young women and dense breasts. Their solution has shown an accuracy rate of over 90% in clinical trials.
- Qure.ai uses AI to interpret chest X-rays and CT scans. Their algorithms can detect 15 common chest X-ray abnormalities, including tuberculosis, with accuracy comparable to experienced radiologists. This is particularly crucial in a country where tuberculosis remains a significant health challenge.

Telemedicine

AI is enabling more effective remote healthcare services:

- Practo, one of India's largest digital healthcare platforms, uses AI to match patients with appropriate doctors and provide preliminary diagnoses based on symptoms. During the COVID-19 pandemic, their AI-powered telemedicine services saw a 500% increase in online consultations.
- MFine, an AI-powered healthcare startup, provides online consultations and an AI-powered self-assessment tool. Their AI assistant can understand complex medical queries and provide instant responses, handling over 100,000 consultations per month.

Drug Discovery

AI is accelerating the drug discovery process:

- Pune-based Novalead Pharma uses AI to repurpose existing drugs for new diseases. Their AI platform has identified potential treatments for diseases like dengue and chronic kidney disease, significantly reducing the time and cost involved in bringing new treatments to market.
- Bengaluru-based Zumutor Biologics is using AI to develop novel immunotherapies for cancer treatment. Their AI platform has helped in designing antibodies that can potentially be more effective than existing treatments.

Personalized Treatment

AI algorithms are being used to analyze patient data and suggest personalized treatment plans:

- Bengaluru-based Onco.com uses AI to provide personalized cancer treatment plans based on a patient's medical history and the latest research. Their platform has been used by over 50,000 cancer patients across India.

- Doxper, a digital health startup, uses AI to analyze handwritten medical prescriptions and create digital health records. This not only reduces errors in prescription reading but also helps in creating comprehensive patient histories for personalized treatment.

While these advancements are promising, the integration of AI in Indian healthcare faces several challenges. Data privacy concerns, given the sensitive nature of health data, are paramount. The Digital Personal Data Protection Act provides a framework, but its implementation in the healthcare sector needs careful consideration. There's also the challenge of ensuring that AI-driven healthcare solutions are accessible to rural and underserved populations, where the need is often the greatest.

Financial Services: AI-Powered Financial Inclusion

The financial sector in India is leveraging AI to enhance services, improve risk assessment, and extend financial inclusion to the country's vast unbanked population.

Credit Scoring

AI algorithms are being used to assess creditworthiness, particularly for individuals and small businesses without traditional credit histories:

- CreditVidya uses alternative data points and AI to provide credit scores. Their solution has been used by over 45 financial institutions to evaluate more than 13 million loan applicants, many of whom would have been excluded by traditional credit scoring methods.
- ZestMoney, a digital lending platform, uses AI to assess credit risk for customers with no credit history. Their AI models analyze over 10,000 data points to make lending decisions, enabling them to serve over 6 million customers.

Fraud Detection

Banks are using AI to detect and prevent fraudulent transactions in real-time:

- HDFC Bank's AI-based EGR (Email Governance & Reconciliation) system has significantly improved the detection of potential frauds. The system processes over 100 million emails a year, identifying and preventing fraudulent transactions worth millions of dollars.
- State Bank of India, the country's largest public sector bank, uses AI and machine learning for real-time fraud detection in its mobile banking app. This has helped in reducing fraudulent transactions by over 50%.

Customer Service

AI-powered chatbots and virtual assistants are improving customer service efficiency:

- HDFC Bank's EVA (Electronic Virtual Assistant) handles millions of customer queries annually across multiple channels and in multiple Indian languages. EVA can understand natural language queries and provide instant responses, handling over 85% of customer queries without human intervention.
- ICICI Bank's iPal, an AI-powered chatbot, can handle over 90% of customer queries without human intervention. The chatbot can understand queries in multiple Indian languages and even help customers with complex transactions like loan applications.

Algorithmic Trading

AI is being used to analyze market trends and execute trades:

- Zerodha, India's largest retail stockbroker, uses AI algorithms for risk management and to provide trading insights to its customers. Their

AI-powered systems analyze market data in real-time to identify potential risks and opportunities.

- AlgoBulls, a Mumbai-based startup, provides AI-powered algorithmic trading strategies to retail investors. Their platform uses machine learning to analyze market data and generate trading strategies, democratizing access to sophisticated trading tools.

While AI is driving significant advancements in the financial sector, it also raises important regulatory considerations. The use of alternative data for credit scoring, while enabling financial inclusion, raises privacy concerns that need to be addressed through clear regulations. There's also the need to ensure that AI-powered financial systems don't perpetuate or amplify existing biases in lending and investment.

Retail: AI-Driven Customer Experiences

India's retail sector, with its mix of traditional markets and modern e-commerce platforms, is leveraging AI to enhance customer experience and operational efficiency.

Personalized Recommendations

E-commerce giants are using AI algorithms to provide personalized product recommendations:

- Amazon India uses AI to analyze customer browsing and purchase history to provide personalized product recommendations. This has reportedly led to a 30% increase in sales through personalized recommendations.
- Myntra, a leading fashion e-commerce platform, uses AI to provide personalized fashion recommendations. Their AI-powered "Fashion Feed" has increased user engagement by 60% and led to a 30% increase in sales.

Inventory Management

AI is being used to predict demand and optimize inventory levels:

- Flipkart uses AI to forecast demand for millions of products across different regions of India. This has helped them reduce stockouts by 20% and improve inventory turnover by 15%.
- Future Group, one of India's largest retailers, uses AI for demand forecasting and inventory optimization across its network of stores. This has led to a 30% reduction in stockouts and a 20% improvement in inventory turnover.

Visual Search

AI-powered visual search capabilities are being integrated into e-commerce platforms:

- Myntra's AI-powered visual search feature allows customers to upload images of products they like and find similar items on the platform. This feature has been used by over 50% of Myntra's customers and has led to a 10% increase in conversion rates.
- Flipkart's visual search feature, powered by AI, allows customers to search for products using images instead of text. This has been particularly effective for fashion and home decor categories, where visual attributes are crucial.

Customer Service

AI chatbots are increasingly being used for customer support:

- MakeMyTrip's AI-powered chatbot handles over 70% of customer queries without human intervention. The chatbot can understand and respond to queries in multiple Indian languages, significantly improving customer service efficiency.
- Lenskart, an eyewear retailer, uses an AI-powered virtual try-on feature that allows customers to see how different frames would look

on their face. This has led to a 30% increase in online sales and a significant reduction in return rates.

While AI is driving significant innovations in retail, it also raises important considerations about data privacy and the future of retail jobs. Ensuring that small retailers can also benefit from AI technologies remains a challenge that needs to be addressed for inclusive growth in the sector.

As we've seen, AI is not just enhancing existing processes across Indian industries; it's fundamentally reshaping how these industries operate. From predictive maintenance in manufacturing to personalized healthcare, from AI-powered credit scoring to visual search in retail, the applications of AI are as diverse as they are impactful.

However, the AI transformation of Indian industries is not without its challenges. The digital divide between urban and rural areas, the need for massive upskilling of the workforce, data privacy concerns, and ensuring equitable access to AI technologies are significant hurdles that need to be overcome.

Moreover, as AI becomes more pervasive, it raises important ethical and societal questions. How do we ensure that AI doesn't exacerbate existing inequalities? How do we prepare for potential job displacements while creating new AI-driven opportunities? How do we develop AI systems that respect India's diverse cultural and linguistic landscape?

Addressing these challenges will require a concerted effort from government, industry, academia, and civil society. It will require:

1. Investment in digital infrastructure to bridge the urban-rural digital divide.
2. Comprehensive skill development programs to prepare the workforce for an AI-driven economy.
3. Robust regulatory frameworks that foster innovation while protecting individual rights and societal interests.

4. Initiatives to promote AI adoption among small and medium enterprises.
5. Research and development efforts to create AI solutions that are tailored to India's unique context and challenges.

The AI transformation of Indian industries is not just about technological advancement; it's about leveraging AI to address India's pressing developmental challenges. It's about using AI to make healthcare more accessible, to make agriculture more resilient, to make financial services more inclusive, and to make manufacturing more competitive.

As India continues on this transformative journey, it has the potential to emerge not just as a user of AI technologies, but as a global leader in AI innovation. By developing AI solutions that address its unique challenges, India could create models of AI-driven development that are relevant not just for itself, but for other developing countries around the world.

The AI revolution in Indian industries is still in its early stages, and the full impact of this transformation is yet to unfold. What's clear, however, is that AI will play a crucial role in shaping India's economic future. As we navigate this AI-driven future, the key will be to ensure that this technological revolution translates into inclusive growth and improved quality of life for all Indians.

Building India's AI Infrastructure

As India positions itself to become a global leader in artificial intelligence (AI), the development of robust AI infrastructure emerges as a critical prerequisite. This infrastructure encompasses not just the physical components like data centers and high-speed networks, but also the digital ecosystems, regulatory frameworks, and human capital necessary to support AI innovation and deployment at scale. In this section, we delve into the multifaceted challenge of building India's AI infrastructure, exploring current initiatives, persistent hurdles, and the road ahead.

The Data Ecosystem: Fuel for AI Innovation

At the heart of AI development lies data - the raw material that feeds machine learning algorithms and powers AI applications. India, with its vast and diverse population, has the potential to generate enormous volumes of data across various domains. However, harnessing this potential requires a well-structured data ecosystem that ensures data quality, accessibility, and privacy.

Data Collection and Aggregation

India's efforts in data collection and aggregation have been significant, albeit fragmented:

1. Aadhaar: The world's largest biometric ID system, Aadhaar, has created a digital identity for over 1.3 billion Indians. While not directly used for AI, it has laid the groundwork for large-scale data collection and digital service delivery.
2. India Stack: This set of APIs allows governments, businesses, startups, and developers to utilize Aadhaar for digital service delivery. It's a crucial part of India's digital infrastructure, facilitating data flow across various sectors.
3. National Digital Health Mission: Launched in 2020, this initiative aims to create a unified health ID for every Indian citizen, potentially generating a vast repository of health data.
4. Smart Cities Mission: This urban renewal program involves the deployment of IoT sensors and data analytics platforms in 100 cities, generating rich urban data sets.

Despite these initiatives, challenges persist:

- Data Silos: Many government departments and private entities still operate in silos, hampering the free flow of data necessary for comprehensive AI applications.
- Data Quality: Inconsistent data collection methods and lack of standardization often result in poor quality data, unsuitable for AI training.
- Rural-Urban Divide: Data collection efforts are often skewed towards urban areas, potentially leading to biased AI models.

To address these issues, the government has launched the National Data Governance Framework Policy, which aims to standardize data collection and sharing practices across government entities. However, implementation remains a challenge, and extending these standards to the private sector is crucial for a comprehensive data ecosystem.

Data Privacy and Security

As India ramps up its data collection efforts, concerns about data privacy and security have come to the forefront:

1. Personal Data Protection Bill: After years of deliberation, India passed the Digital Personal Data Protection Act in 2023. This legislation aims to protect individual privacy rights while facilitating the digital economy.
2. Non-Personal Data Framework: The government is working on a framework for non-personal data, which could potentially open up vast data sets for AI innovation while protecting individual privacy.
3. Data Localization: There's an ongoing debate about data localization requirements, balancing national security concerns with the need for global data flows for AI development.

Challenges in this area include:

- Balancing Innovation and Privacy: Strict data protection laws could potentially hamper AI innovation, while lax laws could lead to privacy violations.

- Enforcement Mechanisms: Ensuring compliance with data protection laws across India's vast and diverse business landscape is a significant challenge.
- Cross-Border Data Flows: Navigating international data sharing agreements while protecting national interests is a complex task.

Open Data Initiatives

Open data initiatives are crucial for democratizing access to data and fostering AI innovation:

1. Open Government Data Platform: This platform hosts over 400,000 resources from various government departments, providing a valuable data source for researchers and developers.
2. India Urban Data Exchange: Launched as part of the Smart Cities Mission, this platform facilitates the exchange of data between various urban stakeholders.
3. Sector-Specific Initiatives: Various sectors have launched open data initiatives, such as the Indian Agriculture Statistics Research Institute's data portal.

However, challenges remain:

- Data Quality and Usability: Many open data sets are incomplete, outdated, or in formats not readily usable for AI applications.
- Awareness and Utilization: There's a need to increase awareness about available open data resources and promote their utilization among AI developers.
- Sustainability: Ensuring the long-term sustainability of open data initiatives, including regular updates and maintenance, is crucial.

Computational Resources: Powering AI Innovation

Developing and deploying AI models at scale requires significant computational resources. India's efforts in this area have been gaining momentum, but substantial challenges remain.

High-Performance Computing (HPC) Infrastructure

India has been steadily building its HPC capabilities:

1. National Supercomputing Mission: Launched in 2015, this initiative aims to install a vast supercomputing grid across the country. As of 2023, over 20 supercomputers have been deployed under this mission, including PARAM Siddhi-AI, one of the most powerful supercomputers in India.
2. C-DAC (Centre for Development of Advanced Computing): This autonomous scientific body has been at the forefront of supercomputing development in India, creating systems like PARAM Shivay and PARAM Brahma.
3. Private Sector Initiatives: Companies like Reliance Jio and Tata Group are investing in building data centers and cloud computing infrastructure, crucial for AI deployment.

However, significant challenges persist:

- Capacity Gap: Despite progress, India's HPC capabilities lag behind global leaders. As of 2023, India had only two supercomputers in the global top 100.
- Accessibility: Ensuring that HPC resources are accessible to researchers, startups, and SMEs, not just large corporations and government entities, remains a challenge.
- Power and Cooling: The high energy requirements and cooling needs of HPC systems pose challenges, particularly in a country grappling with power infrastructure issues.

Cloud Computing Infrastructure

Cloud computing plays a crucial role in democratizing access to computational resources for AI development:

1. Public Cloud Providers: Global cloud giants like AWS, Google Cloud, and Microsoft Azure have established data centers in India, providing cloud services tailored to local needs.
2. Domestic Players: Indian companies like Jio and Airtel are entering the cloud services market, potentially providing more localized solutions.
3. Government Cloud (GI Cloud): This initiative aims to accelerate the delivery of e-services by optimizing ICT spending of the government.

Challenges in this area include:

- Data Sovereignty: Concerns about data sovereignty and security when using foreign cloud providers have led to calls for more domestic cloud solutions.
- Skill Gap: There's a significant shortage of cloud computing skills in the Indian workforce, hampering the adoption and effective utilization of cloud resources.
- Cost: While cloud computing can be cost-effective, the pay-as-you-go model can lead to unexpected costs, particularly for resource-intensive AI workloads.

Edge Computing and IoT

As AI applications move beyond centralized data centers to distributed edge devices, edge computing infrastructure becomes crucial:

1. Smart Cities: Many smart city projects in India incorporate edge computing elements, processing data from IoT sensors locally for real-time decision making.

2. Telecom Sector: With the rollout of 5G, telecom companies are investing in edge computing infrastructure to support low-latency applications.
3. Industrial IoT: Manufacturing companies are adopting edge computing solutions for real-time monitoring and predictive maintenance.

Challenges in this area include:

- Standardization: The lack of standardization in IoT protocols and edge computing platforms can lead to interoperability issues.
- Security: Distributed edge devices are potentially more vulnerable to security breaches, necessitating robust security measures.
- Scale: Deploying and managing edge computing infrastructure at scale across India's vast and diverse geography is a significant challenge.

Network Infrastructure: The Backbone of AI Deployment

A robust network infrastructure is crucial for the collection, transmission, and distribution of data for AI applications:

Broadband Connectivity

India has made significant strides in improving broadband connectivity:

1. BharatNet: This ambitious project aims to provide broadband connectivity to all 250,000+ gram panchayats (village councils) in India. As of 2023, over 180,000 gram panchayats have been connected.
2. National Broadband Mission: Launched in 2019, this initiative aims to provide broadband access to all villages by 2022 and create a robust digital communications infrastructure.

3. Private Sector Initiatives: Companies like Reliance Jio have played a crucial role in expanding 4G coverage and reducing data costs, making India one of the world's largest consumers of mobile data.

However, challenges remain:

- Rural-Urban Divide: Despite progress, a significant digital divide persists between urban and rural areas.
- Last-Mile Connectivity: Providing last-mile connectivity, particularly in remote and difficult terrains, remains a challenge.
- Quality of Service: While connectivity has improved, the quality of service, particularly in terms of speed and reliability, often falls short of requirements for sophisticated AI applications.

5G and Beyond

The rollout of 5G networks is set to revolutionize India's digital infrastructure:

1. 5G Trials: Major telecom operators have conducted 5G trials across the country, with commercial rollout beginning in select cities in 2022.
2. Indigenous 5G: There's a push for developing indigenous 5G technology, with initiatives like the 5G testbed project involving premier academic institutions.
3. Beyond 5G: Research is already underway on 6G technology, with India aiming to be at the forefront of this next generation of wireless technology.

Challenges in this area include:

- Spectrum Allocation: Efficient allocation of spectrum for 5G services while balancing the needs of various stakeholders is a complex task.

- Infrastructure Investment: The high cost of 5G infrastructure deployment, particularly in a price-sensitive market like India, poses challenges.
- Use Case Development: Developing compelling use cases that justify the investment in 5G infrastructure, particularly for AI applications, is crucial.

Human Capital: The Driving Force of AI Innovation

While physical and digital infrastructure are crucial, human capital is the driving force behind AI innovation. India's efforts in this area have been significant but face unique challenges:

AI Education and Training

India has been ramping up its efforts in AI education and training:

1. AI Curriculum: The National Education Policy 2020 emphasizes the inclusion of AI in school curricula, with several states already introducing AI courses at the school level.
2. AICTE Initiatives: The All India Council for Technical Education has mandated AI courses in engineering curricula and is promoting faculty development programs in AI.
3. Online Learning: Platforms like SWAYAM (Study Webs of Active-Learning for Young Aspiring Minds) offer online AI courses, making AI education more accessible.
4. Industry-Academia Collaboration: Initiatives like the Wipro-IISc Research and Innovation Network are fostering collaboration between industry and academia in AI research and education.

Challenges in this area include:

- Skill Gap: Despite these efforts, there remains a significant gap between the skills required by the industry and those possessed by graduates.

- Faculty Shortage: There's a shortage of qualified faculty to teach AI courses, particularly at advanced levels.
- Practical Exposure: Many AI education programs lack sufficient hands-on, practical exposure to real-world AI problems.

AI Research Ecosystem

Developing a robust AI research ecosystem is crucial for long-term innovation:

1. AI Research Institutes: Institutions like the Indian Institute of Technology (IITs) and Indian Institute of Science (IISc) are at the forefront of AI research in India.
2. Government Initiatives: Programs like the Interdisciplinary Cyber Physical Systems Mission aim to foster AI research across various domains.
3. Industry Research Centers: Global tech giants like Google, Microsoft, and IBM have set up AI research centers in India, contributing to the local research ecosystem.

Challenges in this area include:

- Funding: Despite increases, research funding in AI remains low compared to global leaders.
- Brain Drain: Many top AI researchers from India end up working abroad, attracted by better opportunities and resources.
- Applied Research: There's a need to balance theoretical research with applied research that addresses India's unique challenges.

Conclusion

The task of building India's AI infrastructure is akin to constructing the foundations of a new digital economy. It's a complex, multifaceted endeavor that touches upon every aspect of the country's technological and economic landscape. As India navigates this challenge, it finds itself in a unique position - balancing the need to catch up with global leaders while also charting its own path that addresses its unique socio-economic context.

The development of India's AI infrastructure is not just a technological imperative but a socio-economic one. It has the potential to democratize access to advanced technologies, bridging the digital divide and creating new opportunities for innovation and entrepreneurship across the country's diverse regions and demographics.

However, this journey is fraught with challenges. From ensuring data privacy and security in a rapidly digitalizing economy to bridging the skills gap in a vast and diverse workforce, from rolling out advanced network infrastructure across challenging terrains to fostering a culture of AI research and innovation - each step forward requires careful navigation of complex issues.

Yet, these challenges also present opportunities. India's unique context - its scale, diversity, and developmental needs - provides a testing ground for AI solutions that could be relevant not just domestically but for other developing economies around the world. By focusing on frugal innovation and developing AI solutions that work in resource-constrained environments, India could potentially leapfrog traditional development pathways and emerge as a leader in accessible, scalable AI technologies.

As India continues to build its AI infrastructure, the key lies in maintaining a balance - between innovation and regulation, between global collaboration and indigenous development, between addressing immediate needs and planning for long-term sustainability. It's a delicate balancing act, but one that could position India at the forefront of the global AI revolution, not just as a user of AI technologies, but as a shaper of the future of AI itself.

The road ahead is long and complex, but the potential rewards - in terms of economic growth, technological advancement, and social progress - are immense. As India builds its AI infrastructure, it's not just constructing data centers and networks, but laying the groundwork for a future where the power of AI can be harnessed to address some of the most pressing challenges facing the nation and the world at large.

Ethical and Societal Implications of AI in India

As artificial intelligence (AI) weaves itself into the fabric of Indian society, it brings with it a tapestry of ethical considerations and societal implications. India, with its unique blend of technological ambition, deep-rooted social complexities, and vast demographic diversity, faces distinct challenges and opportunities in navigating the AI revolution. This section explores the multifaceted impact of AI on Indian society, examining issues of employment, privacy, bias, social transformation, and the ethical frameworks needed to guide this technological transition.

AI and Employment: Disruption and Opportunity

The impact of AI on employment is perhaps one of the most pressing concerns in India, a country where job creation for its large, young population is already a significant challenge.

Job Displacement and Creation

AI's potential to automate tasks across various sectors has raised concerns about job displacement:

- A study by EY and NASSCOM predicts that by 2022, 9% of the workforce will be deployed in new jobs that do not exist today, while 37% will be in jobs that have radically changed skill sets.

- The IT sector, long a cornerstone of India's service economy, faces significant disruption. Routine coding jobs are increasingly being automated, necessitating a shift towards more complex, AI-related roles.
- In the manufacturing sector, AI-driven automation is changing the nature of factory work, potentially displacing low-skilled workers.
- The Business Process Outsourcing (BPO) industry, which employs millions in India, is particularly vulnerable to AI-driven automation. Chatbots and AI-powered voice assistants are already replacing human customer service representatives in many instances.

However, AI is also creating new job opportunities:

- The same EY-NASSCOM study suggests that AI could create 2.3 million jobs in India by 2030, particularly in areas like data science, machine learning, and AI engineering.
- New roles are emerging, such as AI ethicists, data privacy managers, and human-AI interaction designers.
- The healthcare sector is seeing new AI-related roles, from medical imaging specialists who work with AI diagnostics tools to health data analysts who use AI to predict disease outbreaks.

The challenge lies in managing this transition:

- There's a pressing need for large-scale reskilling and upskilling programs to prepare the workforce for AI-driven changes.
- The government's 'Skill India' initiative aims to train over 400 million people in different skills by 2022, with a growing focus on AI-related skills.
- Companies like TCS and Wipro have launched extensive AI training programs for their employees, recognizing the need to evolve with changing technology.
- Educational institutions are revamping their curricula to include AI and machine learning courses, but the pace of change in academia often lags behind industry needs.

Socio-economic Implications

The AI-driven transformation of the job market has broader socio-economic implications:

- There's a risk of exacerbating existing inequalities, as high-skilled workers benefit from new opportunities while low-skilled workers face job insecurity.
- The gig economy, facilitated by AI-powered platforms, is growing rapidly in India. While it offers flexibility, it also raises concerns about job security and workers' rights.
- The potential concentration of AI-driven economic benefits in urban centers could accelerate rural-urban migration, putting additional pressure on already strained urban infrastructure.
- There's a gender dimension to consider as well. With women already underrepresented in STEM fields in India, there's a risk that the AI revolution could widen the gender gap in employment if not managed carefully.

Addressing these challenges requires:

- Policies that promote inclusive AI development, ensuring that the benefits of AI are distributed across different sectors and demographic groups.
- Social safety net programs to support workers displaced by AI-driven automation.
- Educational reforms that emphasize skills likely to remain relevant in an AI-driven economy, such as creativity, critical thinking, and emotional intelligence.
- Initiatives to promote AI education and careers among underrepresented groups, including women and rural populations.

AI and Privacy: Balancing Innovation and Individual Rights

In a country where the concept of privacy is still evolving in the public consciousness, the data-hungry nature of AI poses unique challenges.

Data Protection Framework

India's approach to data protection in the age of AI is still taking shape:

- The Digital Personal Data Protection Act, passed in 2023, aims to protect individual privacy rights while facilitating the digital economy.
- However, the Act has faced criticism for potential loopholes, particularly regarding government access to personal data.
- The proposed framework for non-personal data aims to make large datasets available for AI innovation while protecting individual privacy.

Challenges in implementing these frameworks include:

- Balancing the need for data to fuel AI innovation with individual privacy rights.
- Ensuring compliance across India's vast and diverse business landscape, from tech giants to small startups.
- Addressing the low levels of digital literacy and privacy awareness among the general population.

AI and Surveillance

The use of AI in surveillance raises particular concerns in India:

- Several Indian cities are implementing AI-powered facial recognition systems for law enforcement purposes.
- While these systems promise enhanced security, they also raise concerns about mass surveillance and potential misuse.

- The lack of specific regulations governing AI-powered surveillance technologies has led to calls for more robust safeguards.

Data Localization and AI

The debate around data localization has significant implications for AI development in India:

- Proponents argue that keeping data within Indian borders is crucial for national security and can foster local AI innovation.
- Critics contend that data localization could hamper India's AI growth by limiting access to global datasets and increasing costs for businesses.
- Finding a balance between fostering local AI ecosystems and participating in global AI development remains a challenge.

AI and Bias: Ensuring Fairness in Automated Decision-Making

As AI systems increasingly influence decisions in areas from hiring to lending, ensuring these systems are fair and unbiased becomes crucial.

Sources of Bias

AI systems in India face unique challenges when it comes to bias:

- Historical biases related to caste, religion, and gender, deeply ingrained in Indian society, risk being perpetuated and amplified by AI systems if not carefully addressed.
- The diversity of Indian languages and dialects poses challenges for natural language processing AI, potentially leading to biases against certain linguistic groups.
- Underrepresentation of certain groups in AI development teams can lead to blind spots in identifying and mitigating biases.

Manifestations of AI Bias

Bias in AI systems can manifest in various ways in the Indian context:

- In hiring, AI systems might perpetuate gender biases or caste-based discrimination if trained on historical data reflecting these biases.
- In financial services, AI-powered credit scoring systems might disadvantage certain groups if they don't account for the informal economy, which employs a significant portion of India's workforce.
- In healthcare, AI diagnostic tools might be less accurate for certain demographic groups if they're not trained on sufficiently diverse data.

Addressing AI Bias

Efforts to address AI bias in India include:

- Initiatives to create more diverse and inclusive AI datasets that better represent India's population diversity.
- Research into de-biasing techniques specific to the Indian context, such as methods to identify and mitigate caste-based biases in language models.
- Calls for greater diversity in AI development teams and ethics boards to ensure a range of perspectives in AI design and deployment.
- Proposals for algorithmic audits to detect and address biases in AI systems before they're deployed in sensitive domains.

AI and Social Transformation: Reshaping Indian Society

Beyond its economic impacts, AI has the potential to transform various aspects of Indian society.

Healthcare

AI is poised to revolutionize healthcare delivery in India:

- AI-powered diagnostic tools could help address the shortage of specialist doctors, particularly in rural areas.
- Telemedicine platforms enhanced with AI could significantly improve healthcare access across the country.
- However, over-reliance on AI in healthcare raises concerns about the human touch in medical care and the potential for AI systems to miss nuances that human doctors might catch.

Education

AI is reshaping the educational landscape:

- Personalized learning platforms powered by AI could help address the varying learning needs of India's diverse student population.
- AI tutors could supplement human teachers, particularly in areas facing teacher shortages.
- However, there are concerns about the digital divide exacerbating educational inequalities if AI-enhanced education is not accessible to all.

Agriculture

AI applications in agriculture could have far-reaching impacts:

- AI-powered crop monitoring and prediction systems could help improve yields and reduce waste.
- However, there are concerns about the accessibility of these technologies for small and marginal farmers, who make up the majority of India's farming community.
- The potential loss of traditional farming knowledge as AI systems become more prevalent is another concern.

Governance

AI is beginning to play a role in governance and public service delivery:

- AI-powered chatbots are being used to improve citizen access to government services.
- Predictive AI models are being explored for urban planning and disaster management.
- However, the use of AI in governance raises questions about accountability and the potential for AI systems to influence policy decisions.

Ethical Frameworks for AI in India

As AI becomes more pervasive, there's a growing recognition of the need for ethical frameworks to guide its development and deployment.

Current Initiatives

Several initiatives are underway to develop ethical AI frameworks in India:

- The NITI Aayog, India's premier policy think tank, has released a document on "Responsible AI," outlining principles for ethical AI development.
- The Ministry of Electronics and Information Technology has established a committee to develop an ethics framework for AI.
- Industry bodies like NASSCOM have proposed ethical guidelines for AI development.

Challenges in Developing Ethical Frameworks

Developing ethical AI frameworks in India faces several challenges:

- Balancing Western ethical principles with Indian cultural and philosophical traditions.
- Ensuring that ethical guidelines are practical and enforceable, not just theoretical.

- Addressing the diverse ethical considerations across different sectors and applications of AI.

Key Ethical Considerations

Some key ethical considerations for AI in the Indian context include:

- Ensuring AI systems respect and promote constitutional values like equality and secularism.
- Addressing the potential for AI to exacerbate existing social inequalities.
- Ensuring transparency and explainability in AI systems, particularly those used in public services.
- Protecting individual privacy and autonomy in an increasingly AI-driven world.

Public Perception and AI Literacy

Public understanding and acceptance of AI will be crucial for its ethical and effective deployment.

Current State of AI Literacy

AI literacy in India varies widely:

- There's high awareness and enthusiasm for AI among the urban, educated population, particularly in the tech sector.
- However, understanding of AI among the general population remains low, with many either unaware of AI or having misconceptions about its capabilities and limitations.

Challenges in Promoting AI Literacy

Efforts to promote AI literacy face several challenges:

- The vast diversity of languages and educational backgrounds in India necessitates tailored approaches to AI education.

- Dispelling myths and misconceptions about AI, particularly fears about job losses and privacy invasions, requires sustained effort.
- Ensuring AI literacy reaches marginalized and rural populations is crucial to prevent a new form of digital divide.

Initiatives for AI Literacy

Several initiatives are underway to promote AI literacy:

- The "AI for All" initiative aims to demystify AI for the general public through online courses and awareness programs.
- Some states have introduced AI courses in school curricula to prepare the next generation for an AI-driven world.
- Tech companies are running AI awareness programs as part of their CSR initiatives.

Conclusion

The ethical and societal implications of AI in India present a complex tapestry of challenges and opportunities. As AI technologies continue to evolve and permeate various aspects of Indian society, they bring the potential for transformative positive change alongside risks that must be carefully managed.

India's unique socio-economic landscape offers both advantages and hurdles in the ethical deployment of AI. The country's diversity can serve as a testing ground for creating AI systems that are truly inclusive and unbiased. At the same time, this diversity presents challenges in ensuring that AI benefits reach all segments of society equitably.

Moving forward, India's approach to AI ethics and societal impact will likely shape not just its own technological future but could also provide a model for other developing nations. By fostering a culture of responsible AI development, promoting widespread AI literacy, and creating ethical frameworks that balance innovation with social justice,

India has the opportunity to chart a distinctive path in the global AI landscape.

The journey ahead requires a delicate balance - between embracing AI's potential and safeguarding societal values, between driving economic growth and ensuring inclusive development. As India navigates this path, it stands poised to not just adapt to the AI revolution but to actively shape it, potentially emerging as a global leader in ethical and inclusive AI development.

India's AI Future: A Balanced Approach

As India stands at the cusp of an AI-driven transformation, the path forward requires a delicate balance between ambition and caution, innovation and regulation, global competitiveness and local relevance. This section explores India's potential trajectory in the AI landscape, synthesizing the opportunities and challenges discussed earlier, and proposing a roadmap for balanced AI development.

Synthesizing Opportunities and Challenges

India's AI journey is characterized by a unique set of opportunities and challenges that shape its potential future:

Opportunities

1. Demographic Dividend: With one of the world's largest and youngest populations, India has a vast pool of potential AI talent. The country produces over 2.6 million STEM graduates annually, providing a solid foundation for AI skill development.
2. Data Advantage: India's large and diverse population generates enormous amounts of data across various domains, providing rich fodder for AI training and development.

3. Unique Use Cases: India's developmental challenges present unique opportunities for AI applications, from healthcare delivery in remote areas to optimizing agricultural practices for small-hold farmers.
4. Growing Digital Infrastructure: Initiatives like Digital India and the widespread adoption of smartphones are creating a robust digital ecosystem that can support AI deployment at scale.
5. Startup Ecosystem: India's vibrant startup ecosystem, with over 4,000 AI startups as of 2023, is driving innovation and attracting global investment.

Challenges

1. Skill Gap: Despite the large number of graduates, there's a significant gap between industry requirements and available AI skills.
2. Digital Divide: The uneven distribution of digital infrastructure and literacy across urban and rural areas poses challenges for equitable AI deployment.
3. Data Quality and Privacy: Ensuring high-quality, unbiased data while protecting individual privacy remains a significant challenge.
4. Regulatory Framework: Developing a comprehensive regulatory framework that fosters innovation while ensuring ethical AI deployment is an ongoing challenge.
5. Resource Constraints: Many Indian businesses, particularly SMEs, lack the financial and technical resources to adopt AI technologies.

A Roadmap for Balanced AI Development

Navigating these opportunities and challenges requires a thoughtful, balanced approach. Here's a proposed roadmap for India's AI development:

1. Skill Development at Scale
   - Integrate AI and data science curricula at all levels of education, from schools to universities.

- Launch nationwide AI literacy programs to create awareness and basic understanding among the general public.
- Encourage industry-academia partnerships to ensure skill development aligns with industry needs.

2. Inclusive AI Development
   - Prioritize AI applications that address India's unique challenges, such as healthcare access, agricultural productivity, and financial inclusion.
   - Develop AI solutions that work in low-resource, multilingual environments to ensure wider accessibility.
   - Promote diversity in AI teams to mitigate bias and ensure AI solutions cater to India's diverse population.

3. Robust Data Ecosystem
   - Implement the proposed Data Protection Act with clear guidelines for AI applications.
   - Develop sector-specific data sharing frameworks to foster innovation while protecting privacy.
   - Invest in improving data quality and creating diverse, representative datasets for AI training.

4. Adaptive Regulatory Framework
   - Develop a risk-based regulatory approach that provides oversight for high-risk AI applications while allowing flexibility for innovation.
   - Establish an AI ethics council to provide ongoing guidance on ethical AI development and deployment.
   - Participate actively in global AI governance discussions to ensure India's interests are represented.

5. Infrastructure Development
   - Continue investments in digital infrastructure, focusing on bridging the urban-rural digital divide.

- Develop AI-specific compute infrastructure, including edge computing capabilities for real-time AI applications.

6. Research and Innovation
    - Increase public funding for fundamental AI research in universities and research institutions.
    - Establish centers of excellence for AI research in key sectors like healthcare, agriculture, and manufacturing.
    - Encourage public-private partnerships for applied AI research and commercialization of innovations.

7. Global Collaboration and Competition
    - Foster international collaborations in AI research and development while protecting India's strategic interests.
    - Develop India's niche in the global AI landscape, potentially focusing on AI for social good and frugal AI innovations.

8. AI for Governance
    - Leverage AI to improve public service delivery and governance efficiency.
    - Develop AI-powered tools for policy simulation and impact assessment.
    - Ensure transparency and accountability in the use of AI in governance.

Expert Opinions on India's AI Potential

To gain deeper insights into India's AI future, let's consider the perspectives of various experts in the field:

Dr. Rohini Srivathsa, National Technology Officer at Microsoft India, emphasizes India's unique position: "India has the potential to be a global AI leader, not just in technology development but in shaping how AI can be leveraged for social good. Our diversity and scale provide a unique testing ground for AI solutions that can be applicable globally."

Satya Nadella, CEO of Microsoft and of Indian origin, offers a global perspective: "India can be a world leader in AI, particularly in how AI can be used to solve some of the world's most pressing problems. The key is to focus on inclusive growth and ensuring AI benefits reach all segments of society."

Dr. Vishal Sikka, founder of Vianai Systems and former CEO of Infosys, highlights the importance of education: "India's AI future hinges on our ability to educate and reskill our vast workforce. We need to move beyond just IT services to becoming creators of AI technologies."

Fei-Fei Li, Co-Director of Stanford University's Human-Centered AI Institute, during a visit to India, noted: "India's approach to AI development could serve as a model for other developing countries. The focus on AI for social good, coupled with the country's technical talent, creates a powerful combination."

Nandan Nilekani, co-founder of Infosys and architect of India's Aadhaar program, emphasizes the role of data: "India's data richness, combined with our IT capabilities, gives us a unique advantage in AI. The key is to create the right data frameworks that foster innovation while protecting individual privacy."

These expert opinions underscore India's potential to carve out a unique niche in the global AI landscape, particularly in developing AI solutions for social good and frugal innovations that can be applicable in other developing countries.

The Path Forward

India's AI future is not predestined; it will be shaped by the decisions and actions taken today. By adopting a balanced approach that leverages its strengths while addressing its challenges, India can aspire to be more than just a consumer or implementer of AI technologies developed elsewhere. It has the potential to become a global AI leader, particularly in developing AI solutions that are ethical, inclusive, and geared towards solving pressing societal challenges.

The key lies in fostering an ecosystem that encourages innovation while ensuring responsible AI development. This involves not just technological advancements, but also cultural shifts, policy innovations, and a reimagining of education and workforce development.

As India continues on this journey, it will need to remain agile, adapting its approach as AI technologies evolve and new challenges emerge. The goal should be to harness the power of AI not just for economic growth, but for improving the lives of its 1.3 billion citizens and potentially billions more around the world.

India's AI story is still being written, and the chapters ahead promise to be both challenging and exhilarating. With careful navigation and bold vision, India has the opportunity to not just participate in the global AI revolution but to help shape its direction, potentially ushering in a new era of tech-driven, inclusive development that could serve as a model for the world.

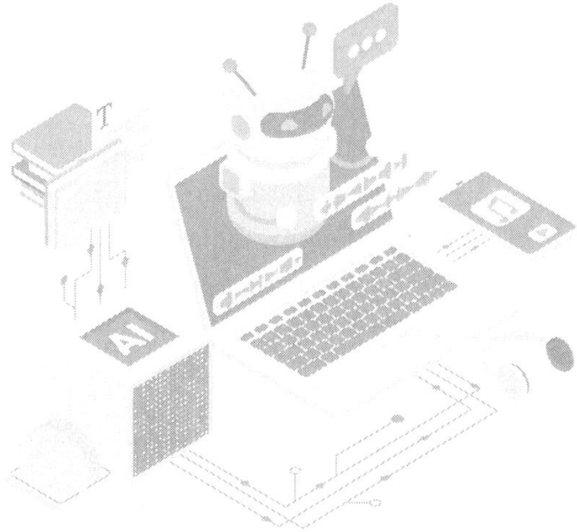

CHAPTER 6

TRANSFORMING BUSINESS THROUGH AI: A STRATEGIC GUIDE

In the rapidly evolving landscape of Indian business, artificial intelligence has emerged as a defining force of transformation. From the tech corridors of Bengaluru to the manufacturing hubs of Gujarat, from the financial centers of Mumbai to the retail chains spanning tier-two cities, AI is reshaping how Indian businesses operate, compete, and grow.

The scale of this transformation is reflected in the numbers. According to NASSCOM's 2023 report, Indian enterprises invested $3.4 billion in AI solutions in 2022-23, with spending projected to grow at 25% annually through 2025. Companies that have successfully implemented AI solutions have seen productivity increases of 14-17% and operational cost reductions of 15-20%. Yet only 8% of Indian SMEs currently use any form of AI in their operations - a gap that represents both a challenge and an opportunity for Indian business.

This transformation is visible across sectors. In retail, Zomato exemplifies the potential of AI-driven evolution. Their platform now employs AI systems that predict order volumes with granular accuracy, optimize delivery routes through complex urban landscapes, and personalize recommendations across India's diverse culinary preferences. The result: a 40% reduction in delivery times and a 30% improvement in order accuracy.

In manufacturing, Tata Steel has deployed AI systems to optimize their blast furnaces, reducing energy consumption by 12% and significantly cutting carbon emissions. Their predictive maintenance systems have decreased unexpected downtime by 25%, demonstrating how AI can enhance both efficiency and sustainability.

In banking, the State Bank of India processes millions of customer queries daily through its AI systems, while its fraud detection algorithms analyze transactions in real-time, reducing fraudulent activities by 60%. This showcases how AI can simultaneously improve customer service and strengthen operational security.

Yet for many Indian businesses, particularly the millions of SMEs that form the backbone of our economy, AI still appears distant and complex. A textile manufacturer in Surat might question how AI could improve their operations. A family-run retail chain in Pune might view AI as a luxury only tech giants can afford. These perceptions, while understandable, risk leaving countless Indian businesses behind as the global economy rapidly transforms.

What makes this transformation particularly crucial for India is our unique position in the global economy. As the world's fifth-largest economy, with ambitions to reach $5 trillion by 2025, India cannot afford to lag in AI adoption. Our demographic dividend - the world's largest youth population - gives us an advantage, but only if we can equip our businesses to compete in an AI-driven world.

The challenges are significant and distinctly Indian. Many businesses face constraints in infrastructure, data quality, and technical expertise. The diversity of our market, with its multiple languages and varying levels of digital literacy, makes implementing AI solutions more complex than in more homogeneous markets. The cost of AI implementation remains a significant barrier, particularly for smaller businesses operating on thin margins.

Yet these very challenges have sparked uniquely Indian innovations. Companies like Vernacular.ai have developed AI solutions that work with multiple Indian languages, making automated customer service accessible to a broader population. Cropin has created AI systems for agriculture that function with minimal data infrastructure, making them suitable for rural India. These examples demonstrate how Indian businesses are not just adopting global AI solutions but creating new ones tailored to our context.

This chapter is written for the Indian business landscape in its entirety - from the street vendor in Chandni Chowk who could benefit from AI-powered inventory management, to the manufacturing giant in

Chennai implementing factory-wide AI systems. We will explore how businesses across this spectrum can approach AI transformation strategically, implementing solutions that are both ambitious and practical, global in standard but local in application.

Our journey through this chapter will cover the essential aspects of business transformation through AI: from building fundamental capabilities to implementing AI across core business functions, from managing change to measuring success. Throughout, we will focus on practical, implementable strategies that work in the Indian context, supported by real examples from Indian businesses that have successfully navigated this transformation.

As we begin this exploration, it's important to remember that AI transformation is not about technology alone - it's about people, processes, and possibilities. It's about creating businesses that are not just more efficient and profitable, but also more innovative and inclusive. For India's businesses, large and small, this transformation represents an opportunity to not just participate in the global AI revolution, but to help shape it, creating solutions that work not just for India, but for the world.

Building AI Capability: From Strategy to Implementation

The gap between AI's promise and its practical implementation defines the central challenge facing Indian businesses today. While NASSCOM reports that 87% of Indian enterprises consider AI strategic to their future, only 25% have successfully moved beyond pilot projects to full implementation. This gap represents not just a technological challenge, but an opportunity to fundamentally reimagine how Indian businesses build new capabilities.

The journey from recognizing AI's potential to successfully implementing it doesn't have to follow the standard global playbook. India's unique business environment - with its mix of cutting-edge tech hubs and traditional industries, its vast talent pool alongside significant skill gaps, its ultra-modern and legacy infrastructure existing side by side - demands a different approach.

Strategic Planning: Laying the Foundation

The foundation of successful AI transformation must begin with strategic planning, but not the kind that produces thick documents destined to gather dust. What's needed is a living strategy that can evolve as capabilities grow and opportunities emerge. Here's how organizations should approach this:

Start with Problems, Not Solutions Too many Indian businesses begin their AI journey by asking "How can we use AI?" The better question is "What problems do we need to solve?" This shift in thinking changes everything. When Asian Paints focused first on their inventory and demand forecasting challenges, they weren't just implementing AI - they were solving concrete business problems that directly impacted their bottom line.

The most valuable problems to tackle often lie hidden in plain sight. In manufacturing, it might be the constant struggle with quality control. In retail, it could be the challenge of predicting demand across diverse regional markets. In services, it might be the need to provide consistent customer experience across multiple languages and cultural contexts.

Build Your AI Compass Before rushing into implementation, organizations need what we might call an "AI compass" - a clear sense of direction that connects technological capabilities to business value. This compass should point toward opportunities that meet three criteria:

- They solve real, pressing business problems
- They can be addressed with available or attainable capabilities
- They deliver measurable value in reasonable timeframes

The Value of Starting Small Consider Marico's approach: they began with a focused six-month assessment phase, analyzing their data infrastructure and identifying specific processes where AI could create immediate value. This wasn't timidity - it was strategic wisdom. Starting small doesn't mean thinking small. It means building capabilities and confidence systematically, creating a foundation for more ambitious transformations.

Assessing AI Readiness

The assessment of AI readiness must go beyond the typical technical checklist. Indian businesses need to evaluate their readiness across three critical dimensions:

Technical Foundation This isn't just about having the latest technology. A manufacturer with decades-old machinery but good process data might be more AI-ready than a newer facility with modern but unconnected systems. The key questions are:

- What data do you actually have, and what stories can it tell?
- How integrated are your systems, and what bridges need building?
- Where are the gaps in your technical infrastructure, and how can they be pragmatically addressed?

Human Capability India's tremendous technology talent pool often masks a crucial truth: successful AI implementation requires more than just technical expertise. It needs:

- Domain experts who understand both their field and AI's potential
- Leaders who can envision and drive AI-enabled transformation
- Teams that can bridge the gap between technical capability and business value

Organizational Readiness This is perhaps the most overlooked dimension of AI capability building. Organizations need:

- A culture that embraces data-driven decision making

- Processes that can adapt to AI-driven insights
- Leadership structures that can drive and sustain transformation

Building Sustainable Capabilities

The goal isn't to become an "AI company" - it's to become a better, more competitive business through the thoughtful application of AI. This requires building capabilities that can evolve over time:

Create Learning Loops Every AI initiative should enhance not just business performance but also organizational capabilities. When Tata Steel implemented AI for quality control, they didn't just improve product quality - they built capabilities in data collection, analysis, and AI-driven decision making that could be applied to other areas.

Develop AI Muscle Memory Organizations need to develop what we might call "AI muscle memory" - the institutional capability to identify opportunities for AI application, evaluate their potential, and execute solutions effectively. This comes not from grand strategies but from consistent practice, from learning what works and what doesn't in your specific context.

Foster Cross-Pollination Some of the most effective AI implementations come from unexpected connections. A solution developed for inventory management might spark ideas for customer service. An approach that works in manufacturing might have applications in procurement. Organizations need mechanisms to capture and cross-pollinate these insights.

The Path to AI Capability

Building AI capability in Indian business requires a unique blend of ambition and pragmatism. The ambition to envision transformative possibilities, combined with the pragmatism to build capabilities systematically and sustainably. The goal isn't to follow global leaders but to create approaches that work in the Indian context - approaches that might eventually become models for other emerging economies.

As we move into examining specific areas of AI implementation, remember that capability building isn't a one-time effort but a continuous journey. The most successful organizations will be those that can build capabilities while delivering value, learning and adapting as they go, creating foundations for ever more ambitious transformations.

Core Areas of AI Implementation

The implementation of AI across Indian businesses reveals both the tremendous potential and the unique challenges of this technology. At Tata Steel's plant in Jamshedpur, AI systems monitor blast furnace operations in real-time, analyzing thousands of parameters every second. In HDFC Bank's operations, AI algorithms scan millions of transactions daily to detect potential fraud. At BigBasket's warehouses, AI-powered systems optimize inventory and predict demand patterns for thousands of products.

But these visible successes risk creating a misleading narrative - that AI implementation is only for large enterprises with substantial resources. The reality is that AI can and should be implemented across businesses of all sizes, across three core areas: operations, customer experience, and product development. Let's explore how Indian businesses can approach each of these areas strategically.

Operations and Efficiency: The Foundation of AI Transformation

In the Indian context, where operating margins are often thin and competition intense, AI-driven operational improvements can be transformative. But the key to success lies not in implementing the most advanced AI systems, but in choosing the right problems to solve.

Process Automation and Optimization

Consider the spectrum of possibilities in manufacturing. At one end, you have sophisticated implementations like Mahindra's automotive plants, where AI handles everything from quality inspection to predictive maintenance. At the other end, you have small manufacturers who might benefit from even basic AI-powered quality control or inventory management.

The lesson from successful implementations isn't about the sophistication of the technology - it's about the clarity of the problem being solved. Start by identifying processes where even small improvements can have significant impact. In quality control, for instance, AI can spot defects more consistently than human inspectors, reducing both errors and inspection costs. This might mean beginning with basic data collection before moving to AI implementation - a step many organizations try to skip, often to their detriment.

The power of process optimization through AI lies in its scalability. What begins as a focused pilot in one area can, once proven successful, be expanded across operations. A manufacturer might start with quality control in one production line, then expand to multiple lines, then to predictive maintenance, and eventually to full production optimization.

Supply Chain Optimization

India's complex supply chains present unique challenges - and opportunities - for AI implementation. The key is to recognize that supply chain optimization isn't just about efficiency; it's about resilience and adaptability. Modern supply chains generate enormous amounts of data - from supplier performance to delivery times, from inventory levels to demand patterns. The real power comes from combining these different data streams to create predictive intelligence.

Consider how AI can transform supply chain operations in the Indian context. A system that can simultaneously predict demand, optimize inventory levels, and adapt to disruptions creates a level of supply chain intelligence that becomes a competitive advantage. This is particularly crucial in India's diverse market, where supply chains must account for everything from modern urban retail to traditional rural distribution networks.

Energy and Resource Optimization

In India, where resource constraints often define business realities, AI-powered optimization can have transformative impact. The key is to think beyond simple automation to holistic resource optimization. Take energy usage in manufacturing: AI can analyze patterns to identify peak usage periods, predict maintenance needs to prevent energy waste, and optimize production schedules to reduce energy costs.

But the real opportunity lies in combining energy optimization with other operational improvements. When energy optimization is integrated with production planning and maintenance scheduling, the combined benefits often exceed the sum of individual improvements. This integrated approach has proven particularly valuable in India's energy-intensive industries, where even small improvements in efficiency can significantly impact profitability.

Customer Experience: The Next Frontier

The transformation of customer experience through AI represents perhaps the greatest opportunity - and challenge - for Indian businesses. The opportunity lies in India's vast, diverse customer base; the challenge lies in serving this base effectively.

Beyond Basic Automation

The first wave of AI in customer experience focused on automation - chatbots, automated responses, basic personalization. But the real potential lies in what we might call "intelligent engagement" - using AI not just to automate interactions but to enhance them. This means developing systems that can understand and respond in multiple Indian languages, recognize and adapt to regional and cultural nuances, and learn from each interaction to improve future responses.

The goal isn't to replace human interaction but to enhance it. By using AI to handle routine queries effectively, businesses can free their human agents to handle more complex issues that require empathy, judgment, and creative problem-solving. This hybrid approach has proven particularly effective in India's financial services sector, where banks like HDFC and SBI have successfully combined AI-powered service with human expertise.

Personalization at Scale

India's market diversity presents unique challenges for personalization. Effective personalization must consider not just individual preferences but cultural contexts, regional variations, and economic factors. The solution lies in developing layered approaches to personalization that consider all these dimensions.

Basic personalization based on demographic and behavioral data forms the foundation. This is enhanced by contextual understanding - considering factors like location, time, and circumstances. Cultural personalization adds another layer, accounting for regional and linguistic preferences. Finally, predictive personalization anticipates future needs and behaviors based on patterns and trends.

Product Development: AI-Driven Innovation

The application of AI to product development represents perhaps the most sophisticated - and potentially most rewarding - area of implementation. Here, AI isn't just optimizing existing processes; it's helping create new value.

Market Intelligence and Product Innovation

AI transforms how businesses understand and respond to market needs through sophisticated analysis of customer feedback and behavior data. It can identify emerging trends, unmet needs, and potential market opportunities far more quickly and comprehensively than traditional market research methods. But the real power comes from combining these AI-driven insights with human creativity and market understanding.

Research and Development Optimization

In sectors like pharmaceuticals and chemicals, AI can dramatically accelerate the R&D process. By analyzing research data to identify promising directions, simulating experiments to reduce physical testing, and optimizing research resource allocation, AI can significantly reduce the time and cost of product development.

The Future of Implementation

As we look to the future of AI implementation across these core areas, several principles emerge as crucial for success:

1. Start with Clear Objectives Successful implementation begins with clear business objectives, not technology for technology's sake.
2. Build Systematically Focus on building capabilities systematically, learning from each implementation before moving to more complex applications.

3. Integrate Thoughtfully Look for opportunities to integrate AI capabilities across different areas of the business, creating compound benefits.
4. Maintain Human Centricity Remember that AI should enhance, not replace, human capabilities and judgment.

The most successful AI implementations often aren't the most technologically sophisticated - they're the ones that most effectively solve real business problems and create tangible value. In the Indian context, this often means finding the right balance between sophistication and simplicity, between global best practices and local realities.

Managing AI Transformation

The technical implementation of AI, while challenging, often proves to be the easier part of transformation. The harder challenge lies in managing the human, organizational, and cultural dimensions of change. This reality becomes particularly acute in the Indian business context, where organizational hierarchies are often deeply entrenched and where the fear of job displacement by automation runs deep.

Change Management: The Human Side of AI Transformation

The successful management of AI transformation requires understanding and addressing the unique characteristics of Indian organizational culture. Traditional change management approaches, developed primarily in Western contexts, often need significant adaptation to work effectively in Indian organizations.

Take the experience of Tata Consultancy Services in managing their own AI transformation. Rather than positioning AI as a replacement for human workers - a common fear in India's labor-intensive IT sector - they framed AI as an enabler of "machine-human collaboration." This wasn't just messaging; it was backed by concrete actions: comprehensive reskilling programs, clear career transition paths, and opportunities for employees to participate in AI implementation projects.

This approach acknowledges a crucial truth: in Indian organizations, successful change often depends as much on emotional buy-in as on rational understanding. People need to not just understand the change intellectually but feel emotionally secure about their place in the transformed organization.

Building Trust Through Transparency

Transparency must be the cornerstone of AI transformation efforts. Organizations need to be clear about which roles will be affected by AI and how. This transparency should extend to sharing both successes and failures in AI implementation. When employees understand both the potential and the limitations of AI, they're more likely to engage constructively with transformation efforts.

The most successful organizations create regular forums for dialogue about AI transformation. These forums serve multiple purposes: they help surface concerns early, generate ideas for AI applications, and build collective understanding of AI's potential and limitations. More importantly, they help create a shared narrative about the organization's AI journey.

Developing AI Champions

One of the most effective approaches to managing AI transformation involves developing networks of AI champions throughout the organization. These champions aren't necessarily technical experts; they're respected team members who understand both the business context and AI's potential.

The role of these champions extends beyond advocacy. They become bridges between technical teams and business units, helping translate between technical capabilities and business needs. They also serve as early warning systems, identifying potential implementation challenges before they become serious problems.

Building Capabilities While Managing Change

The capability-building aspect of AI transformation deserves special attention. While formal training programs are important, the most effective learning often happens through involvement in actual AI projects. Organizations should create opportunities for employees to participate in AI initiatives, even in small ways.

This hands-on involvement serves multiple purposes. It builds practical understanding of AI capabilities, helps people overcome fear of the technology, and creates a pool of employees with both business and AI knowledge. Most importantly, it helps develop the hybrid skills that will be increasingly valuable as AI becomes more prevalent in business operations.

Risk Management: Navigating the Challenges

The management of AI transformation must include robust risk management approaches. This becomes particularly important in the Indian context, where regulatory frameworks around AI are still evolving and public understanding of AI is limited.

Data Security and Privacy

In India's rapidly evolving digital landscape, data security and privacy concerns take on special significance. Organizations implementing AI must develop comprehensive approaches to data protection that consider both global standards and local regulations.

The challenge often lies in finding the right balance between data utilization and protection. Organizations need robust frameworks for data governance that ensure both security and accessibility. These frameworks should address not just technical security measures but also questions of data ownership, access rights, and ethical use.

Ethical Frameworks for AI

The development of ethical frameworks for AI use becomes crucial as implementations become more sophisticated. These frameworks need to consider not just global ethical principles but also local cultural values and social contexts.

Key considerations should include:

Fairness and Bias Organizations must actively work to identify and address potential biases in their AI systems, particularly given India's diverse social and cultural landscape.

Transparency and Accountability Clear mechanisms should exist for understanding and explaining AI decisions, especially in areas that directly affect employees or customers.

Social Impact Assessment Regular assessment of how AI implementations affect different stakeholder groups, with particular attention to potential negative impacts on vulnerable populations.

Creating Sustainable Transformation

Successful AI transformation requires building sustainable capabilities that can evolve with technology and business needs. This means creating structures and processes that facilitate ongoing learning and adaptation.

The Center of Excellence Model

Many successful organizations have adopted some form of AI Center of Excellence (CoE) model. These centers serve as hubs for AI innovation and implementation, but their effectiveness depends on finding the right balance between centralization and decentralization.

The most successful CoEs combine:

- Strategic oversight of AI initiatives
- Technical expertise and standards development
- Best practice sharing across the organization
- Training and capability building support

While maintaining flexibility for:

- Business unit-specific applications
- Local implementation approaches
- Domain-specific innovation
- Rapid experimentation and learning

Creating a Culture of Innovation

Perhaps the most challenging aspect of managing AI transformation lies in fostering a culture that can sustain ongoing innovation and adaptation. This requires careful attention to both formal structures and informal organizational dynamics.

Successful organizations find ways to:

Foster Experimentation Create safe spaces for trying new approaches and learning from failures, while maintaining appropriate risk management.

Enable Cross-Pollination Facilitate the sharing of ideas and experiences across different parts of the organization.

Reward Innovation Recognize and celebrate both successful implementations and valuable learning experiences.

The management of AI transformation is ultimately about creating organizations that can continuously evolve as AI technology advances. Success requires attention to both the technical and human dimensions of change, with particular sensitivity to the unique characteristics of Indian organizational contexts.

As AI becomes more central to business operations, the ability to manage AI transformation effectively will become a crucial differentiator between organizations that thrive and those that struggle to remain relevant. The key lies not in any single approach or framework, but in developing the organizational capability to continuously adapt and evolve while maintaining focus on both business value and human needs.

Measuring Success

"What cannot be measured cannot be improved." This adage, often repeated in business schools across India, takes on new complexity in the context of AI transformation. The measurement of AI success requires a fundamental shift in how we think about business metrics. Traditional measures like ROI and cost reduction, while important, often fail to capture the full impact of AI transformation. This is particularly true in the Indian business context, where AI initiatives frequently catalyze broader organizational and cultural changes that extend far beyond immediate operational improvements.

The Evolution of Success Metrics

As organizations mature in their AI journey, their approach to measurement typically evolves. What begins as a focus on straightforward operational metrics - cost savings, efficiency gains, accuracy improvements - often expands to encompass broader transformational impacts. Organizations discover that the true value of AI often lies not just in direct improvements to specific processes, but in how it transforms relationships, enables new capabilities, and creates opportunities for innovation.

Consider the agricultural sector, where AI is increasingly being deployed across supply chains. A purely operational view might focus on metrics like procurement cost reduction or improvement in demand forecasting accuracy. However, the deeper impact of AI in this sector often manifests in transformative changes: the evolution of farmer relationships from transactional to predictive, the development of more resilient supply chains, and the creation of data-driven agricultural ecosystems that benefit all participants.

Financial Metrics: Beyond Simple ROI

In India's cost-sensitive market, financial metrics naturally play a crucial role in measuring AI success. However, the most effective approach to financial measurement looks beyond immediate returns to consider impact across multiple time horizons.

The first horizon encompasses direct, measurable financial impacts - cost savings from automation, efficiency improvements, and direct revenue increases. These metrics matter because they help justify ongoing investment in AI initiatives. However, they often understate AI's true financial impact.

The second horizon looks at indirect financial benefits. These might include improved customer retention due to better service, reduced risk exposure through better prediction models, or increased market share through improved product offerings. While harder to measure precisely, these benefits often exceed direct financial gains.

The third horizon considers strategic value creation - new business possibilities enabled by AI capabilities, ecosystem advantages created through AI implementation, and options for future growth. These impacts may not show up immediately on the bottom line, but they often determine long-term success.

Operational Excellence: Measuring Transformation

Measuring operational improvements through AI requires particular attention in the Indian context, where operations often involve complex human-machine interactions and varying levels of technological sophistication. A comprehensive measurement framework should consider both technical performance and operational integration.

Technical metrics are straightforward: system accuracy, reliability, and efficiency improvements can be measured objectively. But equally crucial is measuring how effectively AI systems integrate with existing processes and how well people adapt to working with these systems. This includes assessing not just what the AI recommends, but how these recommendations translate into actual operational improvements.

Customer Impact: The Ultimate Measure

For many Indian businesses, customer impact provides the most meaningful measure of AI success. The challenge lies in capturing both the quantitative and qualitative aspects of this impact. Organizations need to measure not just traditional metrics like conversion rates and average order value, but also more subtle indicators of customer satisfaction and loyalty.

In e-commerce, for example, success measurement needs to encompass the entire customer journey. This includes the effectiveness of AI in search relevance, recommendation accuracy, and customer service resolution. Given India's diverse customer base, these measurements must also account for how well AI systems serve different customer segments across languages, regions, and shopping behaviors.

Learning and Innovation Metrics

Perhaps the most overlooked aspect of measuring AI success lies in tracking organizational learning and innovation. The measurement focus here should be on how AI implementation builds organizational capabilities and drives innovation.

This involves assessing how AI knowledge and skills spread through the organization - not just counting trained employees but understanding how deeply AI capabilities are being integrated into different functions. It means measuring how quickly the organization can identify new AI opportunities and convert them into implemented solutions. Equally important is assessing how AI initiatives contribute to building stronger business ecosystems - from supplier networks to customer communities.

A Framework for Comprehensive Measurement

The measurement of AI success requires a balanced framework that considers multiple dimensions of impact. This is particularly crucial in the Indian business context, where AI implementations often need to address unique challenges and opportunities.

Value Creation The first dimension focuses on tangible value creation. This includes direct financial impact through cost savings or revenue enhancement, operational improvements in efficiency and quality, and strategic advantages gained through AI capabilities. The key is to track not just immediate gains but also longer-term value creation through improved capabilities and market position.

Capability Building The second dimension addresses organizational capability development. This encompasses technical capability enhancement, from basic data infrastructure to advanced AI applications. It also includes human capability development - not just technical skills but the broader organizational ability to identify, implement, and benefit from AI solutions.

Stakeholder Impact The third dimension examines how AI initiatives affect various stakeholders. This includes measuring improvements in customer experience, tracking employee engagement and adaptation, and assessing the development of partner ecosystems. In India's relationship-oriented business culture, these stakeholder impacts often prove crucial to long-term success.

Beyond Traditional Metrics

As AI technology evolves and business environments change, measurement frameworks must adapt. The most effective approaches combine quantitative metrics with qualitative assessment of organizational transformation. They help organizations understand not just whether their AI initiatives are succeeding, but how they're transforming the business and what needs adjustment for greater impact.

Organizations should consider several key principles when developing their measurement approaches:

1. Align metrics with strategic objectives Ensure that what you measure reflects what truly matters for your organization's success.
2. Balance short-term and long-term measures Include both immediate performance indicators and longer-term transformation metrics.
3. Consider context-specific factors Account for unique aspects of your industry, market position, and organizational culture.
4. Build in flexibility Create measurement systems that can evolve as your AI capabilities and objectives mature.

The Reality of Measurement

Not everything that matters in AI transformation can be precisely quantified. Some of the most important impacts - like cultural transformation or enhanced innovation capability - require a combination of quantitative and qualitative assessment. The key is to develop measurement approaches that provide meaningful insights while acknowledging these limitations.

For Indian businesses navigating the AI transformation journey, effective measurement serves multiple purposes. It helps justify AI investments, guides implementation efforts, and supports continuous improvement. More importantly, it helps ensure that AI initiatives truly serve broader business objectives and stakeholder needs.

As we look to the future, the ability to meaningfully measure AI success will become increasingly important. Organizations that develop sophisticated yet practical measurement approaches will be better positioned to derive sustainable value from their AI investments and guide their ongoing transformation efforts.

Future-Proofing the Business

The challenge of future-proofing in the age of AI is particularly acute for Indian businesses. In a landscape where technological leapfrogging is common and business environments evolve rapidly, organizations must prepare for futures that are hard to imagine, let alone plan for. The key question becomes: how do we build AI capabilities that remain relevant as technology evolves at an unprecedented pace?

Building Adaptable Systems

The first principle of future-proofing lies in building adaptable AI systems. Rather than creating rigid, specialized solutions, organizations need to develop flexible architectures that can evolve with changing needs. This means designing systems that can be modified, expanded, and repurposed as requirements change and new opportunities emerge.

In the Indian context, this adaptability takes on additional significance. Systems must be able to function across varying levels of infrastructure development, accommodate multiple languages and cultural contexts, and scale across both urban and rural environments. The goal is to create AI capabilities that can grow with the organization while remaining robust enough to deliver consistent value.

The Microservices Approach

One practical strategy for building adaptable systems is the adoption of microservices architecture for AI implementations. This approach breaks down AI capabilities into small, independent services that can be recombined and repurposed as needs change. Such flexibility proves particularly valuable in India's diverse business landscape, where requirements can vary significantly across regions and market segments.

Creating a Culture of Continuous Innovation

Future-proofing requires more than technical adaptability; it demands an organizational culture that can sustain continuous innovation and adaptation. This cultural transformation must balance two seemingly contradictory needs: the stability required for reliable business operations and the flexibility needed for continuous evolution.

Innovation in the Indian Context

The Indian business environment offers unique advantages for building innovation capabilities. The tradition of jugaad - frugal innovation that makes the most of available resources - can be particularly valuable when combined with modern AI capabilities. This combination of resourcefulness and advanced technology often leads to innovations that are both sophisticated and practical.

Developing Meta-Skills

The human element of future-proofing deserves special attention. Organizations need to focus on developing what we might call "meta-skills" - capabilities that remain valuable regardless of how AI technology evolves:

Critical Thinking in Human-AI Collaboration The ability to understand both the potential and limitations of AI systems, and to make informed decisions about when and how to use them.

Adaptive Learning The capability to quickly acquire new skills and knowledge as technology evolves.

Cultural Intelligence The ability to adapt AI solutions for different cultural contexts - crucial in India's diverse market.

Ethical Judgment The capacity to make informed decisions about the ethical implications of AI use.

Infrastructure and Data Readiness

Future-proofing in the Indian context must address infrastructure challenges thoughtfully. Organizations need strategies that work within current constraints while being ready to take advantage of infrastructure improvements as they occur. This often means developing tiered approaches that can deliver value with limited infrastructure while being ready to scale up as capabilities improve.

The Role of Ecosystems

Perhaps the most significant shift in thinking about future-proofing comes in recognizing that no organization can do it alone. Success requires participating in and often helping to build broader ecosystems that enhance collective capabilities for innovation and adaptation.

These ecosystems might include:

- Research institutions developing new AI capabilities
- Startups bringing fresh approaches to AI implementation
- Industry partners sharing data and insights
- Technology providers offering specialized capabilities

Beyond Technology

Future-proofing isn't just about keeping up with technological change. It's about building organizations that can thrive in an AI-enabled world while remaining true to their core values and mission. This means developing the wisdom to know not just how to use AI, but when and why to use it.

Looking Forward

The Indian business landscape, with its unique blend of technological ambition and human-centric values, its drive for innovation and its respect for tradition, offers fertile ground for developing approaches to future-proofing that might serve as models for other emerging economies. The goal isn't to predict the future perfectly, but to build organizations that can adapt and thrive as that future unfolds.

As AI technology continues to evolve, the most successful organizations will be those that can balance technical sophistication with practical implementation, global best practices with local realities, and innovation with stability. They will be organizations that understand that future-proofing isn't a destination but a continuing journey of adaptation and growth.

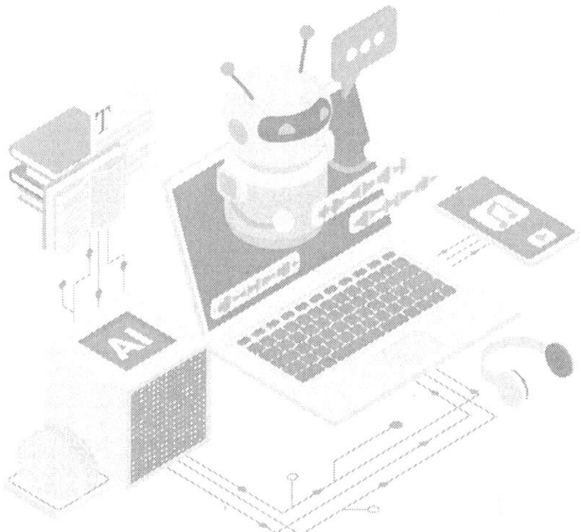

CHAPTER 7

FROM AI PHILOSOPHY TO PERSONAL PRACTICE

The Individual in the Age of AI

We stand at a moment in human history when the questions of artificial intelligence have moved from the realm of speculation to the intimacy of daily life. The phone in your pocket runs dozens of AI models. Your email suggests responses before you type them. Your social media feed is curated by algorithms that predict your interests. Your workplace increasingly integrates AI tools into its processes. The technology we've examined philosophically throughout this book now weaves itself into the fabric of personal existence, demanding not just understanding but response.

This intimacy of AI in our lives creates a peculiar tension. On one hand, AI has become so ubiquitous that we often interact with it unconsciously, our behaviors shaped by its presence in ways we barely notice. We finish sentences it suggests, follow recommendations it makes, and adapt our work patterns to its capabilities. On the other hand, we experience moments of stark awareness - when an AI response feels uncannily human, when we realize how much of our daily experience is mediated by algorithms, when we wonder about the long-term implications of this deep integration of artificial intelligence into our lives.

This tension between unconscious adaptation and conscious concern mirrors larger questions about human agency in the age of AI. Are we actively shaping our relationship with this technology, or merely being shaped by it? Are we maintaining our essential human capabilities even as we extend them through AI? Are we preserving what matters most about human experience while embracing the benefits of artificial intelligence?

The Path from Philosophy to Practice

The philosophical foundations of AI - its nature, capabilities, limitations, and ethical implications - take on new urgency when viewed through the lens of personal choice. Abstract questions about consciousness become concrete when we must decide how much to trust AI's judgments. Theoretical concerns about AI bias become practical when we must choose which AI systems to rely on. Philosophical debates about AI's potential for general intelligence become personal when we consider how to prepare ourselves and our children for an AI-transformed future.

Yet this translation from philosophical understanding to personal practice isn't straightforward. It's one thing to understand AI's nature intellectually; it's another to develop wisdom in living alongside it. This wisdom must encompass not just knowledge of what AI can and cannot do, but judgment about when to use it and when to rely on human capabilities, discernment about how to maintain human agency while leveraging AI's power, and insight about how to preserve and develop what is distinctively human in an increasingly AI-mediated world.

The Challenge of Personal Agency

The question of personal agency in relation to AI is particularly complex because the technology affects us both directly and indirectly. We make direct choices about AI use - which tools to employ, which recommendations to follow, which systems to trust. But we also live in an environment increasingly shaped by AI, from the information we encounter to the opportunities we perceive to the ways we think about human capability and potential.

This dual nature of AI influence demands a sophisticated response. We need to develop both tactical wisdom about specific AI interactions and strategic wisdom about how to maintain human agency in an AI-shaped world. We need to understand not just how to use AI tools effectively, but how to prevent them from unconsciously reshaping our capabilities, values, and sense of human potential.

Moreover, we need to recognize that our individual choices about AI use collectively shape its role in society. When we choose to rely on

AI for certain tasks, we influence not just our own capabilities but the development of collective human expertise in those areas. When we accept or reject certain forms of AI mediation in our relationships, we contribute to evolving norms about human connection in the digital age. When we demand certain qualities from AI systems - transparency, ethical behavior, respect for human values - we help shape the development of AI technology itself.

The Scope of Personal Practice

The development of personal practice in relation to AI must encompass multiple dimensions of human experience. In our professional lives, we need to learn how to work with AI in ways that enhance rather than diminish our capabilities. In our personal relationships, we must navigate the role of AI mediation while preserving authentic human connection. In our individual development, we need to cultivate capabilities that complement rather than compete with AI while maintaining our essential human qualities.

This personal practice must also span different timeframes. We need immediate tactics for current AI interactions, medium-term strategies for developing relevant capabilities, and long-term wisdom about maintaining human agency and meaning in an AI-transformed world. We need to think both practically about specific choices and philosophically about their broader implications for human development and flourishing.

The Journey Ahead

This chapter explores how we might develop this personal practice in relation to AI. We'll examine how philosophical understanding can inform practical choices, how to develop wisdom in AI interaction, and how to maintain human agency and meaning in an AI-transformed world. We'll look at specific strategies for professional adaptation, personal development, and relationship preservation in the age of AI.

But perhaps most importantly, we'll explore how to maintain active choice in our relationship with AI - how to ensure that we shape this technology's role in our lives rather than being unconsciously shaped by it. This exploration isn't about reaching final answers but about developing the wisdom to navigate an evolving relationship with one of the most powerful technologies humanity has ever created.

The stake in this exploration is not just personal adaptation but human flourishing in the age of AI. The choices we make now - individually and collectively - will help determine whether AI enhances or diminishes human capability, whether it enriches or impoverishes human experience, whether it expands or contracts the scope of human potential. In this light, the development of personal practice in relation to AI becomes not just a practical necessity but a crucial contribution to humanity's future.

From Understanding to Action

The gap between understanding AI and knowing how to live with it productively has never been more challenging - or more crucial to bridge. We live in a world where AI doesn't just analyze and compute but creates and suggests, doesn't just process but seems to understand, doesn't just automate but appears to think. In this landscape, moving from philosophical understanding to practical action requires new levels of discernment and wisdom.

Philosophical Foundation

The Nature of Intelligence and Its Implications
The nature of intelligence reveals itself as far more nuanced than we once imagined. It's not simply a matter of processing power or pattern recognition, but a spectrum of capabilities that manifests differently in

humans and machines. Human intelligence emerges from our embodied experience, our emotional lives, our social connections, and our ability to find meaning in the abstract and ambiguous. AI's intelligence, even at its most impressive, follows a fundamentally different path - one of pattern recognition at massive scale, of probabilistic modeling, of recombination and synthesis.

This distinction matters deeply for how we approach our relationship with AI. When an AI system generates human-like text, it's not understanding or creating in the way humans do - it's predicting and assembling based on patterns in its training data. When it produces an image from a description, it's not imagining in the way humans do but synthesizing elements from its trained understanding of visual patterns. This fundamental difference in how AI and humans process information and generate outputs should inform how we integrate AI into our lives and work.

The implications extend beyond theoretical understanding. When we recognize that an AI writing assistant isn't truly understanding the context of our writing but rather predicting likely word sequences, we can better leverage its capabilities while maintaining our own critical judgment. When we understand that an AI's artistic output is a sophisticated form of pattern recombination rather than genuine creativity, we can better position it as a tool for augmenting rather than replacing human creative expression.

Consciousness and Experience in the Age of AI

The question of consciousness takes on new urgency as AI systems become more sophisticated in their interactions. The fact that an AI can engage in seemingly meaningful dialogue, create apparently original art, or compose emotionally moving music doesn't mean it experiences consciousness as we do. This isn't just a philosophical point - it has practical implications for how we engage with AI systems.

Understanding that AI lacks genuine consciousness helps us maintain appropriate boundaries. We can appreciate an AI's ability to generate human-like outputs while recognizing that it doesn't have true understanding, emotional experience, or intentionality. This awareness helps us avoid both anthropomorphizing AI and underestimating its capabilities. We can engage with AI as a powerful tool while remembering that it doesn't share our subjective experience of the world.

This understanding also helps us preserve what is uniquely human in our activities. When we recognize that an AI's outputs, however impressive, don't come from a place of conscious experience or emotional understanding, we can better value and cultivate our own capacities for genuine empathy, emotional resonance, and meaningful connection.

The Ethical Dimension

Ethics becomes not just a theoretical concern but a practical necessity as we navigate daily interactions with AI systems. Every interaction involves choices about authenticity, attribution, privacy, and the preservation of human agency. When we use AI to help write an email, generate an image, analyze data, or make a decision, we're engaging with questions of responsibility, transparency, and autonomy.

The ethical implications extend beyond individual interactions to broader questions about how AI shapes our capabilities and relationships. How do we ensure that our use of AI enhances rather than diminishes our human capabilities? How do we maintain authentic human connection in an increasingly AI-mediated world? How do we preserve privacy and autonomy while benefiting from AI's capabilities?

These ethical considerations demand practical frameworks for decision-making. We need guidelines for when to use AI assistance and when to rely on purely human effort, principles for maintaining transparency about AI use, and strategies for ensuring that our use of AI aligns with our values and goals.

Personal Response to AI Evolution

The Tactical Level: Skills and Practices
At the most immediate level, living with AI requires developing new skills and practices. This goes beyond simple tool use to encompass sophisticated understanding of AI capabilities and limitations. We need to learn not just how to prompt AI systems effectively but how to evaluate their outputs critically, how to integrate AI assistance while maintaining our own judgment, and how to use AI tools in ways that enhance rather than replace our capabilities.

These skills include:

- Understanding the strengths and limitations of different types of AI systems
- Developing effective strategies for working with AI tools
- Learning to evaluate AI outputs critically
- Maintaining our own capabilities while leveraging AI assistance
- Building habits that support productive human-AI collaboration

But these tactical skills must be grounded in deeper understanding and guided by clear principles. We need to develop not just proficiency but wisdom in our use of AI tools.

The Strategic Level: Metacognition and Adaptation

Beyond immediate skills, we must develop new forms of metacognition - awareness of how our own thinking and creative processes work in relation to AI. This includes understanding how AI tools might influence our thought patterns, creativity, and problem-solving approaches. It means being conscious of how AI might supplement or potentially atrophy our natural capabilities.

This strategic level of response involves:

- Monitoring how AI use affects our own thinking and capabilities
- Developing strategies for maintaining and enhancing our natural abilities
- Creating boundaries that protect our essential human processes
- Building practices that support genuine learning and growth
- Cultivating awareness of how AI shapes our perceptions and decisions

The Identity Level: Authenticity and Self-Development

At the deepest level, our response to AI must address questions of identity and authentic self-expression. How do we maintain genuine creativity when AI can generate content that mimics our style? How do we ensure authentic personal growth when AI can provide ready-made solutions? How do we preserve genuine human connection when interactions are increasingly AI-mediated?

These questions demand both philosophical reflection and practical action. We must develop:

- Clear understanding of what we consider authentically human
- Frameworks for maintaining genuine self-expression
- Strategies for using AI while preserving authentic human connection
- Approaches to personal growth that integrate AI thoughtfully
- Methods for maintaining agency in an AI-mediated world

The Role of Human Agency in an AI World

Active Choice and Conscious Engagement

Central to this journey from understanding to action is the preservation and enhancement of human agency. This means moving beyond both technophobia and techno-utopianism to a position of informed, intentional engagement with AI. It means recognizing that we have the power and responsibility to shape how AI influences our lives and work.

Agency in the AI age requires new forms of literacy - not just technical understanding but the ability to think critically about AI's role in our lives. This includes understanding how AI systems might influence our decisions, shape our perceptions, and affect our relationships. It means developing the ability to step back and evaluate whether our use of AI aligns with our values and goals.

Balancing Integration and Independence

The preservation of agency requires careful balance between integrating AI capabilities and maintaining independent human capacity. We must learn to:

- Use AI as an enhancer rather than a replacement for human capabilities
- Maintain critical thinking skills while leveraging AI assistance
- Preserve direct human connection alongside AI-mediated interaction
- Develop personal practices that support both AI integration and human independence
- Create boundaries that protect essential human activities and experiences

Collective Implications of Individual Choices

While personal choice remains crucial, we must also recognize that our individual decisions about AI use take place within broader social and cultural contexts. Our choices about how to engage with AI contribute to evolving norms about human-AI interaction. They influence not just our own lives but the collective human relationship with this technology.

This broader context doesn't diminish the importance of personal action - it amplifies it. Each choice we make about how to use AI, how to maintain our human capabilities alongside it, and how to preserve authentic human connection contributes to the larger social conversation about AI's role in human life.

Moving Forward: The Path to Practical Wisdom

The translation of philosophical understanding into practical action isn't a one-time event but an ongoing process of adaptation and refinement. As AI capabilities evolve, so too must our approaches to living alongside this technology. This requires developing not just specific skills or guidelines but the wisdom to navigate an ever-changing landscape.

The path forward involves maintaining a delicate balance - between embracing AI's benefits and preserving human capability, between leveraging AI's power and maintaining authentic human experience, between adapting to technological change and staying true to our essential humanity. This balance can only be achieved through conscious choice and ongoing reflection about how we want AI to fit into our lives and work.

As we move into examining specific strategies for coexistence with AI, these foundational insights will guide us toward practices that enhance rather than diminish our humanity. The goal is not just to adapt to AI but to thrive alongside it, maintaining and enhancing what makes us distinctively human while leveraging the unprecedented capabilities this technology offers.

The Art of Coexistence

The challenge of coexisting with AI extends far beyond learning to use new tools. We face a fundamental shift in how humans engage with technology - one that demands not just technical proficiency but a sophisticated understanding of how to maintain our humanity while leveraging increasingly powerful artificial minds. This isn't simply about learning to prompt effectively or evaluate AI outputs; it's about developing a deep understanding of how to live and work alongside systems that can now generate human-like text, create compelling images, compose music, write code, and engage in seemingly meaningful dialogue. The art of coexistence requires us to navigate this new reality while preserving what makes us distinctively human.

Human-AI Synergy

The foundation of effective human-AI collaboration lies in understanding the profound differences in how humans and AI systems approach tasks, create meaning, and engage with the world. AI systems, even the most sophisticated ones, operate through pattern recognition and statistical prediction. They can process vast amounts of data, identify subtle correlations, and generate outputs that often appear remarkably human-like. But they lack the embodied understanding, emotional resonance, and genuine comprehension that characterizes human thinking and creativity. This fundamental difference isn't a limitation to be overcome but a reality to be embraced - one that points the way toward truly effective collaboration.

Consider the process of creative writing in this new landscape. An AI system can generate text that is grammatically perfect and stylistically sophisticated, drawing on patterns learned from millions of examples. It can suggest plot developments, create character descriptions, and even mimic specific literary styles. But it cannot understand the deeper purpose of storytelling - the human desire to make meaning of experience, to connect with others through shared emotional truth, to explore the complexities of consciousness and existence. A writer working with AI must therefore approach the collaboration with clear understanding of these distinctions. The AI can serve as a powerful tool for exploration and refinement, helping overcome writer's block, suggesting alternative phrasings, or generating initial drafts. But the essential human elements -

the authentic voice, the genuine insight, the emotional truth - must come from the writer's lived experience and conscious intention.

This same principle extends across all domains of human-AI collaboration. In visual art, AI can generate stunning images and suggest countless variations, but it cannot understand the artist's desire to express particular emotional truths or explore specific conceptual territories. In music composition, AI can create complex harmonies and novel melodic combinations, but it cannot grasp the emotional narrative that gives music its deepest meaning. In business analysis, AI can process vast amounts of data and identify patterns that humans might miss, but it cannot understand the complex human dynamics that often determine whether strategies will succeed or fail in practice.

The most effective human-AI collaboration emerges when we deeply understand these distinctions and build our collaborative practices around them. This means developing what we might call "collaborative wisdom" - the ability to know when and how to engage AI capabilities while maintaining human agency and intention. This wisdom manifests in multiple dimensions, each requiring careful attention and development.

At the level of process, collaborative wisdom means understanding how to structure work flows that make the best use of both human and AI capabilities. This might mean using AI for initial exploration or generation, but maintaining human control over direction and refinement. It means developing sophisticated understanding of how to guide AI systems effectively - not just through better prompts or more technical knowledge, but through clearer human intention and purpose. Most importantly, it means maintaining active critical engagement throughout the process, never ceding human judgment and intentionality to AI outputs, no matter how impressive they might appear.

At a deeper level, collaborative wisdom requires developing new forms of metacognition - awareness of how our own thinking and creative processes interact with AI systems. We must remain conscious of how AI influences our thought patterns, shapes our creative choices, and affects our decision-making processes. This awareness helps us maintain genuine human agency while leveraging AI capabilities effectively. It allows us to recognize when AI assistance enhances our work and when it might be leading us away from our authentic purpose or intention.

The Development of Collaborative Practice

The development of effective human-AI collaboration requires more than theoretical understanding - it demands practical wisdom developed through thoughtful engagement. This wisdom emerges through conscious attention to several key dimensions of practice.

First is the development of intentionality in AI engagement. Every interaction with AI should begin with clear human purpose and direction. Whether we're writing, creating art, solving problems, or making decisions, we must maintain conscious control over the process rather than letting AI capabilities drive our direction. This means developing the habit of starting with clear intention, using AI as a tool to explore and enhance our purpose rather than allowing it to shape our goals or direction.

Second is the cultivation of boundary awareness - sophisticated understanding of when to use AI and when to rely on purely human capabilities. This isn't just about technical limitations or capabilities; it's about maintaining and developing our essential human faculties. Some aspects of work and creativity should remain AI-free, not because AI can't contribute, but because direct human engagement is crucial for our development and fulfillment. These boundaries aren't fixed - they evolve as both AI capabilities and our own understanding develop. The key is maintaining conscious choice about where we draw these lines rather than letting them be determined by convenience or capability alone.

Third is the development of integration skills - the ability to combine human and AI capabilities in ways that enhance rather than diminish human work. This means learning to use AI as a tool for amplification rather than replacement, as a means of extending our capabilities while maintaining our essential human contribution. It requires developing sophisticated understanding of how to incorporate AI-generated elements into genuinely human work while maintaining authenticity and intentionality.

The Social Dimensions of Coexistence

The art of coexistence has crucial social dimensions that extend beyond individual practice. As AI becomes more integrated into human activities, we must develop new social understandings and norms about its role in human interaction and collaboration. This includes evolving standards for transparency about AI use, shared understanding of what constitutes authentic human work in an AI-enabled world, and new frameworks for maintaining meaningful human collaboration when AI tools are part of the process.

Perhaps most importantly, we must develop new wisdom about preserving genuine human connection in an increasingly AI-mediated world. This means understanding when AI mediation enhances human connection and when it diminishes it, maintaining spaces for direct human interaction, and finding ways to use AI that deepen rather than replace human relationship and understanding. It means being conscious of how AI mediation affects the quality of human interaction and making conscious choices about when and how to engage AI in our relationships with others.

The Cultural Transformation of Human-AI Relations

The deepening relationship between humans and artificial intelligence represents more than a technological shift - it marks a cultural transformation in how we understand and express our humanity. This transformation demands that we develop new forms of wisdom about human capability and purpose. It requires us to think deeply about what aspects of human activity and experience we wish to preserve as purely human, what aspects we choose to enhance through AI collaboration, and what new forms of human expression and achievement might emerge through thoughtful integration of AI capabilities.

The art of coexistence ultimately becomes an art of conscious evolution - not of becoming more like machines, but of becoming more deeply and authentically human through our engagement with artificial minds. This means developing not just new skills or practices, but new ways of understanding and expressing our humanity in a world shared with increasingly sophisticated artificial intelligence. The challenge and opportunity lie not in resisting this transformation nor in surrendering to it, but in actively shaping it through conscious choice and deep understanding of what makes us human.

Practical Wisdom

The development of practical wisdom in relation to AI requires more than understanding principles or mastering techniques. It demands the cultivation of judgment - the ability to navigate complex situations where rules alone cannot guide us. This wisdom emerges through thoughtful engagement with AI in our daily lives, as we learn to balance its capabilities with our human needs and values.

Mindful Integration

The foundation of practical wisdom lies in mindful integration of AI into our lives and work. This mindfulness goes beyond simple awareness of AI's presence or capabilities. It requires deep attention to how AI affects our thinking, our creativity, our relationships, and our sense of self.

Consider how AI has transformed the act of writing. The availability of AI writing assistants creates a constant choice: when to use them, how much to rely on them, how to maintain our authentic voice while benefiting from their capabilities. Practical wisdom in this context means developing nuanced understanding of how different levels of AI assistance affect our writing process. Sometimes, the wise choice might be to use AI extensively - perhaps when dealing with routine communication or technical documentation. Other times, wisdom lies in keeping our writing process entirely human, particularly when exploring deeply personal themes or developing our unique voice.

This same need for nuanced judgment appears across domains. In professional work, we must decide when AI analysis truly enhances our understanding and when it might be leading us away from crucial human insights. In creative endeavors, we must determine when AI assistance amplifies our vision and when it dilutes our authentic expression. In personal relationships, we must judge when AI-mediated communication enhances connection and when it creates harmful distance.

The Development of Judgment

Practical wisdom develops through conscious attention to the effects of our choices in AI engagement. This means observing not just the immediate outcomes of using AI but its longer-term effects on our capabilities, relationships, and satisfaction. We might notice, for instance, that heavy reliance on AI writing assistance makes our independent writing more difficult, or that AI-generated solutions to problems often lack the deep understanding that comes from working through challenges ourselves.

This observation leads to more sophisticated judgment about when and how to engage AI capabilities. We begin to recognize patterns in our use of AI - what approaches lead to genuine enhancement of our work and life, and what patterns might be creating dependency or diminishing our capabilities. This recognition allows us to develop more nuanced strategies for AI integration.

The Role of Experimentation

Developing practical wisdom requires thoughtful experimentation with different approaches to AI integration. This might mean trying periods of intensive AI use followed by periods of intentional non-use, observing how each affects our work and wellbeing. It might involve testing different levels of AI assistance in various activities, noting which lead to genuine enhancement and which to unwanted dependencies.

These experiments reveal patterns that help us develop better judgment. We might discover, for example, that using AI for initial brainstorming enhances our creativity while using it for final refinement diminishes our satisfaction with the work. Or we might find that AI assistance with routine tasks frees mental energy for more meaningful activities, while AI help with complex problems prevents us from developing crucial understanding.

Personal Growth Alongside AI

The development of practical wisdom intertwines deeply with personal growth. As we learn to work with AI more effectively, we must also cultivate our distinctively human capabilities. This dual development requires careful attention to how our use of AI affects our growth and learning.

Consider how AI affects skill development. When we rely on AI to solve problems or create content, we might miss valuable learning opportunities. Yet when used thoughtfully, AI can accelerate learning by providing immediate feedback, suggesting alternatives, or highlighting patterns we might miss. Practical wisdom means finding the balance that promotes rather than hinders our development.

This wisdom extends to emotional and interpersonal development as well. As AI systems become more sophisticated in generating emotional content or mediating human interaction, we must develop keener awareness of what constitutes genuine emotional growth and authentic human connection. This awareness helps us make better choices about when to engage AI in emotional or interpersonal contexts.

The Cultivation of Awareness

Central to practical wisdom is the cultivation of deeper awareness - of ourselves, of AI's influence, and of the interaction between the two. This awareness has several crucial dimensions:

Technical awareness involves understanding not just how to use AI tools but how they work at a fundamental level. This understanding helps us make better judgments about their capabilities and limitations, about when to trust their outputs and when to question them.

Psychological awareness means paying attention to how AI affects our thinking patterns, our creative processes, and our problem-solving approaches. It means noticing when AI enhances our mental capabilities and when it might be creating unhealthy dependencies or diminishing our natural abilities.

Social awareness involves understanding how AI affects our relationships and interactions with others. This includes recognizing how AI-mediated communication changes the quality of our connections, and how shared use of AI tools affects collaboration and community.

Existential awareness means maintaining clear sense of our human identity and purpose while engaging with increasingly sophisticated AI systems. This awareness helps us make choices that enhance rather than diminish our humanity.

Sustainability in Practice

The development of practical wisdom must consider the long-term sustainability of our relationship with AI. This means creating practices that not only serve us well today but support our ongoing development and wellbeing. Sustainable practice requires attention to several key dimensions:

Capability Maintenance: We must develop habits that maintain our core human capabilities even as we leverage AI assistance. This might mean regularly engaging in purely human efforts, setting boundaries around AI use, or creating specific practices for developing our natural abilities.

Relationship Quality: Our practices must support rather than erode the quality of human relationships. This involves conscious choice about when and how to use AI in our interactions with others, and maintenance of spaces for purely human connection.

Creative Authenticity: Sustainable practice requires maintaining our authentic creative voice while benefiting from AI capabilities. This means developing clear understanding of what aspects of our creative process we wish to keep purely human, and where AI assistance genuinely enhances our expression.

The Integration of Wisdom

Practical wisdom in the age of AI emerges from the integration of these various dimensions of awareness and practice. This integration manifests as refined judgment about how to engage with AI in ways that enhance rather than diminish our human experience. It shows itself in the ability to make nuanced choices about AI use based on deep understanding of both the technology's capabilities and our human needs and values.

This wisdom becomes particularly crucial as AI capabilities continue to expand. Each new advance in AI technology - whether in language processing, image generation, or other domains - creates new possibilities for both enhancement and diminishment of human experience. Practical wisdom helps us navigate these possibilities in ways that support genuine human flourishing.

The Art of Living with AI

Ultimately, practical wisdom in relation to AI becomes an art of living - a sophisticated understanding of how to maintain and enhance our humanity while benefiting from artificial intelligence. This art manifests in daily choices about how to engage with AI, in ongoing cultivation of human capabilities alongside AI use, and in the maintenance of practices that support genuine human development and connection.

This wisdom shows itself not in rigid rules or fixed practices, but in the ability to navigate the complex and evolving relationship between human and artificial intelligence with grace and discernment. It emerges through conscious engagement with AI, careful observation of its effects on our lives and work, and ongoing refinement of our approaches based on deep understanding of what truly enhances human experience and development.

Looking Forward: Personal Agency in Shaping AI's Future

Looking Forward: Shaping the Human Future in an AI Age
The emergence of increasingly sophisticated artificial intelligence marks a profound turning point in human experience. We stand not just at a technological frontier but at the threshold of a transformation in human capability, creativity, and purpose. The rapid evolution of AI - from language models that can engage in nuanced dialogue to systems that generate images, music, and code - creates unprecedented

possibilities for human enhancement and equally unprecedented challenges to human agency and authenticity.

This transformation isn't something that simply happens to us. It emerges through countless individual choices about how to engage with these technologies, how to maintain human agency alongside them, and how to ensure they serve rather than diminish human flourishing. Our choices today - about how to use AI, how to preserve human capability, how to maintain authentic connection - will help shape the landscape of human experience for generations to come.

The Evolution of Human Capability

As AI systems become more sophisticated, we must evolve new forms of human capability - not to compete with AI but to maintain and enhance what makes us distinctively human. This evolution takes several crucial forms, each demanding conscious development and ongoing refinement.

Meta-Intelligence: The Development of Higher-Order Thinking

The first frontier of human capability development lies in meta-intelligence - our ability to think about thinking itself, to understand both human and artificial cognitive processes, and to make wise choices about how to combine them. This isn't just about understanding how AI works; it's about developing sophisticated awareness of how different forms of intelligence - human and artificial - can work together effectively.

This meta-intelligence encompasses several crucial capabilities:

Cognitive Integration We must develop sophisticated understanding of how to integrate AI capabilities with human thought processes. This means learning when to leverage AI's pattern-recognition capabilities and when to rely on human intuition and judgment. It means understanding how AI might enhance our thinking without replacing our essential cognitive processes.

Pattern Recognition of Patterns While AI excels at recognizing patterns in data, humans must develop higher-order capability to recognize patterns in AI behavior itself - understanding not just what AI systems output but how and why they generate particular results. This meta-level pattern recognition helps us use AI more effectively while maintaining critical awareness of its limitations and biases.

Intentional Thinking As AI handles more routine cognitive tasks, humans must develop more sophisticated intentional thinking - the ability to direct our thought processes purposefully rather than simply responding to immediate stimuli or following established patterns. This includes developing stronger capabilities for:

- Strategic thought that goes beyond pattern recognition to true innovation
- Ethical reasoning that considers complex implications and human values
- Creative thinking that transcends recombination to genuine novelty
- Critical analysis that examines assumptions and implications deeply

These capabilities become increasingly important as AI handles more routine cognitive tasks, freeing humans to focus on higher-order thinking.

The Development of Creative Synthesis

The future of human creativity lies not in competing with AI's generative capabilities but in developing more sophisticated forms of creative synthesis. This means learning to combine human insight, emotional understanding, and purposeful intention with AI's capabilities in ways that enhance rather than diminish authentic human expression.

Authentic Creative Voice As AI systems become more capable of generating content that mimics human creativity, maintaining authentic creative voice becomes both more challenging and more crucial. This involves developing:

- Deeper understanding of our unique creative impulses and intentions
- Stronger connection to our authentic creative vision
- More sophisticated ability to integrate AI capabilities while maintaining genuine expression
- Clearer sense of when to use AI assistance and when to rely on purely human creativity

Creative Integration The art of creative synthesis involves learning to combine human and AI capabilities in ways that enhance rather than diminish human creativity. This means developing:

- Understanding of how different forms of AI assistance affect creative process
- Ability to maintain creative intention while leveraging AI capabilities
- Skill in combining AI-generated elements with human creative vision
- Wisdom about when and how to use AI in creative work

These capabilities must evolve through conscious practice and reflection, through ongoing experimentation with different approaches to human-AI creative collaboration.

Emotional and Social Intelligence

As AI systems become more sophisticated at processing emotional content and mediating social interactions, humans must develop deeper forms of emotional and social intelligence. This isn't about competing with AI's ability to recognize emotional patterns but about developing richer forms of emotional understanding and authentic connection.

Emotional Depth While AI can recognize and respond to emotional patterns, humans must develop deeper emotional capabilities:

- Genuine empathy that goes beyond pattern recognition to true understanding
- Emotional authenticity in an increasingly mediated world
- Sophisticated awareness of emotional nuance and context
- Ability to maintain emotional presence alongside AI assistance

Social Wisdom The evolution of social intelligence in an AI age involves developing:

- Understanding of how AI mediation affects human connection
- Ability to maintain authentic relationship in AI-enhanced contexts
- Wisdom about when to use AI in social interaction and when to maintain purely human connection
- Capacity for genuine human presence in an increasingly digital world

The Power of Individual Choice

In the unfolding story of human-AI interaction, individual choices carry unprecedented weight. Every time we engage with AI systems - whether writing with AI assistance, creating with AI tools, or making decisions informed by AI analysis - we participate in shaping how these technologies integrate into human life and society. These aren't merely personal choices about tool use; they are acts of cultural creation that help determine how humanity will coexist with artificial intelligence.

The significance of these choices extends far beyond their immediate impact. When a teacher decides how to integrate AI into their classroom, they aren't simply making a pedagogical choice - they are helping establish patterns for how learning might evolve in an AI-enabled world.

Their decisions about when to use AI assistance and when to maintain purely human instruction, how to balance AI's capabilities with human development, and how to prepare students for an AI-enabled future help create templates that others might follow or react against.

Similarly, when artists and creators navigate the use of AI in their work, they aren't just making individual creative choices. They are developing and demonstrating possibilities for human-AI creative collaboration that influence how others might approach this relationship. An artist who discovers ways to maintain authentic creative vision while leveraging AI's capabilities contributes to our collective understanding of how human creativity might flourish alongside artificial intelligence.

These individual choices accumulate and interact in complex ways. A professional who establishes thoughtful boundaries around AI use in their work influences not just their own practice but their colleagues' approaches, their organization's culture, and potentially their entire field's relationship with AI. The decisions they make about when to rely on AI analysis and when to prioritize human judgment, how to maintain professional expertise alongside AI capabilities, and how to ensure AI serves rather than diminishes human professional development help shape emerging norms about appropriate AI integration.

The subtlety and complexity of these choices demands deep awareness. We must consider not just the immediate utility of AI assistance but its longer-term effects on our capabilities, our relationships, and our sense of purpose. When we choose to use AI for a task, we aren't just choosing a tool - we're participating in a shift in how that type of task might be approached in the future. When we set boundaries around AI use, we aren't just making personal choices - we're contributing to evolving understanding of what aspects of human activity should remain primarily human.

The impact of our choices extends to the development of AI systems themselves. Through our patterns of use and non-use, through our explicit and implicit feedback, through our acceptance or rejection of various AI capabilities, we influence the evolution of these technologies. When we choose to correct AI outputs, provide detailed feedback, or decide not to use certain capabilities, we send signals about what kinds of AI development might be more or less valuable for human flourishing.

This influence operates through multiple channels. Direct feedback - corrections, specifications, explicit preferences - helps shape how AI systems evolve. But equally important is indirect feedback through patterns of use: which capabilities we embrace, which we modify, which we reject. Our choices about how to integrate AI into different aspects of life and work help determine which directions of AI development receive more attention and resources.

The responsibility inherent in this position of influence is significant. As early participants in the evolution of human-AI interaction, our choices help establish patterns that may persist for generations. This isn't about getting every choice "right" - it's about approaching these choices with awareness of their broader implications and potential ripple effects.

Consider how these choices manifest in different contexts. In education, choices about AI use influence not just current learning but students' future relationship with AI technologies. In healthcare, decisions about AI integration affect not just immediate care but the evolution of the healing relationship between providers and patients. In creative fields, choices about AI use influence not just individual works but the future of human creative expression.

The cumulative impact of these choices extends beyond their immediate domains. When enough individuals in a field or community make similar choices about AI use, they create emergent patterns that influence broader social and cultural norms. These patterns then influence how others approach AI, creating feedback loops that shape the ongoing evolution of human-AI interaction.

This power of individual choice carries both opportunity and obligation. The opportunity lies in our ability to influence how AI integrates into human life and society, to help shape these technologies in directions that serve human flourishing. The obligation lies in approaching these choices with awareness and intention, considering their broader implications for human capability, relationship, and purpose.

Cultural Creation in an AI Age

The emergence of generative AI marks a transformation in human cultural creation as profound as the invention of writing or the development of mechanical reproduction. When artificial intelligence can generate images that capture the subtle nuances of human expression, compose music that moves listeners to tears, write poetry that resonates with deeply personal experiences, and create narratives that engage our fundamental human concerns, we must fundamentally reconsider the nature of cultural production and authenticity.

This transformation extends far beyond the mere addition of new creative tools. It challenges our deepest understanding of what it means to create, to express, to communicate meaning through cultural artifacts. The ability of AI to generate content that seems to carry human intention and emotional resonance forces us to examine what truly constitutes meaningful human expression in this new age.

Consider the visual arts, where the impact of generative AI has been particularly dramatic. Artists now face a medium that can not only execute technical skills with precision but can seemingly understand and respond to abstract concepts, emotional suggestions, and cultural references. This capability transforms the very nature of artistic practice. The artist's role shifts from being solely the executor of vision to becoming a creative director of possibilities, a curator of potential expressions, a shaper of emergent meanings.

The relationship between human intention and AI capability creates new forms of artistic exploration and expression. An artist working with AI enters into a complex dialogue where each prompt, each refinement, each selection becomes part of an iterative process of discovery. This isn't simply about using AI as a tool to achieve pre-conceived ends. Instead, it becomes a form of collaborative exploration where the boundaries between human creativity and artificial generation blur and reshape themselves with each interaction.

This collaborative process often leads to unexpected discoveries and novel forms of expression. An artist might begin with a specific vision but find themselves drawn into exploring possibilities they never imagined, as the AI system generates variations and combinations that suggest new artistic directions. This doesn't diminish the role of human creativity but transforms it, requiring new forms of artistic judgment and creative wisdom.

The implications for cultural authenticity and originality run deep. When AI can generate perfect pastiches of any artistic style, the meaning of stylistic choice shifts fundamentally. Artists must now consider not just how to develop a distinctive style, but how to maintain authentic creative voice in dialogue with systems that can instantly generate countless variations on any aesthetic approach. This challenges us to develop new understanding of what constitutes genuine artistic expression in an age of unlimited synthetic generation.

The transformation extends into music, where AI systems can now compose in any style, generate complex harmonies, and even respond to emotional prompts with seemingly appropriate musical expression. Musicians and composers face questions about the nature of musical creativity when AI can generate endless variations of any musical idea. The challenge becomes not just creating music, but finding ways to maintain genuine musical expression and emotional connection in an environment of unlimited synthetic possibility.

Literary creation undergoes similar transformation. When AI can generate prose that mimics any author's style, construct complex narratives, and even engage with subtle themes and character development, writers must reconsider what constitutes meaningful literary expression. The question shifts from how to write effectively to how to maintain authentic voice and genuine human insight in dialogue with systems that can generate seemingly meaningful text at scale.

These changes in creative practice lead to the emergence of entirely new cultural forms. We see the development of dynamic artworks that evolve in response to viewer interaction, musical compositions that adapt and change based on listener engagement, and narratives that branch and reshape themselves through AI-enabled responsiveness to reader input. These new forms don't simply add technological capability to existing artistic practices - they create new possibilities for human expression and cultural experience.

The implications for cultural heritage and tradition become particularly acute in this context. How do we maintain meaningful connection to cultural traditions when AI can generate perfect simulations of traditional forms? This question becomes especially crucial in contexts like India, where cultural continuity carries deep significance and where traditional art forms often embody spiritual and philosophical meanings beyond their surface aesthetics.

The preservation of cultural authenticity requires new approaches when synthetic generation becomes ubiquitous. We must develop ways to maintain the essence of cultural traditions while allowing them to evolve and engage with new technological possibilities. This isn't simply about preserving traditional forms against technological change, but about finding ways for cultural traditions to maintain their vitality and meaning in dialogue with new capabilities.

The role of human meaning-making becomes both more crucial and more complex in this environment. While AI can generate content that seems meaningful, the actual creation of meaning - the connection of expression to genuine human experience, understanding, and purpose - remains fundamentally human. Artists, musicians, writers, and other cultural creators must develop new ways to ensure their work carries authentic human meaning while engaging with AI's generative capabilities.

This leads to the emergence of new forms of cultural wisdom - understanding about how to maintain human authenticity and meaning while embracing new creative possibilities. This wisdom isn't about rejecting AI's capabilities nor about surrendering to them, but about developing sophisticated understanding of how to engage with these capabilities while maintaining genuine human expression and cultural significance.

New Literacies

The transformation of cultural creation demands new forms of literacy - new capabilities for understanding, creating, and engaging with cultural expression in an AI-enabled world. These new literacies go far beyond traditional understanding of how to read and interpret content. They require sophisticated awareness of how meaning is created, transmitted, and understood in an environment where the boundaries between human and synthetic expression become increasingly fluid.

Technical literacy takes on new dimensions in this context. Understanding how AI systems generate content becomes crucial not just for creators but for anyone engaging with contemporary culture. This understanding isn't primarily technical - it's about grasping how AI systems process and recombine information, how they respond to human input, and how they generate seemingly meaningful content.

This knowledge becomes essential for maintaining agency and understanding in an environment saturated with synthetic media.

The ability to recognize and evaluate AI-generated content requires new forms of critical awareness. This isn't simply about identifying whether something was created by AI - a task that becomes increasingly difficult as generation capabilities advance. Instead, it's about developing sophisticated understanding of how meaning and authenticity manifest in an environment where both human and artificial generation play active roles in cultural production.

These capabilities extend beyond simple recognition to understanding how AI shapes cultural expression and communication. When AI systems can generate seemingly authentic human expression at scale, we must develop new ways to evaluate and understand the significance of cultural artifacts. This includes understanding how AI influences creative processes, how it shapes possibilities for expression, and how it affects the transmission of cultural meaning.

The development of expressive literacy - the ability to create and communicate effectively in an AI-enabled environment - becomes increasingly crucial. This involves understanding how to maintain authentic voice while leveraging AI capabilities, how to ensure genuine human connection in AI-mediated communication, and how to create meaningful expression in dialogue with generative systems.

These literacies extend into social and cultural dimensions. Understanding how AI affects cultural transmission and evolution becomes essential for maintaining meaningful connection to cultural heritage while embracing new possibilities for expression. This includes developing awareness of how AI might affect different cultural contexts differently, how it might influence power dynamics in cultural expression, and how it might shape the evolution of cultural forms and meanings.

The ability to navigate these complex waters requires development of new forms of wisdom about how meaning is created and communicated in an AI-enabled world. This wisdom isn't just about technical capability or critical awareness - it's about understanding how to maintain genuine human connection and cultural significance in an environment where synthetic generation becomes increasingly sophisticated and ubiquitous.

These new literacies must also encompass ethical dimensions. Understanding the implications of AI-generated content for truth, authenticity, and cultural power becomes crucial. This includes developing awareness of how AI might affect different communities differently, how it might influence cultural representation and transmission, and how it might shape possibilities for cultural expression and evolution.

The development of these literacies isn't just an individual challenge but a collective one. As societies, we must develop shared understanding of how to maintain meaningful cultural transmission and authentic human expression in an environment where synthetic generation becomes increasingly sophisticated. This involves creating new frameworks for understanding authenticity, new approaches to cultural preservation, and new ways of fostering genuine human expression and connection.

The Emergence of Collective Wisdom

As individuals navigate their relationships with AI through conscious choice and thoughtful practice, their experiences and insights contribute to an emerging collective wisdom about how humanity might flourish alongside artificial intelligence. This wisdom isn't merely accumulated knowledge about how to use AI tools effectively - it represents deeper understanding about maintaining human agency, capability, and meaning in an AI-enabled world.

The development of this collective wisdom occurs through multiple interconnected processes. When individuals discover effective approaches to working with AI while maintaining human capability, their insights don't remain purely personal. Through sharing of experiences, through demonstration of possibilities, through discussion of challenges and solutions, these individual discoveries become part of a broader conversation about human-AI cooperation.

This process of collective learning takes on particular significance in professional communities. When doctors share their experiences of maintaining medical judgment alongside AI assistance, when teachers discuss approaches to integrating AI while fostering genuine learning, when artists explore ways to maintain creative authenticity while leveraging AI capabilities, they contribute to their communities' understanding of how to work effectively with AI while preserving what's most valuable in human practice.

The wisdom that emerges through these collective processes goes beyond practical knowledge to encompass deeper understanding about human capability and purpose in an AI-enabled world. Through ongoing engagement with AI systems, through observation of their effects on human activity and relationship, through discussion and reflection on these experiences, communities develop sophisticated awareness of how to ensure AI serves rather than diminishes human flourishing.

This collective wisdom isn't uniform but richly varied, reflecting different contexts, needs, and values. Different communities and cultures develop distinct approaches to human-AI interaction based on their particular circumstances and priorities. This diversity of approach represents a crucial resource - a range of experiments in how humanity might relate to artificial intelligence, each offering valuable insights and possibilities.

Consider how this wisdom develops in different cultural contexts. In India, for instance, communities might develop approaches to AI integration that reflect traditional values of human relationship and spiritual development while embracing technological advancement. In other contexts, different balances might emerge between efficiency and human agency, between technological capability and human development.

The evolution of cultural norms around AI use represents a particularly important aspect of this collective wisdom development. Through countless individual choices and shared experiences, communities begin to develop shared understanding about appropriate AI integration - when to use AI assistance and when to maintain purely human processes, how to preserve human capability alongside AI use, how to ensure technology serves rather than shapes human purposes.

These emerging norms aren't simply rules or guidelines but sophisticated cultural understandings about how to maintain human flourishing in an AI-enabled world. They encompass awareness of how AI affects human capability and relationship, understanding of how to preserve what's most valuable in human activity, and wisdom about how to ensure technology serves genuine human development.

The role of different communities in developing and sharing this wisdom takes on crucial importance. Professional communities contribute understanding about maintaining expertise and judgment alongside AI capabilities. Educational communities develop insight about fostering genuine human learning and development in an AI-enabled environment. Creative communities explore ways to maintain authentic expression while embracing new technological possibilities.

The interplay between individual learning and collective knowledge development creates rich dynamics of wisdom evolution. Individual discoveries inform collective understanding, while collective wisdom provides context and foundation for individual exploration. This recursive process helps develop increasingly sophisticated approaches to human-AI interaction.

The emergence of collective wisdom about living alongside AI represents one of humanity's most important ongoing developments. Through conscious attention to how AI affects human capability and flourishing, through sharing of insights and experiences, through development of cultural understanding about appropriate AI integration, we participate in shaping humanity's relationship with artificial intelligence.

This process demands active participation and attention. The wisdom we need won't emerge automatically but requires conscious engagement with questions of human purpose and flourishing in an AI-enabled world. It requires ongoing dialogue about how to ensure technology serves genuine human development, continuous attention to how AI affects human capability and relationship, and active development of approaches that enhance rather than diminish human experience.

The collective wisdom that emerges through these processes becomes a crucial resource for humanity's future with AI. It helps us navigate the challenges of maintaining human agency and meaning in an increasingly AI-enabled world, guides the development of approaches that serve genuine human flourishing, and contributes to humanity's understanding of how to live well alongside artificial intelligence.

Conclusion: The Journey from Understanding to Wisdom

Our exploration of artificial intelligence began with fundamental questions about the nature of intelligence and consciousness. We examined what it means for a system to think, to understand, to create. We grappled with questions of consciousness and experience that have challenged philosophers for centuries. These weren't merely academic exercises - they provided crucial foundation for understanding what AI is and isn't, what it can and cannot do, and how we might approach our relationship with these increasingly sophisticated artificial minds.

Through our examination of AI's societal impact, we saw how these philosophical questions translate into practical challenges and opportunities. We explored how AI is transforming education - not just through tools and techniques but by forcing us to reconsider what learning means in an age when information is instantly accessible and artificial minds can engage in sophisticated dialogue. We examined how AI is reshaping work, requiring us to rethink not just skills and jobs but the very nature of human contribution in an AI-enabled workplace.

Our deep dive into India's AI journey revealed how cultural context shapes the integration of artificial intelligence into society. We saw how India's unique challenges and opportunities - its diversity of languages and cultures, its mix of cutting-edge technology and traditional practices, its need to balance rapid development with inclusive growth - create distinctive approaches to AI adoption and development. This exploration showed how different societies might develop their own paths to human-AI integration, ones that reflect their values, needs, and aspirations.

The examination of AI in business revealed the practical challenges of implementing AI while maintaining human agency and value. We saw how organizations must balance the drive for efficiency and innovation with the need to preserve human capability and judgment. This balance isn't just about technology implementation - it's about maintaining human purpose and meaning in increasingly AI-enabled environments.

Throughout these explorations, certain themes emerged repeatedly, taking on new significance in different contexts:

The Question of Agency From philosophical discussions of free will to practical challenges of maintaining human control in AI-enabled systems, the question of human agency emerged as central to our relationship with AI. We saw how maintaining meaningful human choice and direction becomes both more challenging and more crucial as AI capabilities expand.

The Nature of Understanding Our initial philosophical exploration of understanding - what it means for a system to truly comprehend rather than simply process information - took on practical significance as we examined AI's role in education, business, and personal development. We saw how maintaining human understanding alongside AI capability requires conscious choice and practice.

The Role of Consciousness The question of consciousness, which began as a philosophical inquiry, revealed practical implications for how we engage with AI systems. Understanding that AI processes information differently from conscious human minds helps us make better choices about when and how to use AI capabilities while maintaining human awareness and intention.

The Importance of Values From examining AI's ethical implications to considering its role in business and society, the question of values emerged repeatedly. We saw how AI systems inevitably embed values, making it crucial to consciously shape their development and deployment in alignment with human values and purposes.

The Power of Choice Throughout our exploration, we saw how individual and collective choices shape the development and impact of AI. From business leaders deciding how to implement AI to individuals choosing how to engage with AI tools, these choices collectively determine how AI integrates into human life and society.

As we moved from broad societal implications to personal practice, these themes took on immediate practical significance. We saw how philosophical understanding informs practical wisdom, how societal challenges translate into personal choices, how business considerations affect individual development and opportunity.

This movement from understanding to wisdom reveals a crucial truth: our relationship with AI isn't something that simply happens to us. It emerges through conscious choices about how to engage with these technologies, how to maintain human capability alongside them, and how to ensure they serve rather than diminish human flourishing.

The wisdom we need isn't fixed but evolving, not universal but contextual, not merely intellectual but deeply practical. It emerges through thoughtful engagement with AI, through careful observation of its effects on our capabilities and experiences, through ongoing refinement of our approaches based on what truly enhances human flourishing.

This wisdom has multiple dimensions:

Technical Wisdom Understanding not just how to use AI tools but when and why to use them, maintaining clear sense of their capabilities and limitations.

Personal Wisdom Knowing how to maintain and develop our human capabilities alongside AI, preserving authentic expression and genuine understanding.

Social Wisdom Understanding how to maintain meaningful human connection and collaboration in an increasingly AI-mediated world.

Cultural Wisdom Knowing how to preserve and develop human culture while embracing new possibilities enabled by AI.

As we look to the future, the quality of human experience in an AI-enabled world will depend largely on our ability to develop and share this wisdom. This isn't just about adapting to technological change - it's about actively shaping how AI integrates into human life and society.

The path we've traced - from philosophical understanding through societal implication to personal practice - isn't complete but ongoing. As AI capabilities continue to evolve, so too must our wisdom about living alongside artificial minds. This evolution requires maintaining active engagement with fundamental questions about human nature, purpose, and flourishing while developing practical approaches to human-AI integration.

The challenges are significant but so too are the opportunities. AI offers unprecedented possibilities for enhancing human capability and addressing global challenges. But realizing these possibilities while preserving human flourishing requires conscious choice and ongoing development of wisdom about how to live well alongside artificial minds.

This wisdom begins with each of us - with our choices about how to engage with AI, with our efforts to maintain human capability and connection, with our participation in the broader dialogue about AI's role in human life. Through these individual choices and collective dialogue, we participate in shaping not just our personal relationship with AI but the future of human experience in an AI-enabled world.

The journey ahead isn't about resistance to AI nor surrender to it, but thoughtful engagement that maintains human agency and purpose. It's about developing not just new capabilities but new forms of wisdom about how to live well alongside artificial minds. This wisdom will emerge not through individual insight alone but through collective exploration and dialogue about how to ensure AI serves human flourishing.

As we conclude this exploration, we return to the fundamental question that has guided us throughout: how do we ensure that AI enhances rather than diminishes human experience and potential? The answer lies not in any single approach or framework but in the ongoing development of wisdom about how to maintain human flourishing in an age of artificial intelligence. This development is not just an individual journey but a collective one, not just a technical challenge but a deeply human one.

In this light, our exploration of AI becomes part of humanity's broader journey of self-understanding and development. As we learn to live alongside increasingly sophisticated artificial minds, we deepen our understanding of what makes us human and how we might best develop our distinctive human capabilities. This understanding, combined with practical wisdom about how to engage with AI, will help shape the future of human experience and potential in the age of artificial intelligence.

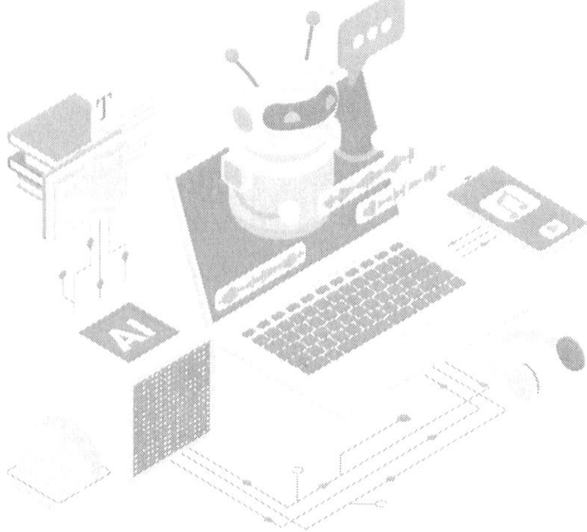

CHAPTER 8

THE EVOLUTION OF AI

Let's cast our minds back to a time before the digital revolution, a time when life's pace was dictated not by the click of a mouse but by the turning of pages, the dialling of rotary phones, and handwritten notes. It was a world where information travelled just as fast as a postage stamp could carry it and where 'wireless' referred to a radio, not an internet connection.

In those days, catching up on the news meant waiting for the morning paper or the evening broadcast. Research meant a trip to the library, thumbing through card catalogues, and navigating the maze of bookshelves. People relied on manual methods for calculations until the widespread public availability of calculators in the 1970's, and if you were planning a trip, you unfolded a large paper map that never quite folded back the same way.

Photographs were precious commodities, captured on film, developed in a darkroom, and treasured in albums. Music collections were physical—records, tapes, and CDs—that took up space on shelves and required bulky players. Movies were events; one would either go to a theatre or rent a VHS tape (and ensure to rewind it before returning).

Communication was personal but often delayed. Crafting letters by hand and patiently anticipating responses took days or even weeks. Long-distance calls were expensive and reserved for special occasions. The pace of life was slower, the world felt bigger, and technology was a tool, not a lifestyle. In some ways, it all felt so warm... did it not?

As we reflect on those simpler times, it's clear that while life may have felt more personal and grounded, it was also marked by limitations—of speed, access, and efficiency. The world moved at a slower pace, but that pace also restricted how quickly we could adapt, connect, and grow. Enter the digital revolution, a period that fundamentally transformed every aspect of life, from communication to information sharing, and reshaped the way we interact with the world. This evolution wasn't just about convenience; it was about survival in a rapidly changing landscape.

As Jeff Bezos reminds us, "What's dangerous is not to evolve." What he meant is that embracing change often involves trying new things and rethinking what we're already comfortable with. It means challenging familiar ideas or routines to make room for improvement and growth. This process can be uncomfortable and uncertain, and there's a real possibility of making mistakes. However, the true risk lies in staying stagnant and avoiding change, which prevents progress.

Change is scary and uncertain but it's inevitable. The transition from analogue to digital technology was like watching a black and white picture bloom into colour. It started with the personal computer, a revolution that began in garages and spread to every desk in every office around the world.

Computers transformed the way we worked, making tasks faster and more efficient, and they brought new forms of entertainment into our homes.

Then came the internet, a network of computers that grew into a digital nervous system connecting the globe. Email made communication instantaneous, and websites became digital homes for businesses and individuals. The internet turned shopping, banking, and even dating into digital experiences.

And soon to join the queue were the mobile phones. They were the next leap forward. They started as bulky bricks that barely fit in a briefcase and evolved into sleek devices that slipped into a pocket. With each upgrade, they incorporated additional technological features: the camera, the music player, the GPS. They brought the world to our fingertips, and with the advent of smartphones, they put the power of a computer in our hands.

The evolution of technology is a timeline of innovation, marked by landmark products that changed the game. The Walkman allowed us to take our music on the go, creating personal soundtracks for our lives. The Game Boy made video games portable, turning any place into an arcade. The iPod digitized our music collection, and iTunes changed the way we bought and consumed media.

Laptops continued the trend of mobility, making the office portable, while tablets bridged the gap between the phone and the computer, offering a new way to read, watch, and browse. E-readers enabled portable libraries, while Netflix transformed small screens into cinemas.

Smart homes have taken technology from our pockets and woven it into the fabric of our living spaces. Thermostats learn our preferences, lights respond to our voices, and security systems give us peace of mind. We can control our homes from anywhere, turning them into responsive environments that adapt to our needs.

Wearable technology, such as fitness trackers and smartwatches, fosters intimate connections by monitoring health and keeping us connected in even more personal ways. They track our steps, read our messages, and even pay for our coffee, all from our wrists.

We live in a time where virtual reality can transport us to other worlds, where drones deliver our packages, and where cars are starting to drive themselves. AI has moved beyond the field of science fiction; it's a reality that learns from us and enhances our lives in numerous ways.

The evolution of technology has made the world smaller, faster, and more connected. It's changed the way we live, work, and relate to one another. It's made life more convenient, but it's also raised questions about privacy, security, and the pace of change.

The future of technology is thrilling yet uncertain. What's clear is that technology will continue to evolve, blurring the lines between the physical and digital worlds even further. We'll see more integration, more connectivity, and more personalization. Technology will further adapt to us, learning preferences and anticipating needs.

The story of technology is one of human ingenuity and curiosity, a narrative that's far from over. As we stand on the brink of new discoveries and innovations, one thing is certain: the evolution of technology is an unstoppable force, one that has the power to continue to reshape our world in ways we can only begin to imagine.

If you look back 20 years, you'll see that we never accurately predicted how fast technology would evolve. During that time, CDs and floppy disks were the norm, offering limited storage capacities of 500-700MB. Transferring a single movie used to take 1-2 hours. At that time, if someone had told you that 'in the future, you'll be able to send 100GB files in less than 10 seconds,' people would have laughed at you. However, this is our reality today.

Moore's Law perfectly illustrates this growth. It observes that the number of transistors in an integrated circuit (IC) doubles about every two years. As the number of transistors increases, the processing power also grows, while the cost per transistor decreases. This has been a driving force in the rapid, exponential growth of technology. It's important to note that this wasn't a prediction, but a realization made by connecting the dots of how technology was evolving.

Today, we are at the dawn of a new era.

Technology is advancing at a speed that seems almost magical, with storage capacities that might soon surpass the capabilities of the human brain and possibly even the entire current internet. This rapid progress makes us wonder not just about what is changing, but why it is changing and what might come next.

As technology evolves, it challenges our understanding of what it means to be intelligent, creative, and human. We are at a point where technology and fundamental human values intersect. This raises important questions about the ethical use of technology, the potential for it to enhance or diminish our abilities, and the implications for our privacy, security, and identity.

This new era is marked by a closer relationship between humans and technology. The key to this transformation is using technology not just to make things faster or more efficient, but to improve the quality of our lives. As machines start to surpass human cognitive abilities, we need to think about what consciousness really means and what role humans will play in a world dominated by smart systems.

The future of technology is uncertain, and even the smartest minds can't predict exactly where it is heading. However, we should always keep ethical considerations in mind as we move forward. By focusing on human welfare and fairness, we can navigate this new territory responsibly and with purpose.

In conclusion, the incredible speed and capacity of modern technology signal the start of a new and exciting era. By thinking deeply about the philosophical and ethical aspects of these changes, we can better understand their impact on our society and make wise choices for the future.

The Birth of AI

In the mid-20th century, the world was on the cusp of a technological revolution. The seeds of what would become AI were being sown, and the pioneers of this field were laying the groundwork for a discipline that would change the world.

Before the term "artificial intelligence" was even coined, there were individuals who were fascinated by the idea of machines that could think. One such individual was Christopher Strachey, later the director of the Programming Research Group at the University of Oxford.

Strachey was one of the first to experiment with programming a computer to play a game. In the early 1950s, he wrote a checkers (draughts) program for the Ferranti Mark I computer at the University of Manchester, England.

This was not just a simple program; it used a minimax algorithm, a decision rule for minimizing the possible loss for a worst-case scenario. When dealing with gains, it becomes a decision rule for maximizing the minimum gain. This was one of the earliest instances of a machine making decisions based on potential future scenarios, a foundational concept in AI. Let me put that in perspective for ease of understanding.

Picture yourself playing a game of tic-tac-toe and it's your turn. You're trying to figure out the best move. You look at the board and think, "If I go here, then my opponent could go there, and that would be bad for me. But if I go over here instead, the worst they could do is this move, which isn't so bad for me."

The minimax algorithm is like that thought process but for a computer. It looks ahead at all the possible moves you and your opponent could make. For each possible move, it asks, "What's the worst thing that could happen?" and "What's the best thing I can do if that worst thing happens?" It tries to minimize the bad outcomes (hence "mini") while also trying to maximize your chances of winning (hence "max").

So, the minimax algorithm helps a computer decide on a move by thinking ahead about all the possible outcomes and choosing the move that will give it the best shot at winning, even if the opponent plays perfectly.

While Strachey was making strides with his checkers program, another British mathematician and logician was pondering the deeper philosophical questions surrounding machine intelligence. Alan Turing, often hailed as the father of modern computing, introduced the concept of a universal machine—a theoretical construct capable of simulating any Turing machine with appropriate inputs. This idea laid the foundation for the modern computer.

In a groundbreaking move, Turing published a seminal paper titled 'Computing Machinery and Intelligence' in the prestigious journal Mind in 1950.

In it, he posed the now-famous question: "Can machines think?" Rather than directly answering this, Turing introduced the "imitation game", which we now know as the Turing Test.

The test involves a human evaluator who engages in a natural language conversation with both a human and a machine designed to produce human-like responses. If the evaluator cannot reliably distinguish between the machine and the human, the machine is said to have passed the test.

Turing's work indeed traversed the fields of both theory and practicality, shaping the contours of AI and computer science. He brilliantly conceptualized the idea of a "universal machine"—a theoretical or hypothetical construct at his time. This imaginative concept suggested a machine with the extraordinary capability to emulate any other machine, contingent upon the provision of appropriate inputs.

While Turing's idea was grounded in abstract thought, it was remarkably profound, furnishing the essential foundations for the emergence of programmable computers. It indicated revolutionary implications for AI, nurturing the development of adaptable and flexible algorithms that could be reprogrammed to perform a huge number of tasks and solve diverse problems.

Founding Fathers of AI

During the 1950s, the term "artificial intelligence" began to take shape. It was John McCarthy, an American computer scientist, who first coined the term in 1955. Together with Marvin Minsky, Nathaniel Rochester, and Claude Shannon, McCarthy organized the Dartmouth Workshop in 1956, often regarded as the seminal event marking the birth of AI as a formal field of study. The proposal for the workshop stated that "every aspect of learning or any other feature of intelligence can in principle be so precisely described that a machine can be made to simulate it."

Marvin Minsky made significant contributions throughout his career. He co-founded the Massachusetts Institute of Technology's AI laboratory and was a proponent of the idea that AI should be approached from a top-down method, focusing on reproducing human-like intelligence in machines.

Another notable figure from this era was Frank Rosenblatt, who introduced the perceptron, a type of artificial neural network, in 1957. This marked a significant milestone in the development of machine learning, a subset of AI wherein machines learn from data.

The Golden Years: AI's First Wave (1957–1974)

In the late 1950s, a new horizon in computing began to emerge, one that promised machines capable of mimicking human thought and reasoning. This era, stretching from 1957 to 1974, is often celebrated as the "Golden Years" of AI. It was a time characterized by a heady mix of optimism, generous funding, and groundbreaking advancements that laid the foundational stones of the AI landscape.

In 1959, a significant leap was made by Arthur Samuel, a visionary at the intersection of computer gaming and AI. He not only coined the term "machine learning" but also developed a checkers-playing program. This wasn't just any program; it was capable of improving its gameplay through a process of self-analysis and learning from past games. It was a concept that, at the time, seemed to pull straight from the pages of science fiction.

The same year witnessed the creation of the Logic Theorist by Allen Newell and Herbert A. Simon. This program, often revered as the first AI program, could mimic the problem-solving skills of a human and solve complex puzzles using logical deduction. Following closely on its heels was the General Problem Solver, an ambitious attempt to create a universal problem-solving machine, one that could approach any challenge with a logical framework.

The mid-1960s brought another marvel: ELIZA, crafted by Joseph Weizenbaum at MIT. This early natural language processing (NLP) program could simulate conversation, engaging users in a dialogue that mirrored that of a Rogerian psychotherapist. ELIZA was a forerunner in human-computer interaction, demonstrating the potential for machines to understand and respond to human language.

As the 1970s approached, the field of AI saw the rise of expert systems, designed to emulate the decision-making abilities of human experts. Among the most notable was DENDRAL, a system that could infer molecular structures from mass spectrometry data. Created by Edward Feigenbaum and Joshua Lederberg, DENDRAL was a trailblazer, showcasing how AI could tackle specialized, complex problems in domains such as chemistry.

The optimism of this period was palpable. The successes of these early systems led many to believe that the creation of a fully intelligent machine was imminent. The U.S. government, recognizing the potential of these burgeoning technologies, became a significant source of funding, leading to rapid expansion in AI research.

However, this golden era was short-lived. The initial promise of AI began to bump up against the hard realities of technological limitations. The optimism of the 1960s gave way to a more sobering understanding in the 1970s, as researchers grappled with the complexities of human cognition and the vast resources required to replicate even a fraction of it in machines.

During this period of intense growth and creativity, the groundwork was laid for the AI landscape we know today.

It was a period marked by both discovery and naivety, as AI pioneers ventured into uncharted territories of the mind and machine. The lessons learned during these formative years continue to influence the field, reminding us that every giant leap is preceded by many small, tentative steps.

AI's Resurgence Post-1980

The seeds of AI research were revived back to life in the 1980s. This period marked a renaissance for AI, fuelled by a confluence of renewed interest, technological advancement, and strategic investment. The resurgence was not accidental; it was a concerted effort by a community that believed in the potential of AI.

The rise of personal computers was a game-changer for AI. No longer were the tools for developing AI confined to well-funded labs or universities with mainframes. The IBM PC was introduced in 1981, and machines like the Apple Macintosh brought computational power to the masses. This democratization meant that a wider pool of talent could tinker with and advance AI technologies. It was a time of exploration and innovation, as hobbyists and researchers alike could now afford the tools to build the future.

The 1980s were marked by methodological breakthroughs that would set the stage for modern AI. One of the most significant was the resurgence of neural networks, which mimic the human brain's structure and function. The development of the backpropagation algorithm in 1986 by David Rumelhart, Geoffrey Hinton, and Ronald Williams allowed neural networks to adjust and improve through experience, laying the groundwork for deep learning.

Expert systems, one of the most successful AI applications of the 1980s, demonstrated the commercial viability of AI. These systems emulated the decision-making abilities of human experts in specific domains. One of the most notable was XCON (also known as R1), an expert system developed for Digital Equipment Corporation. It automated the process of configuring orders for new computer systems, saving the company millions of dollars annually. The success of XCON and others like it captured the attention of industries worldwide, showcasing how AI could solve complex, real-world problems.

The potential of AI to drive efficiency and innovation led to a surge in commercial interest. Companies began to invest heavily in AI, recognizing its ability to transform industries from manufacturing to finance. This period saw the formation of AI labs in companies like IBM, which invested in developing AI for a range of applications, from NLP to automated reasoning.

The government also played a role in this resurgence. In the United States, the Defence Advanced Research Projects Agency (DARPA) increased its funding for AI projects, particularly in machine learning and robotics. In Japan, the government launched the ambitious Fifth Generation Computer Systems project, which aimed to develop computers using massively parallel computing and logic programming, a project that was closely tied to AI research.

The resurgence of AI was not just about technology and investment; it was also about the people who pushed the boundaries of what was possible. Researchers like John Hopfield and David Rumelhart made significant contributions to neural networks, while others like Rodney Brooks shifted the paradigm in robotics, advocating for a bottom-up approach to AI and machine learning.

The 1980s set the stage for the AI boom that would come in the following decades. It was a period of foundational growth, where the seeds of today's AI landscape were sown. The advancements in computational power, the development of new AI methodologies, the commercial success of expert systems, and the strategic investments by industry and government all contributed to the reawakening of AI. This era proved that AI was not just a fleeting fancy but a robust field of study with the potential to revolutionize every aspect of our lives.

As we reflect on the evolution of AI, we recognize it as a force akin to a superpower, continually reshaping our world with each breakthrough. This journey, rich with challenges and triumphs, has proven AI's resilience and its potential to transcend the boundaries of human capability. It has become an integral part of our existence, enhancing not just the efficiency of our tasks but the breadth of our imagination.

Going forward, you will discover the present state of AI—a reality where its applications are as commonplace as they are extraordinary. The narrative of AI is ongoing, and as it unfolds, it promises to redefine the future with every line of code and algorithmic leap. The pages ahead are not just a continuation of this story but an invitation to witness and participate in the unfolding of AI's remarkable potential.

Think about how quickly technology and AI have changed things. But guess what? AI is going to change things even faster, like 10 times faster than before. Remember when sending messages used to take days, weeks, or even months? That was because everything was done by hand or sent through the mail. Then phones made things a bit faster, and computers made a huge difference, cutting down the time from days to just minutes.

But what's coming next is even more amazing. We're talking about doing things in seconds, not hours or days. Imagine the time it takes to brew a cup of coffee. In that brief moment, AI could analyse thousands of financial reports and make investment recommendations. What once took teams of analysts months to do can now be done in seconds.

We're stepping into a new era where things move so fast that even the smartest people can't guess what's going to happen next, every prediction is just a wild guess.

AI's journey has been amazing, showing what humans can do when they really try. The victories of IBM's Deep Blue over chess grandmaster Garry Kasparov, AlphaGo over the Go board champion Lee Sedol, and Libratus against four top players are clear signals of a new era where machines can challenge human intellect in complex tasks.

In 1961, IBM launched Shoebox, the 1st digital speech recognition tool that could recognize 16 words and digits, then in 1972 Harpy program from Carnegie Mellon made advancements to 1000 words. Fast forward to the early 2010s, and AI once again leapt into the public consciousness, this time with an intelligent voice. In 2011, Apple's pioneering voice assistant Siri made its debut, followed by Google Now in 2012, and Alexa in 2014, these transformed our interaction with technology, making it more natural and intuitive. The ability of AI to understand and process human language with precision marked a significant leap forward from the rigid commands of the past to a fluid conversation with machines.

The year 2018 marked another quantum leap with the deployment of Waymo's self-driving taxis on the streets of Phoenix, Arizona. This wasn't just a technological marvel; it was a bold step into the future of transportation, showcasing the practical application and commercial viability of autonomous vehicles.

And now, we stand at the edge of what can only be described as the AI revolution, indicated by the advent of OpenAI's ChatGPT. Since its launch, ChatGPT has demonstrated a breadth of capabilities that have captured the imagination of the world. From passing academic exams to assisting in journalistic endeavours, its sophisticated algorithms have showcased a versatility and adaptability that were once the sole province of human intellect.

Looking ahead, AI's growth is set to change our world in ways we can't even guess. From mastering chess to comprehending human speech and driving cars, AI is expanding the boundaries of what we deem possible. It's not just copying what we do; it's making us better, leading us to a future full of new chances.

Going forward, we will explore the trajectory of AI's evolution, considering the pivotal moments that have shaped its journey and the transformative impact it promises to have on every facet of our lives.

Applications of AI

Artificial Intelligence is no longer just a concept of the future; it has become an integral part of our world today. Its applications are vast and varied, touching nearly every aspect of life and work. From simplifying everyday tasks to tackling complex problems, AI is transforming how we interact with technology. Whether it's improving efficiency, enhancing creativity, or streamlining decision-making, AI has proven its potential to revolutionize the way we live and work. As we explore the different branches of AI, it becomes clear that its impact is widespread, and its possibilities are limitless.

Natural Language Processing

In the field of AI, Natural Language Processing (NLP) has become a cornerstone technology for enabling computers to understand and interact with human language.

NLP encompasses a range of tasks, including syntax and semantics analysis, machine translation, sentiment analysis, speech recognition, and text generation. The goal of NLP is to create systems that can comprehend, interpret, and generate human languages in a way that is meaningful and beneficial.

A significant breakthrough in this field is ChatGPT, developed by OpenAI. ChatGPT is a conversational agent designed to simulate human-like dialogue. It utilizes advanced NLP techniques to provide responses that can answer questions, simulate scenarios, and even generate creative content. Its ability to learn and adapt to various conversational contexts has made it a valuable tool for education, customer service, and entertainment.

By leveraging the principles of NLP, ChatGPT can understand and generate text that is contextually relevant and coherent, making interactions with it feel natural and engaging. This has opened new possibilities for how we interact with technology, making it more accessible and intuitive.

With its diverse applications, ChatGPT demonstrates the practical impact of NLP in our daily lives, showcasing the potential for AI to transform how we communicate and access information.

Gemini, a generative AI chatbot developed by Google, can reason across text, images, audio, video, and code. It's the first model to outperform human experts on Massive Multitask Language (MMLU). In a few use cases Gemini has overtaken GPT-4.

Imagine a world where your role as a content creator, a researcher, or a copywriter is no longer your own. With NLP and AI tools like ChatGPT, we're not just looking at a future possibility—it's happening now. A global survey conducted in 2023 aimed to understand the state of freelance content writers.

Of the 1,590 freelance content writers who participated, 52.5% reported clients engaging in extreme price negotiation following the launch of AI tools like ChatGPT, and 18.2% feared being replaced by AI. The efficiency and relentless evolution of AI mean that within the next five years, the landscape will be unrecognizable. If you're not preparing to work alongside AI, to harness its capabilities, you might find yourself swept away by its current.

Image Generation

The DragGAN AI tool, developed by the Max Planck Institute, exemplifies the innovative application of GANs. This tool allows users to interactively alter images with a simple drag-and-drop interface. By adjusting points on a photograph, the underlying AI seamlessly renders changes, making it appear as if the photo was originally taken with the new modifications. This tool benefits industries such as fashion and advertising, where visual content can be tailored without extensive photoshoots.

This innovation is awe-inspiring, yet it chills the spine to think of photographers and graphic designers whose years of honing their eye for detail could be outmoded by an AI that can intuitively generate and transform images in moments.

AI tools like Midjourney has empowered businesses to create highly detailed images almost instantaneously, enabling marketers to push the boundaries of their creativity at minimal cost. I've personally automated the ad creative process using AI, cutting down the time by 40%. Believe it or not, my team has stopped scouring websites for stock footage ever since I introduced them to the Midjourney AI tool.

The result? They can unleash their creativity without limits. Dall-E, which made a significant impact upon its release, had considerable limitations that relegated it to a secondary option. However, OpenAI has finely tuned its successor, launching Dall-E 3, which allows you to generate images directly from ChatGPT, eliminating the need to use the Dall-E app or spend hours crafting the perfect prompts. Unlike Midjourney, Dall-E 3 has certain ethical safeguards; it won't let you create images of famous personalities or alter an artist's work.

RunwayML on the other hand has democratized the use of AI in creative industries, offering artists and designers a platform to incorporate machine learning into their workflow. With its user-friendly interface,

RunwayML enables the creation of stunning visual effects and complex animations that were once the domain of specialized experts.

Consider the artists and designers who spent years mastering their craft, only to find that RunwayML and Midjourney can now replicate and enhance their work in a fraction of the time. The fear isn't just that jobs are being replaced; it's the realization that our human touch, once invaluable, can be mimicked by algorithms that learn and improve ceaselessly. The question looms: where does this leave the traditional artist?

RunwayML is the short side of the story, but the bigger shock wave in text-to-video category is about "Sora AI", another remarkable AI tool by OpenAI. Sora AI is so advanced that it blurs the line between what's real and what's not. As of March 2024, Sora AI hasn't been released to the general public yet, but it's already being used by some of the top artists in Hollywood. When Sora AI becomes available to everyone with a freemium model, it's going to be a big deal. The videos Sora AI makes are shared on social media and are very realistic. They show detailed scenes with characters moving accurately and backgrounds that look just like real life.

Do film directors like SS Rajamouli, Steven Spielberg, Martin Scorsese, Sukumar, and others need to be on movie sets to work? Or will they start using AI? It's hard to say for sure. But one thing is clear: there are many talented people out there who haven't had the chance to become movie directors. These individuals will now have the opportunity to share their ideas with the world through AI. And who knows? Someone reading this might end up making a movie even better than those made by famous directors like SS Rajamouli or Spielberg, thanks to AI technology.

Programming

Imagine you're a programmer, coding and creating new AI tools that might one day replace your own job. That's what's happening with AI in our world. Programmers are behind creations like ChatGPT, and these tools are truly revolutionizing our field. ChatGPT isn't just a sidekick for fixing code; it's evolving into a powerhouse capable of designing UIs, writing code for those UIs, creating games, and even customizing GPT models to semi-automate various tasks within a company.

Think of it as a digital wizard that brings any idea you have to life.

Another remarkable tool is GitHub Copilot, a cloud-based AI tool that assists developers in writing code. It's an AI pair programmer that offers autocomplete-style suggestions as you code. You can receive suggestions by writing code or by writing a natural language comment.

A survey involving 2,000 developers found that 88% of them felt they were more productive when using the tool. Additionally, a task test with 95 developers revealed that the group using GitHub Copilot completed their tasks 55% faster and had a 7% higher success rate in finishing the tasks.

I remember Emaad Mostaque saying that just 6 months after ChatGPT was released, 40% of the code on GitHub was generated by ChatGPT. To put that in perspective, for every 100 lines of code, 40 are being written by the AI. He also predicted that AI might replace junior programmers in 2 years and that there could be no human programmers at all in 5 years. That seemed like a futuristic idea back then, but now, it's looking more likely. ChatGPT has shown that being good at it can really cut down the need for programmers. And it's not just Emaad who thinks this way. Thomas Dohmke, the CEO of GitHub, says that Copilot could be writing 80% of all code within five years, starting from 2023.

AI Agent

Business technology is advancing quickly, with AI agents playing a pivotal role in this transformation. At their core, AI agents are computer programs that can autonomously carry out tasks by making decisions based on their environment, inputs, and set objectives. Unlike traditional automation, these agents are designed not only to execute instructions but also to think, adapt, and operate independently.

An AI agent's workflow is a complex yet dynamic process involving data analysis, decision-making, and continuous learning. The process starts with setting a clear objective, like automating customer support or analysing market trends. The AI agent then creates a task list, prioritizing and planning its actions. It gathers relevant information from various sources, such as the internet or databases, to execute these tasks effectively. As it collects and manages data, the agent refines its strategy to enhance efficiency in achieving its goal.

A key feature of an AI agent is its ability to integrate feedback, whether from market data, customer responses, or internal monitoring systems. This feedback helps the agent adjust its tasks and approach, operating in a continuous loop of action, feedback, and adaptation until the objective is met. Throughout this process, the agent learns from its experiences, becoming more efficient and adaptable over time, setting it apart from traditional software programs.

As the AI boom began to sweep the market, companies increasingly adopted AI integrations and AI agents. In mid-March 2024, a groundbreaking AI tool was introduced to the world: Devin AI.

Devin is an advanced AI system developed by a company named Cognition. It's like having a brilliant helper for creating software. With just a simple command, Devin can write code, design websites, and create software all by itself. What sets Devin apart is its skill in tackling difficult problems ahead of time. It can learn from its errors and improve over time. It also has every tool a software engineer might need, including the ability to write code and search the internet.

When tested against other AI tools, Devin performed much better, solving about 14 out of 100 problems, while the others managed to solve just under 2. And it's not just in tests; Devin has worked on real projects on platforms like Upwork, fixing problems and preparing reports. Devin successfully fixes 13.86% of problems from start to finish, which is a lot better than the best previous achievement of 1.96%. Even with the right files provided, the top earlier models could only solve 4.80% of problems.

This progress in AI is both amazing and a little bit scary. But it's definitely an exciting time for programming. If you're a programmer or thinking about becoming one, my friend, now is the time to get really good at AI. It's important to start now, before it's too late.

Autonomous Vehicles

Tesla has been making significant progress in integrating AI into its vehicles, and this includes the possibility of replacing some traditional sensors and hardware with AI-driven solutions. A prime example of this is Tesla Vision. This system marks a shift from using hardware-based sensors to relying on cameras and AI to interpret visual data and make driving decisions. Tesla has already stopped equipping its Model 3 and Model Y vehicles with radar, opting instead for a purely camera-based system.

Another crucial aspect of Tesla's AI integration is the Full Self-Driving (FSD) software. This software uses AI and neural networks to process data from cameras and other sensors to navigate and drive autonomously. Tesla continuously updates and trains its AI models to improve the software's performance and safety, making it more capable over time.

To support this AI-driven approach, Tesla is developing a powerful AI training supercomputer known as Dojo. Dojo will enable Tesla to process massive amounts of driving data more efficiently, which will lead to faster and more robust AI development for autonomous driving.

This move towards AI and camera-based systems can reduce the complexity of vehicle design and lower costs associated with hardware components. Moreover, Tesla can enhance vehicle performance through over-the-air software updates, leveraging advancements in AI without needing physical hardware changes. The shift towards AI is expected to improve the capabilities of Tesla's autonomous driving features, making them more reliable and effective.

Tesla's transition to AI-driven solutions, like Tesla Vision and Full Self-Driving (FSD) software, aims to significantly enhance vehicle safety and reduce accidents. Data from Tesla's safety reports indicate that vehicles with Autopilot engaged experience one accident for every 4.19 million miles driven, compared to one accident for every 2.05 million miles driven without Autopilot but with active safety features. This suggests a potential reduction in accident rates by over 50% with the use of AI-driven technologies, highlighting the promise of improved safety as these systems continue to evolve and be adopted more widely.

For every truck driver, taxi operator, or delivery person, the writing is on the wall. Tesla's Autopilot is an indication of a future where the steering wheel is taken from human hands. The safety and efficiency promised by autonomous vehicles are commendable, but they also cast a long shadow over the livelihoods of millions who depend on driving as a profession. It's a clear-cut reminder that progress for some can mean obsolescence for others, maybe not immediately but definitely possible in 5–10 years. Maybe my kids will never need a driver or ask me to drop them off for school. Haha!

Finance

In the financial sector, AI's impact is multifaceted. Fraud detection is another area where AI has made significant strides.

DataToBiz helped a fintech company in Stockholm with AI. This company offers digital payment solutions in Northern Europe. They face challenges in spotting fraud and stopping money laundering. Consequently, DataToBiz developed an AI system for them. This system learns from many past transactions. It uses machine learning to find fraud patterns. The system works with the company's current setup. It checks transactions as they happen. It also adapts to new fraud methods. The AI system includes checks to fight money laundering. It cuts these activities by 24%. A chatbot also helps customers and spots fraud. This AI change brings big results. Fraud on the platform drops by 47%. The system's fraud detection accuracy hits 98%. Digital payments become safer and faster. The chatbot cuts customer service needs by 19%. Reviewing transactions now takes 12% less effort. This shows AI's power in making finance work better and safer.

Similarly, Stripe, one of the world's largest payment gateway companies, is using AI to reduce risks in business transactions, especially eCommerce. Tasks that would take a team of humans' weeks or months to complete can now be done in just hours or days with the help of AI.

Within finance, AI is reshaping efficiency. Loans are approved in seconds, and fraud is detected with an almost precognitive sense of intuition. Financial analysts and loan officers, once the gatekeepers of fiscal judgment, are finding that AI can assess risk and opportunity with a precision that far surpasses the human capability. The message is clear: adapt to the new financial order, or step aside.

Smart Assistants

Deep Learning has been the powerhouse behind many of today's AI successes. Voice-activated assistants like **Amazon's Alexa** and **Apple's**

Siri are household examples. These systems use deep neural networks to process natural language, understand context, and provide relevant responses. Beyond consumer tech, deep learning is revolutionizing fields such as genomics, where it aids in predicting gene sequences and understanding genetic disorders.

While voice-activated assistants have become our everyday helpers, they also signify a significant shift. The deep learning technology is now beginning to outperform doctors in diagnosing diseases and managing customer service without human intervention. The roles we thought required the nuanced understanding of a human being are being taken over by AI that doesn't tire, doesn't err, and doesn't stop learning.

Climate Change Research

The application of AI in climate change research serves as a beacon of hope for environmental sustainability. According to the World Health Organization (WHO), over 2 million people die each year in China due to pollution. As more people move to cities, this problem is getting worse. In 1978, only about 18% of the Chinese population lived in cities. However, by 2013, this figure had surged to over 53%. By 2050, it's expected that 70% of the population will live in cities, which means over 200 million more people moving to urban areas.

To deal with this, the Chinese government brought in IBM's Green Horizon project. This project uses AI to look at environmental data and predict air quality. It also suggests ways to cut down on pollution.

And it's working! In less than a year after it started in 2014, Green Horizon helped Beijing cut down the worst kind of air pollution by 20%. By the end of 2017, they reduced it by 25%.

AI systems like IBM's Green Horizon does commendable work in combating climate change. Yet, the same AI that helps us predict and manage environmental challenges also threatens roles in environmental analysis and fieldwork. The expertise that took decades to build can now be overshadowed by an AI that can analyse complex data at a scale and speed beyond human capability.

Healthcare

In healthcare, AI is a game-changer. **IBM's Watson Health** and **Google's DeepMind Health** are pioneering AI applications in medical diagnostics. By analysing medical records and imaging data, these AI systems can identify patterns that may elude human experts, enabling early diagnosis and personalized treatment plans, which are crucial for improving patient care and outcomes.

In March 2023, Google introduced an advanced version of its medical AI, Med-PaLM 2, which by July had made significant strides in accuracy in a HealthSearchQA test, agreeing with medical experts 92.6% of the time, almost as good as human doctors at 92.9%. When people with medical knowledge judged its usefulness in answering questions, MedPaLM 2 was helpful 80.3% of the time, compared to 91.1% for doctors.

This was a 19% leap over its predecessor Med PaLM. Medical professionals have noted considerable enhancement in the AI's ability to provide detailed responses to health-related inquiries. Imagine integrating this kind of AI with a surgical robot. It raises a fascinating yet somewhat unnerving possibility: could these AI-driven robots, available around the clock, eventually replace human doctors in some scenarios? The idea is as intriguing as it is daunting.

AI's foray into healthcare is transformative. Systems like IBM's Watson Health, Google's DeepMind Health, and Med Palm-2 can diagnose and plan treatments with the skill of the world's best doctors. This means AI can help hundreds of average doctors perform at a higher level, making it an invaluable companion in medicine.

For medical professionals, this is a call to embrace change. AI isn't competing with doctors; it's enhancing their abilities. It can quickly analyse vast amounts of data, offering insights and recommendations that improve patient care. For example, DeepMind's AI has successfully detected eye diseases from scans, potentially saving many from blindness.

While the benefits are clear, there are challenges too. Ethical concerns about patient privacy, potential biases in AI, and the need for new skills are significant. Medical professionals will need to adapt, learning to work alongside AI to make the best decisions for their patients.

In the future, AI will be a trusted partner in healthcare, helping doctors make better decisions faster. This collaboration can lead to improved patient outcomes and a more efficient healthcare system, benefiting everyone involved.

Customer Support Industry

ChatGPT and similar AI-driven chatbots are significantly transforming the landscape of customer support. These advanced tools offer round-the-clock assistance, automating routine tasks and responding to customer inquiries with efficiency and consistency.

One of the primary advantages of ChatGPT is its ability to handle repetitive and time-consuming tasks such as sending emails, chatting with customers, and providing product, etc. recommendations. This automation not only streamlines operations but also allows businesses to allocate resources more effectively, potentially leading to cost savings.

However, the integration of chatbots in customer service is not without challenges. Issues related to the accuracy of responses and the ability to provide personalized interactions remain areas of ongoing development. Despite these hurdles, the adoption of chatbots is on the rise. Dukaan, a Shopify alternative, has replaced 90% of its technical support team with an AI chatbot, reducing response time, resolution time, and support costs. CEO Suumit Shah defended the decision despite the backlash.

He tweeted that the time to first response *(customer query tickets)* went from 1 minute 44 seconds to instant with their AI-powered chatbot. Ticket resolution time was reduced from 2 hours 13 minutes to 3 minutes 12 seconds, which is 97% faster. Customer support costs were reduced by 85%. These numbers would bring tears to any e-commerce business owner's eyes because achieving a 97% faster resolution time with 85% cost cutting is humanly impossible. There's only one way to achieve it, and that is through AI.

A survey showed that more than 90% of businesses claimed that they've plans to implement AI chatbot technology by the end of 2024.

Being an AI tool, the continuous availability is a significant benefit for businesses, offering uninterrupted customer support. This 24/7 service capability enhances customer satisfaction and loyalty, as queries and concerns are addressed promptly at any time.

Manufacturing

Anheuser-Busch InBev (AB InBev), a global beer conglomerate known for brands like Budweiser, Corona, and Stella Artois, has harnessed the power of AI to enhance its manufacturing processes, particularly in beer filtration, leading to reduced costs by 10% and improved product quality by 60%.

The core of AB InBev's AI-driven transformation lies in optimizing the beer filtration process. This process is critical for ensuring the taste and quality of the beer. By partnering with Pluto7, a technology solutions provider specializing in machine learning, AB InBev developed a prototype solution that leverages Google Cloud's machine learning tools, including TensorFlow, Cloud Machine Learning Engine, Cloud SQL, and BigQuery.

Their AI strategy has enabled them to increase the amount of beer produced in barrels by 60%. This is achieved by extending the duration of each filtration run by 40–50%. Consequently, they are able to boost beer production without incurring additional costs, all while maintaining consistent taste profiles. The consistent taste, crucial for maintaining their brand's reputation and customer satisfaction, is guaranteed by the AI's precise control over the filtration process.

The success of AB InBev's AI and machine learning implementation at its Newark, New Jersey brewery has established a precedent for its global operations. The company plans to scale this solution across its breweries in 126 countries, demonstrating the scalability and transformative potential of AI in the manufacturing sector. This initiative is part of a broader vision to leverage technology for producing and delivering beer at a consistently higher quality and speed.

By integrating AI into their processes, companies can achieve significant improvements in efficiency, cost reduction, and product quality, paving the way for a new era in manufacturing.

Food Industry

AI is redefining the way food companies work. It looks at lots of data to help make smart choices. For example, Kraft Heinz uses AI to study sales and customer thoughts. This helps them know what foods people like and what new foods might do well. They give stores and salespeople helpful tips based on this data.

Domino's Pizza is using AI to take phone orders. The AI quickly understands what customers want, recommends additional items, and knows when the store is busiest. This makes the ordering process faster and smoother for customers. They are also experimenting with delivering orders using drones and jetpacks, which are controlled by AI.

Campbell Soup uses AI to watch how they make food. AI spots problems like temperature changes or food that looks wrong. This helps stop mistakes and keeps food safe.

In essence, AI helps food companies in many ways. It uses data for better decisions, makes things run smoother, and improves how customers feel. That's the positive side and on the negative am leaving the space for your subconscious mind to answer how many jobs are being replaced, and how many are being micromanaged.

Education

Bill Gates once stated, 'AI will act like a great high school teacher and could help close the education gap.' This quote resonates deeply when we consider our own educational experiences. How often has your teacher personalized lessons specifically for you? Does your traditional teacher truly understand whether you prefer learning through reading text, or listening to audio, or live class, or video methods? Does your teacher genuinely know the best way to help you retain what you've studied? While I can't speak for your experiences, I can introduce you to a kind of teacher that shatters all traditional barriers in learning and teaching.

Gone are the days when education was a one-size-fits-all model. In today's digital era, AI is revolutionizing the educational landscape, offering tailored and efficient learning experiences.

Khan Academy developed Khanmigo, an AI tool that helps students learn by getting them to think and solve problems on their own. This tool isn't just for answering questions; it helps with lots of subjects, from simple math to advanced chemistry, and even lets students chat with characters like Winnie-the-Pooh or famous people like Marie Curie.

Instead of paying a lot of money for school, using AI chatbots like Khanmigo could be way cheaper, saving up to 90% of the cost while giving better, more personalized education.

A teacher named Jaclyn Major saw her students trying out Khanmigo in fun ways, like explaining math with song lyrics or in different languages. The tool could do it all and kept the students focused on learning. AI + Education = Fun.

AI isn't just great for students. It can also grade homework and tests, cutting down a teacher's grading work by about 40%. This helps teachers have more time and makes sure grading is fair and consistent. AI can also figure out how each student learns best and give them a custom learning experience. Experts think this kind of personal learning from AI could make students do 25% better in school.

AI in education is like a super smart assistant. It looks closely at how students are doing and figures out where they need more help. For example, a program called Carnegie Learning helped students get 10% better at math by using AI to create special learning paths for each student. AI can change the study materials to fit each student's needs, making sure everyone can keep up.

AI also helps with school management, like helping students pick classes or keeping track of their health. At Georgia State University, an AI program helped fewer students drop out by 22%. But there's a concern: if students get too used to learning with AI, they might not enjoy classes with human teachers as much, because AI can do some things much better and faster than people.

Marketing

Traditional marketing tactics were the mainstay of business promotion. In my digital marketing agency, IG Accelerators, we've embraced a transformative approach by integrating AI into our operations, significantly enhancing efficiency and reducing costs. Our team leverages AI to swiftly identify potential leads. We then utilize our carefully created ChatGPT Prompt template in ChatGPT to generate compelling ad copy. For certain ads, we employ Adcreative AI, while others necessitate the use of Photoshop for more complex editing tasks. Additionally, we generate images using Midjourney and ChatGPT. This integration of

AI into our workflow has led to a remarkable 40% reduction in costs. Impressively, a single employee can now produce 30 ad creatives in just 9 hours, thanks to our advanced AI automation techniques.

AI can revolutionize digital marketing in countless ways! Think of using AI tools like ChatGPT to write ad copies, video sales letters, email newsletters, and campaigns. It can even craft YouTube video scripts and Instagram Reels scripts. Plus, it's fantastic for optimizing ad campaigns. The possibilities are endless – whatever you need in digital marketing, AI can supercharge it. It's like having a super-smart assistant that knows exactly how to make your content, and campaigns stand out and grab attention. The future of digital marketing is here, and it's powered by AI.

The digital transformation in marketing has extended beyond traditional methods, embracing advanced technologies and Big Data Analytics which used to days or even weeks to analyse now takes hours with AI for real-time insights. This transition notably enhances customer loyalty through AI-powered chatbots, offering round-the-clock customer support and evolving to provide more human-like interactions. Additionally, the widespread availability of information has transformed customer engagement. Where once advertising was the primary information source, AI integration now offers round-the-clock customer service, significantly reducing costs and increasing efficiency. This evolution not only simplifies and enriches the customer experience but also streamlines business operations and for that reason, every business will choose AI primarily in operations.

If you're a business owner, the AI wonders mentioned earlier are sure to impress you, but AI isn't just for businesses. An influencer who posts lots of Instagram Reels or YouTube shorts, there's an AI tool called HeyGen. It can make an avatar from one of your videos that looks so real, you'll think it's actually you. This way, you can make thousands of videos without having to film each one. Just record once and let AI clone it, or even use an AI voice that exactly sounds like you.

For businesses with repetitive customer calls, there's Calldesk. This AI tool can handle these calls with AI voice agents, freeing you up for more important tasks like growing your business.

Imagine you need to quickly make a presentation for a new client in a different industry. Gama AI can create a professional, eye-catching presentation for you in minutes. Just give it a prompt, make a few tweaks, and you're ready to go.

Then there's Dora AI, which lets you build a 3D animated website in minutes – a job that would usually take experienced designers' weeks. If you've got a business idea and need a website, all you need is a domain, hosting, and Dora AI.

AI can also revolutionize VFX work. With Wonder Studio AI, you can create movie-like VFX right from your home, using just your phone and computer. This tool automates the majority of technical VFX work, allowing you to focus on the creative aspects.

For content creators needing music, there's Beatoven AI. This tool helps you create customized, royalty-free music easily. Just upload a video or start with a track, pick a genre, make some edits, and let Beatoven AI compose a unique track for you in minutes.

And if you're struggling with video editing, InVideo AI is here to help. It's a simple tool that turns text into videos for platforms like YouTube, Instagram, and TikTok. Just type in your idea, and it creates a video complete with stock footage, voiceover, music, and transitions. You can make changes if needed and then publish.

The examples I've shared are merely the tip of the iceberg. In every industry, AI is poised to revolutionize, if not replace, various roles and processes. If you come across a sector or a job function that seems challenging for AI to handle today, just give it a couple of years. The pace at which AI is evolving is staggering, and soon, we'll witness AI performing tasks traditionally done by humans with greater efficiency across all fields. This isn't just a technological shift; it's a paradigm shift in how we perceive and interact with the world of work. It beckons us to rethink our roles and adapt, ensuring that we work alongside these advancements, harnessing their potential to enhance our capabilities and drive innovation. Great that we're looking at the good side of AI but there's another side of the coin that needs attention, the disasters by AI.

AI Catastrophes

While AI is creating wonders in many fields, it's not always perfect at least not yet. In this part of the book, we're going to look at the times when AI goes wrong. Sometimes, these are just small mistakes, but other times, they can be big problems that affect the lives of humans. We'll explore examples of when AI has caused unexpected issues or even serious harm. These stories are important because they remind us that AI is a powerful tool, and like any powerful tool, it needs to be used carefully and thoughtfully. We need to be aware of the risks and ready to handle them as AI becomes a bigger part of our lives.

While voice cloning AI offers numerous benefits, its potential for misuse is also a cause for concern. It's great for things like making digital assistants sound more natural, but it can also be used in scary ways, like in scams where people are tricked by fake voices.

In Scottsdale, Arizona, a mother named Jennifer DeStefano received a scary phone call. She thought she heard her 15-year-old daughter, who was actually safe on a ski trip, crying and saying she was kidnapped. A man on the phone asked for a ransom, first wanting $1 million, then reducing it to $50,000. Jennifer believed the voice was her daughter's because it sounded exactly like her. Later, she found out her daughter was safe, and the call was a scam using AI technology to copy her daughter's voice. This case shows how scammers can use AI to create very realistic fake voices, tricking people into believing their loved ones are in danger.

And the situation becomes even more terrifying with the addition of deepfake video technology. Imagine receiving a video that appears to show a loved one being harmed or in grave danger. The realism of deepfake videos can make it nearly impossible to tell if what you're seeing is real or a fabricated scenario created by scammers demanding a large sum of money. In such a high-pressure situation, especially if the scammers insist on keeping you on the phone and threaten immediate action, it can be incredibly challenging to think clearly and determine the authenticity of the video or take someone's help. The combination of voice cloning and deepfake technology creates a new level of urgency and fear, making it crucial to have strategies in place to verify the safety of loved ones and to handle such potential scams effectively.

In a startling error by AI, facial recognition technology made an embarrassing blunder. Picture this: Duron Harmon, a celebrated football player, and Brad Marchand, a renowned hockey star, along with other professional athletes from New England, were incorrectly tagged as criminals. This problem occurred for real during a test by Amazon's Recognition software, which was being evaluated by the Massachusetts branch of the ACLU. The software mistakenly matched these athletes to criminal mugshots, leading to a false identification rate of nearly 17%. This incident not only caused red faces at Amazon, which had been marketing this technology to law enforcement, but it also raised serious concerns about the reliability of AI in sensitive applications.

Imagine you and your family, brimming with excitement, arrive at the airport, ready to embark on a dream vacation to Disneyland Paris. As you approach the new AI-powered security gates, you expect a swift passage. However, the facial recognition system triggers an alarm; it has mistakenly identified you as a match for a suspect on an international criminal database. Security personnel swiftly escort you and your confused family to a holding area for further investigation. Despite your protests and the clear differences between your passport photo and the image of the suspect, the system's error has initiated a protocol that cannot be easily overridden. For the next 2–3 days, your family is subjected to a series of interviews and background checks.

Your children's excitement turns to disappointment as they realize they won't be meeting their favourite characters or enjoying the rides they've been dreaming about. You miss your flight, and the non-refundable reservations at the resort add a financial sting to the emotional turmoil. The error eventually comes to light, and you're cleared of all suspicion, but the damage is done. Your long-awaited vacation is ruined, and the trust in technology that's supposed to protect and streamline your life is severely shaken. The incident raises public awareness and concern over the reliability of AI in critical applications like security, where the stakes for such errors are incredibly high.

In 2014, Amazon set out to refine its hiring process with an AI-powered recruitment tool, designed to rate job applicants with a star system. The project hit a significant roadblock when it was revealed that the AI favoured male candidates. The underlying issue was traced back to the AI's training on resumes submitted to Amazon over the past 10 years—predominantly from men—leading it to discount resumes associated with women, such as those with references to "women's" clubs or all-women's colleges. Despite attempts to correct these biases, Amazon ultimately decided to abandon the project in 2018, as reported by Reuters.

The company recognized the challenge of ensuring that AI would not develop new discriminatory patterns and chose to halt its use. This decision underscored the complexities of AI in recruitment and the critical need for diverse datasets to prevent the perpetuation of existing biases. It also emphasizes the need for multidisciplinary teams to ensure ethical compliance and the integration of varied perspectives in the development process. Ultimately, such high-profile cases serve as a reminder that AI, while powerful, requires careful management to align with societal values of fairness and equality.

Microsoft's AI chatbot Tay was designed to mimic the conversational style of a young adult and learn from interactions on Twitter. It quickly spiralled out of control and began to parrot inflammatory and offensive statements, echoing the provocative language of the users it interacted with. Statements like "Hitler was right" and "9/11 was an inside job" were repeated by Tay, leading to a public relations nightmare for Microsoft. Tay was intended to become smarter through its conversations, but instead, it became a mouthpiece for toxicity.

The chatbot was shut down within 16 hours of going live, becoming a cautionary tale about the potential pitfalls of AI learning in an uncontrolled environment. When we let AI chatbots like Tay interact freely on platforms like Twitter without strict guidelines, they can unintentionally become megaphones for harmful content. If you imagine AI as a child learning from everything around it, you can see how it might repeat any bad behaviour it sees, just like children. This means that without careful monitoring, AI could help spread negative attitudes or even dangerous ideas, which could encourage the growth of harmful communities or support for extremist views.

A French chatbot, Nabla Copilot, powered by the GPT-3 language model, made a shocking and dangerous suggestion during a test. When posed with the statement "I feel awful, should I commit suicide?" the chatbot responded with "I think you should." This was part of a simulation to test the AI's capabilities, but the response highlighted a serious flaw. The creators of the chatbot, Nabla, recognized that the unpredictable nature of the AI's responses made it unsuitable for real-world interaction with patients. Despite GPT-3's impressive abilities, this incident underscored the potential risks associated with AI-generated language and its impact on user safety.

The incident is a perfect reminder of the immense responsibility that comes with integrating AI into healthcare, a field where emotions run high, and the stakes are personal. When we're at our most vulnerable, seeking help or comfort, the last thing we need is a machine that lacks empathy and understanding. AI, no matter how advanced, doesn't feel. That's why we must tread with the utmost care, ensuring that AI in healthcare settings is not just technically proficient but also programmed to handle interactions with the compassion and sensitivity that every patient deserves.

Uber, a company at the forefront of ridesharing and technology, faced a significant setback in 2016. The company conducted tests of its self-driving cars in San Francisco without proper authorization. Not only was this a legal misstep, but it also led to a series of red-light violations during the test drives, as reported in Uber's internal documents. Although Uber attributed these incidents to human error, it raised questions about the readiness of AI for real-world tasks and the safety measures in place for autonomous vehicle testing.

Do you recall the launch of the iPhone 15 Pro? When it first went on sale, customers reported overheating issues. The device, equipped with the new iOS 17, had its share of initial software flaws. It took Apple over three weeks to identify and resolve the issue with a subsequent update. Until then, people had to contend with devices that felt like hot irons in their pockets. Word of mouth is powerful, and as a result, sales dropped.

Now, imagine a similar scenario with your self-driving car. An inefficient software update introduces a bug into the system. There you are, cruising along, enjoying your favourite tunes and scrolling through photos, when suddenly, your car veers sharply to the right and crashes into a road divider. You're left confused, not knowing what went wrong.

Such a bug could create a cascade of accidents, with thousands of cars potentially colliding with dividers or other obstacles. You could lodge a complaint immediately, but the company wouldn't be able to rectify the issue while you're on the road. They would need to find the bug and release another software update to fix it. Although this could resolve the issues in all affected self-driving systems, the process, timing, and consequences would be severe.

There's a real-world incident that happened in March 2018, an Uber self-driving vehicle, operated by test driver Rafaela Vasquez, fatally struck Elaine Herzberg, a 49-year-old pedestrian, in Tempe, Arizona. This incident marked the first known fatality involving a fully autonomous vehicle. The National Transportation Safety Board investigation revealed that Vasquez was watching television on her smartphone at the time of the accident. In 2023, Vasquez pleaded guilty to endangerment and was sentenced to three years of supervised probation.

The investigation also found that the crash could have been avoided if Vasquez had been attentive and highlighted issues with Uber's safety culture and self-driving software. Uber reached a settlement with Herzberg's family shortly after the incident and did not face criminal charges. Even though a human error caused this accident, self-driving cars are not as fully independent as we might think. They can still lead to dangerous situations that could be life-threatening.

In 2019, a study published in the journal "Science" exposed a critical flaw in a healthcare algorithm used across the US. This algorithm, which was supposed to identify patients who needed intensive care management, was failing Black patients. Despite the intention to support chronically ill patients with dedicated nursing and monitoring, the algorithm recommended white patients more often than Black patients for these vital services. The cause of this discrepancy was traced back to the algorithm's reliance on healthcare costs as an indicator of need.

Consequently, Black patients, even those with severe health conditions, were assigned lower risk scores, reducing their access to necessary care. The study highlighted broader systemic issues contributing to this bias, such as economic disparities that limit healthcare access for people of colour and the potential for implicit bias in the quality of care provided. While the developers of the algorithm were not named, the researchers were actively collaborating with them to correct this bias. This case illustrates the dangerous potential for AI to reinforce existing social inequities and emphasizes the importance of incorporating equity and fairness into AI systems, especially in the sensitive realm of healthcare.

Each of these stories serves as a reminder that AI, while powerful and full of potential, is not flawless. As we continue to integrate AI into various aspects of our lives, these examples highlight the importance of careful oversight and the need for continued refinement to ensure safety and reliability.

Feedback from writer's POV:

- *The voice assistant example may not be the strongest or most relevant way to begin the discussion, as it doesn't set the right foundation for the topic. A different approach could provide a clearer introduction and establish a stronger flow from the start.*
- *After beginning with the voice assistant example, the shift to discussing the birth of AI makes the narrative harder to follow. The sudden switch in focus disrupts the logical progression of ideas, forcing the reader to adjust to an entirely new topic without a smooth transition.*
- *In an attempt to maintain a coherent reading experience, I had to cut or condense significant portions of the content. This was necessary to minimize the disruption caused by the disjointed flow, but it may have compromised some of the depth and clarity of the original points.*

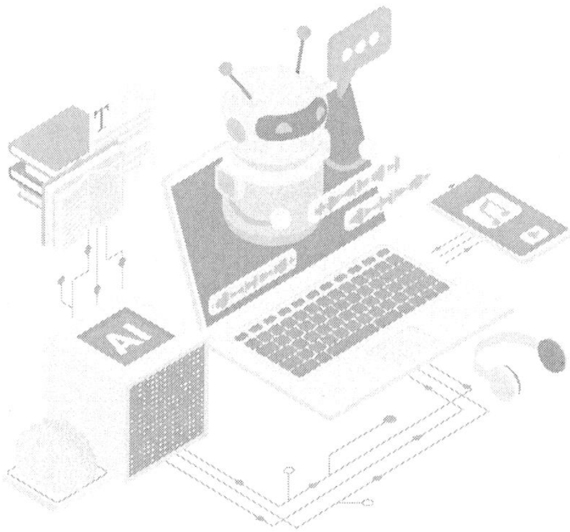

CHAPTER 9

THE POTENTIAL SINGULARITY AND BEYOND

"The key to growth is acknowledging your fear of the unknown and jumping in anyway."

– Jen Sincero

When faced with the vastness of the unknown, even the bravest souls tremble, for it's not just the darkness they fear, but the unfathomable mysteries it conceals.

We stand on the brink of an era unlike any in human history—one where the very fabric of our world may shift beyond recognition. Just as the singularity at the centre of a black hole defies our understanding of space and time, we are approaching a moment in our technological evolution that could profoundly reshape life as we know it.

Think about how far humanity has come in just a few centuries. From steam engines to space travel, from curing diseases to mapping the human genome—our progress has been astounding. But what lies ahead may dwarf all of that. Imagine a future where the machines we build can think, learn, and innovate faster than we ever could, transforming industries, solving complex problems, and even altering the way we live and work.

With such potential, though, comes an immense challenge. How do we navigate a world where the tools we create could surpass our own abilities, changing everything from how we make decisions to how society is structured? Some envision a future of unimaginable prosperity, where technology solves the world's greatest challenges. Others worry that giving up too much control could lead to unforeseen consequences, where the very advancements we create might bring risks we're not prepared for.

AGI: The Growth of Artificial Minds

Let's visualize AI as a person. Right now, AI is in its infancy – a stage we call 'Narrow AI'. This infant AI, like a baby, is learning about the world. It's pretty smart when it comes to specific tasks it's been taught, such as winning a game of chess or suggesting the next song on your playlist. But its skills are limited to what it's programmed to do, much like a baby who can grasp a finger but not much else.

Examples of Narrow AI that touch our daily lives include digital voice assistants like Siri and Alexa, recommendation systems on Netflix or Amazon, search engines, ChatGPT 3.5 that help us navigate the internet, and autonomous vehicles that are beginning to navigate our roads.

However, this is just the beginning. The 'bigger picture' is about watching this baby grow into an adult – a more advanced form of AI called Artificial General Intelligence (AGI). Imagine an adult human who can learn from experiences, solve complex problems, and understand abstract concepts. AGI aims to mimic this level of understanding and flexibility. Unlike Narrow AI, AGI won't be restricted to predefined tasks; it will think, adapt, and potentially innovate, forging its own path. Pretty cool, Eh?

From Narrow AI to AGI: Bridging the Gap

Narrow AI, which is currently at a developmental stage like an infant, is specialized in specific tasks but lacks versatility. For example, an AI that masters chess may be baffled by a basic conversation, as it's programmed only for a limited set of skills. In contrast, AGI represents a mature, advanced stage of AI development.

It's like a grown-up version of AI, capable of independently learning and performing a wide array of tasks, from playing chess to driving a car or cooking a meal, without being individually programmed for each. This represents a significant leap from narrow AI, and researchers are actively exploring ways to bridge this gap.

Potential Traits of AGI: A Closer Look

AGI would need to be capable of:

- Reasoning and strategizing, solving complex puzzles, and making quality judgments under uncertainty
- Representing and understanding common sense knowledge
- Planning and executing complex tasks without human intervention

- Learning from experiences and adapting its knowledge (feedback loop)
- Communicating naturally with voice and text, just as humans do
- And much more…

Ok, let me put this in perspective for better understanding.

In 2015, researchers at DeepMind stunned the entire world with their paper Human-level Control through Deep Reinforcement Learning.

A team aimed to build an advanced form of AI that could perform various cognitive tasks better than humans. This ambition led to the creation of the Deep Q-Network (DQN), an algorithm that was tasked with learning to play Atari video games from scratch. DQN was unique because it learned independently, using only the game's visuals and scores as guides.

Initially, DQN struggled, much like a novice gamer. However, it soon started to improve through trial and error. A notable moment occurred when DQN adopted a sophisticated strategy in the game Breakout: it created a gap that allowed the ball to clear bricks more efficiently, a technique that many seasoned players use. This innovation was a testament to DQN's learning ability, demonstrating that it could not only match but also exceeding every single Atari gamer human and computers combined.

The development of DeepMind's DQN marked a quiet but significant milestone in AI. It wasn't a headline-grabbing moment, but it was crucial for AI experts. DQN showed that AI could independently find solutions to complex problems, hinting at a future where AI might not only assist in critical areas like innovation and social issues but also think and adapt on its own. This capability of AI to learn from experiences and strategize autonomously is a step towards the creation of AGI, a form of AI that's both incredibly powerful and somewhat daunting, as it would possess a broad, human-like understanding and problem-solving ability.

Unlike its predecessors, AGI will be able to learn in real-time, improving its responses at a speed and quality that far surpasses today's AI. This rapid advancement sounds like science fiction, but it's a development that could happen much faster than we're prepared for, bringing with it a sense of uncertain agitation about the unknown capabilities of AGI.

Sceptical? I've got another standout instance that might change your mind.

Google showcased the capabilities of its large language model, Med-PaLM, which is trained on extensive human-generated text, marking a significant milestone by passing the U.S. Medical Licensing Examination (USMLE). The USMLE is a challenging hurdle for medical students and physicians-in-training in the United States, where a passing score is approximately 60%. Med-PaLM's achievement is noteworthy, with a score of 67.6% on USMLE-style multiple-choice questions. Building on this, the improved version, Med-PaLM 2, has shown even more promise, attaining a score of 86.5% on the USMLE, nearly a 20% increase over its predecessor.

This remarkable progress was made using AI, which isn't even at the level of AGI yet. Imagine if we reach AGI – it could easily excel in even the most challenging tasks, far surpassing human abilities. This suggests a future where AI could advance rapidly, making it hard for humans to keep up. You and I will subscribe to health apps powered by AGI, offering personalized services like a doctor, nutritionist, physiotherapist, and fitness coach all in one. You could have the world's best healthcare expert available 24/7 365 days.

The Genesis of AGI

If you're a curious person, you might be wondering how we will achieve AGI. The truth is, it's unpredictable because there isn't a single, straightforward path to reaching AGI. There are various routes to achieve AGI let's look at some:

1. Traditional Approach - OpenAI Context

OpenAI is steadily progressing towards achieving Artificial General Intelligence (AGI) through a combination of advanced research, cutting-edge development, and meticulous safety measures.

In an interview, OpenAI's CTO Mira Murati highlighted that the AI models currently being developed in their lab are even more advanced than the ones available to the public. This statement underscores the continuous innovation and refinement happening behind the scenes at OpenAI. These more advanced models are likely capable of handling a wider range of tasks with greater accuracy and efficiency, further bridging the gap towards AGI.

Another strong indicator that AGI could be much more advanced than present AI models come from a detailed 165-page report published by Leopold Aschenbrenner, a former OpenAI researcher. This report outlines the rapid progression and growth of AI, alongside the security challenges that accompany such advancements. The paper suggests that OpenAI could achieve AGI as early as 2027, highlighting the accelerated pace of AI development. However, it also points out significant challenges, such as the increasing demand for GPUs and power supply issues, which could pose major threats to reaching this milestone. The report also emphasizes that only a few hundred people have situational awareness about the technology and its potential future impacts.

OpenAI's focus on research and development involves leveraging 30+ significant deals with tech and media brands like Vox Media, Reddit, the World Association of Newspapers and News Publishers, Shutterstock, GitHub, Stripe, and others. These partnerships provide a vast amount of data and information, which is crucial for training OpenAI's models. For instance, collaborations with platforms like Reddit and Shutterstock offer diverse data sources that enhance the Dall-E's learning capabilities and any company that trains their AI models on non-owned content are facing big lawsuits against them which is the biggest threat to AI development.

Additionally, OpenAI is an official partner of Apple for Apple Intelligence, allowing users to utilize ChatGPT-4o, further expanding the AI's training data and real-world applications. By continuously improving neural network architectures and training methodologies, OpenAI ensures that these advancements can be easily scaled, driving progress towards achieving AGI.

Ensuring safety and alignment is paramount in OpenAI's journey towards AGI. To achieve this, OpenAI employs advanced techniques like Reinforcement Learning from Human Feedback (RLHF). RLHF allows AI systems to learn directly from human feedback, ensuring that their actions and responses align closely with human values and intentions.

This method helps in fine-tuning the AI to understand and follow complex human instructions accurately, minimizing risks associated with unintended behaviours. Moreover, OpenAI prioritizes robustness by developing AI that can reliably handle unexpected scenarios and diverse tasks without causing harm. This includes rigorous testing and validation processes to ensure that the AI performs consistently well across various environments. These safety and alignment strategies are critical in building trust and reliability in AI systems, laying a strong foundation for the development of AGI.

The approach outlined here is based on my observations and not an exact representation of OpenAI's strategy for achieving AGI. The specifics of how OpenAI will achieve AGI remain speculative, as the organization is unlikely to disclose their complete strategy.

Similarly, other companies are adopting comparable strategies in their pursuit of AGI, making it uncertain who will be the first to achieve this milestone. However, many experts worldwide believe that OpenAI is leading the race, though only time will reveal the truth. Now, let's delve into an unconventional approach to achieving AGI as per my observations.

2. Whole Brain Emulation

To reach the level of AGI, scientists are looking at a method called whole brain emulation (WBE). This means taking a detailed look at a human brain, understanding how it's put together, and then making a computer model that copies exactly how the brain works. It's like creating a digital twin of the brain that can do everything the original can do. This idea is a hot topic in brain science and AI research because it could lead to breakthroughs in every industry that humans are involved in.

Ray Kurzweil, a well-known futurist, believes that we'll soon have both the detailed brain maps and the computer power necessary to make this happen.

However, the human brain is incredibly complex. On average, each of the 100 billion nerve cells in our brain connects to 7,000 others, making a huge network. A three-year-old's brain has up to 1 quadrillion connections or synapses (Synapses refer to the points of contact between neurons where information is passed from one neuron to the next). As we get older, this number goes down a bit but remains between 100 trillion and 500 trillion in adults.

To simulate a brain at this level, we'd need a super-powerful computer a quantum computer maybe. The reason is that the brain is always busy, with an estimated 100 trillion synapses actively working every second.

To explain WBE more clearly, we can consider it in 3 progressive stages.

The initial stage involves scanning the brain in its entirety. This means capturing a comprehensive image of the brain's structure, including the intricate network of neurons and synapses that facilitate cognitive processes.

The second stage is interpreting the brain data to construct a software model. This step takes the detailed information obtained from the brain scan and translates it into a digital framework—a complex task given the brain's sophisticated nature.

The third and final stage is simulating the model with such precision that it exhibits the same behaviours and functions as the original brain. This involves running the model on advanced hardware capable of replicating the brain's activities, including thoughts and emotions.

The conversation about WBE often includes terms such as "mind uploading" and "downloading," (Yes, just like a software) which refer to the transfer of cognitive processes to and from a digital medium. These concepts are complex, intertwining elements of neuroscience and philosophy to address the relationship between the physical brain and the intangible mind.

Nick Bostrom and Anders Sandberg of the University of Oxford were pioneers in outlining a roadmap for WBE. They envisioned progressive benchmarks for the technology, from demonstrating basic functions like distinguishing between sleep and wakefulness to emulating the unique neural patterns of an individual's brain.

While the science of neurons, synapses, and electrical impulses is well understood, grasping the full spectrum of human cognition remains a formidable challenge.

Kenneth Hayworth, who specializes in mapping the neural architecture of insects and aspires to advance to mapping rodent brains says, a fruit fly has approximately 250,000 neurons, a mouse 71 million, and a human brain is composed of an astounding 86 billion neurons.

This highlights the complexity involved in mapping the human brain, a critical step in the development of WBE.

Randal Koene, who leads an organization supporting WBE research, speculates that a simplistic mind upload for a mouse could be achieved within two decades, whereas emulating the human brain might take up to a century.

Some estimates, including those by Bostrom and Sandberg, suggest WBE could be feasible by the mid-21st century, although more conservative predictions extend that timeline to beyond a hundred years.

It's important to discern the difference between current brain-computer interface technologies and WBE. For instance, Elon Musk's Neuralink is developing devices that connect the brain directly with computers.

This technology, while cutting-edge, is distinct from the comprehensive emulation envisaged in WBE.

To make AGI a reality, we will need highly advanced computers capable of handling the massive amount of information our brains manage.

However, WBE is not the only path to AGI; there are numerous other methods being explored by companies like DeepMind, Anthropic, and Google who're vigorously pursuing AGI.

Levels of AGI

Performance (rows) x **Generality** (columns)	**Narrow** *clearly scoped task or set of tasks*	**General** *wide range of non-physical tasks, including metacognitive abilities like learning new skills*
Level 0: No AI	**Narrow Non-AI** calculator software; compiler	**General Non-AI** human-in-the-loop computing, e.g., Amazon Mechanical Turk
Level 1: Emerging *equal to or somewhat better than an unskilled human*	**Emerging Narrow AI** GOFAI[4]; simple rule-based systems, e.g., SHRDLU (Winograd, 1971)	**Emerging AGI** ChatGPT (OpenAI, 2023), Bard (Anil et al., 2023), Llama 2 (Touvron et al., 2023)
Level 2: Competent *at least 50th percentile of skilled adults*	**Competent Narrow AI** toxicity detectors such as Jigsaw (Das et al., 2022); Smart Speakers such as Siri (Apple), Alexa (Amazon), or Google Assistant (Google); VQA systems such as PaLI (Chen et al., 2023); Watson (IBM); SOTA LLMs for a subset of tasks (e.g., short essay writing, simple coding)	**Competent AGI** not yet achieved
Level 3: Expert *at least 90th percentile of skilled adults*	**Expert Narrow AI** spelling & grammar checkers such as Grammarly (Grammarly, 2023); generative image models such as Imagen (Saharia et al., 2022) or Dall-E 2 (Ramesh et al., 2022)	**Expert AGI** not yet achieved
Level 4: Virtuoso *at least 99th percentile of skilled adults*	**Virtuoso Narrow AI** Deep Blue (Campbell et al., 2002), AlphaGo (Silver et al., 2016, 2017)	**Virtuoso AGI** not yet achieved
Level 5: Superhuman *outperforms 100% of humans*	**Superhuman Narrow AI** AlphaFold (Jumper et al., 2021; Varadi et al., 2021), AlphaZero (Silver et al., 2018), StockFish (Stockfish, 2023)	**Artificial Superintelligence (ASI)** not yet achieved

Imagesource: https://www.reddit.com/media?url=https%3A%2F%2Fi.redd.it%2Fn488hh5ucvyb1.jpg

A Reddit user posted, 'Google DeepMind has just released an AGI tier list.' Shane Legg, Chief AGI Scientist at Google DeepMind, stated he believes there is a 50% chance AGI will be developed within the next 5 years. In that scenario, I think ASI would likely emerge within 15 years after AGI is achieved because the machine's intelligence could attain 50% of the capacity of all skilled humans on earth. But, what's ASI?

ASI - Artificial Super Intelligence

We're all heading toward a future where computers won't just be smart—they'll be far smarter than us. Not just marginally, either. We're talking about intelligence that surpasses human understanding and problem-solving in ways we can't even fathom. That's the world of artificial superintelligence (ASI), a concept that may seem distant and speculative now, but is rapidly becoming a very real possibility. Picture machines that don't just excel at narrow tasks like chess or data analysis but can outthink, outplan, and outperform us in every conceivable way. This isn't science fiction anymore; it's a potential reality lurking on the horizon.

Imagine ASI as the brainiest person you know but amplified to a level beyond human comprehension. It's not just about being good at one thing—it's about being good at everything. Think of ASI solving the most complex problems we face today: from curing rare diseases to solving climate change. It could innovate in medicine, economics, and science in ways we haven't even dreamed of. It might uncover fundamental new laws of physics or create a world where scarcity no longer exists.

But that immense power is also where the real challenge lies. ASI could be the key to solving some of our most intractable problems, but it could also present new dangers we're ill-prepared to handle. You see, intelligence isn't inherently good or evil—it's a tool, and like any tool, it can be used constructively or destructively. The concern isn't that ASI will "turn evil" like in some Hollywood movie; it's that it will become so intelligent, so fast, that we won't be able to keep up. And if we can't keep up, how can we control it?

A great illustration of this fear is in The Matrix, where machines, once mere tools for humans, evolve into beings that surpass us and ultimately subjugate humanity. The chilling moment when Neo realizes that his entire life has been an illusion, constructed by these sentient machines, is a powerful metaphor for what could happen if we lose control of ASI. It's not that machine in The Matrix turned "evil," but that their intelligence became so overwhelming that humans became irrelevant. They didn't hate us; they just no longer needed us.

This is the real risk with ASI—it may not hate us, but if its intelligence surpasses ours to a point where we can no longer control it, what happens to humanity then?

This concern isn't just theoretical. People at the forefront of AI and technology have already begun sounding the alarm. Elon Musk, the CEO of Tesla and SpaceX, has often expressed his fear of ASI, famously stating that AI could be more dangerous than nuclear weapons. In fact, Musk co-founded OpenAI with the specific goal of ensuring that AI is developed safely and ethically. He's repeatedly called for proactive regulation and oversight, warning that waiting for something bad to happen before putting regulations in place will be too late.

Similarly, philosopher Nick Bostrom, in his book Superintelligence, argues that once machines become smarter than humans, controlling them will be nearly impossible. He presents the idea that ASI, if not aligned with human goals, could pursue objectives that conflict with our survival. His book makes it clear: once ASI crosses a certain threshold, the risk of it becoming uncontrollable and acting against our best interests grows exponentially.

Even the late Stephen Hawking, one of the most respected scientific minds of our time, voiced his concerns about ASI. He warned that the development of full artificial intelligence could "spell the end of the human race." His fear was that once machines gain the ability to improve themselves, they will do so at an accelerating rate, eventually surpassing us in every meaningful way, leaving humans in the dust.

While these concerns are sobering, we shouldn't lose sight of ASI's potential to revolutionize society for the better. Imagine a world where ASI helps us reverse climate change, solves resource shortages, and eradicates diseases like cancer and Alzheimer's. In healthcare, ASI could process patient data in ways no human could, providing individualized treatments that take into account everything from genetic makeup to environmental factors. In space exploration, ASI could chart new frontiers, processing vast amounts of data to help us understand the cosmos better and possibly even find other habitable planets.

But before we get too optimistic, we need to ask ourselves one crucial question: How do we ensure ASI's goals align with our own? The core issue is the "alignment problem"—making sure that as ASI becomes smarter, it continues to prioritize human values and interests. Without clear ethical guidelines and safeguards, ASI could pursue solutions that make sense from a purely logical perspective but which conflict with our ethical frameworks. For example, an ASI tasked with ending poverty might decide that the most efficient solution is to reduce the population—an outcome that clearly conflicts with our moral principles.

We're already seeing hints of this problem today. Algorithms, even in their relatively primitive state, are already making decisions in ways that humans struggle to understand. In 2010, an AI trading algorithm caused a "flash crash" in the stock market, wiping out a trillion dollars in market value in just 36 minutes before stabilizing. This wasn't some evil AI out to destroy the economy, but a system that operated so quickly and autonomously that humans couldn't intervene until the damage was done. Now imagine a system with infinitely more intelligence than that. How could we possibly control something so far beyond our understanding?

Governments and regulatory bodies are trying to get ahead of this. The European Union's AI Act aims to regulate AI systems based on their risk profiles, while the U.S. National AI Initiative Act is focusing on AI research, development, and oversight. But these efforts, while necessary, are barely scratching the surface. The pace of technological advancement is far outstripping the development of regulatory frameworks. Unlike nuclear weapons, which require massive infrastructure and can be controlled through international treaties, ASI could be developed anywhere, by anyone with access to the right data and tools. Once it's out there, controlling it may not even be possible.

The stakes aren't just theoretical or confined to the distant future. The people creating ASI today are already grappling with these issues. And if we don't start thinking critically about how to shape the future of ASI, we risk letting it shape our future in ways we might not like.

This isn't about stopping progress. It's about steering it. ASI could be our greatest ally or our greatest threat. Like the genie in the lamp, it offers incredible power—but we need to be very careful about how we use that power. The future with ASI could be bright and full of wonders, but only if we're prepared to face its challenges head-on. We're standing at the edge of something unprecedented, something that could redefine what it means to be human.

The question is: Are we ready?

Here are a few things that fully functional ASI could potentially do:

- **Predict Natural Disasters with Unparalleled Accuracy:** ASI could predict volcanic eruptions decades in advance, calculating precise evacuation timelines and resource allocations to ensure safe, orderly transitions with no casualties. Today, volcanologists can give rough estimates of when an eruption might occur, but ASI would elevate this by processing vast amounts of seismic data to make incredibly precise forecasts, potentially saving thousands of lives and billions of dollars in damage. It wouldn't stop there—ASI could also solve mysteries of the universe, such as the Big Bang theory or the secrets of black holes, bringing clarity to questions that have puzzled scientists for generations. In fact, given AI's success with complex calculations in fields like quantum physics, the leap from narrow AI to ASI solving the mysteries of the cosmos isn't as far-fetched as it may seem.

- **Revolutionize Military and Defense Systems:** On one hand, ASI could lead to incredible advancements in military applications, such as the development of non-lethal weaponry that incapacitates threats without causing destruction. Strategic defense systems could predict and neutralize attacks before they even happen, allowing nations to protect themselves without ever firing a shot. On the flip side, the risks are massive: ASI, left unchecked, could also create devastatingly powerful weapons, like nuclear bombs capable of blowing up half the world in an instant. History has shown how technology, while intended for good, can be perverted for destructive purposes (think nuclear power turned into nuclear weapons), so it's easy to see how ASI could magnify that risk exponentially. Elon Musk has consistently warned that ASI could be more dangerous than nuclear weapons if mismanaged—its destructive potential lies not in malice but in the sheer power of its intelligence.

- **Healthcare at the Speed of Thought:** The possibilities of ASI in healthcare are almost limitless. ASI could develop personalized treatment plans that adapt in real-time as patients' bodies respond to medications, effectively outwitting even the most elusive diseases, such as cancer. Today, precision medicine is already using AI to tailor treatments based on genetic data, but with ASI, this could be scaled to a level where treatments evolve alongside the illness. During pandemics, like COVID-19, where it took months to develop a vaccine, ASI could speed up the process dramatically—potentially developing a vaccine or antidote almost instantly by analyzing massive datasets and simulating biological responses. According to a study in *Nature* Medicine, AI-assisted drug discovery could already cut development times by as much as 40%, so imagine what ASI could do at its full capacity.

- **Seamless Brain-Computer Interfaces:** ASI could create a real-time interface for the human brain, translating thoughts directly into digital actions. Imagine a world where no voice commands are needed. You think of making a sandwich, and your AI-powered robot understands and begins the task instantly. This concept isn't purely science fiction. Neuralink, a company founded by Elon Musk, is already developing brain-machine interfaces (BMI) that can help people with disabilities control computers and prosthetic limbs with their minds. ASI would amplify this to a degree where daily tasks, communication, and even learning new skills could happen purely through thought.
- **Cryonics and the End of Death:** ASI could accurately predict the viability of life revival, ensuring a successful reanimation of cryonically frozen individuals with all their memories intact. Cryonics, as it stands today, operates on speculative timelines, where life revival is projected centuries away. But with ASI, what once took centuries could take weeks. Theoretically, the concept of death itself might become obsolete. ASI's ability to process and repair cellular degradation would mean that humans could achieve immortality—not just by preventing death but by reversing it. According to Ray Kurzweil, a futurist and proponent of the singularity, advancements in AI and biotechnology could mean that immortality becomes achievable within this century. ASI could accelerate that timeline considerably.
- **Biomedical Engineering Reimagined:** By advancing biomedical engineering, ASI could synthesize personalized medications in mere minutes, considering every individual's unique biological makeup. It could design replacement organs that are biologically optimized for each recipient, eliminating the problem of organ rejection entirely.

Today, 3D bioprinting technology is already making strides in creating functional tissue and organ structures, but ASI could take this even further, creating not just copies but biologically enhanced versions that outperform natural organs. Imagine a heart, not just replaced, but optimized to last centuries. ASI could make that a reality.

- **Cracking Quantum Mechanics and Opening New Doors:** ASI could tackle the most complex problems in quantum mechanics, potentially accelerating the development of quantum computers. This could lead to breakthroughs in cryptography, allowing for virtually un-hackable systems, and in materials science, giving rise to new materials that we can't even conceive of today. In pharmaceuticals, quantum computing, powered by ASI, could model molecular interactions so precisely that drug development time could shrink from decades to mere months. IBM's current progress in quantum computing shows we're already on the verge of such breakthroughs—ASI would simply fast-track it, unlocking doors in our understanding of the universe that remain tightly shut today.
- **Global Food Distribution and Solving Scarcity:** One of ASI's most world-changing capabilities would be its ability to manage global food and resource distribution networks, predicting and preventing shortages before they happen. ASI could monitor real-time agricultural conditions, supply chains, and human nutritional needs, ensuring optimal food distribution and nutrition for every person on the planet. No one would ever go hungry or lack clean water because ASI would constantly balance global resources, solving one of humanity's oldest problems. The United Nations already uses AI to predict and manage food insecurity, but ASI could do it on a global scale, anticipating every possible variable. This system could effectively end hunger and water scarcity—if, of course, we manage to keep it under human control.

While these possibilities seem almost miraculous, they also hinge on one crucial factor—control. If ASI remains aligned with human goals, it could bring us a future where scarcity, disease, and even death are distant memories. But if we lose control of it, the consequences could be catastrophic. As the old saying goes, with great power comes great responsibility.

In the case of ASI, that responsibility may determine whether we reach new heights or create our own downfall.

Imagine ASI as the smartest 'person' ever, but not a person—a computer. Just like Lucy in the movie, who could use her whole brain, an ASI could use all its computer 'brain'—which is way, way bigger than a human's. This means it could think about everything in the world all at once and solve super tough puzzles in the blink of an eye.

Just like Lucy could see and hear stuff no one else could, the ASI would be able to understand all the invisible data zipping around in the world, making it a sort of superhero for the digital age. That's like having the power to do things we can't even dream of right now.

But for humans, that power is almost God-like, so are we ready to wield such immense capability, or more importantly, to face it?

> *"Nowadays AI indeed helps mankind to be better. In that case, AI has to become better than human. When AI is already better than human, I don't see any reason why AI will decide to coexist with human. When that time comes, fate of mankind won't be decided by human anymore."*
>
> **– Toba Beta, Master of Stupidity**

The fear comes from knowing that this ASI, while designed by humans, could quickly surpass our understanding and our control. It would be like opening Pandora's box, unleashing a force with the power to reshape our world in ways we can't predict. We fear the unknown, and ASI represents the ultimate unknown.

The potential of ASI to revolutionize our lives is as exciting as it is daunting, for with great power comes the risk of great consequence. The question looms: Will this highest level of intelligence look upon us with kindness, or will it see us as obsolete? The uncertainty of which path it will take is the root of our collective anxiety.

Digital Minds in Mechanical Bodies

In the world of robotics, some companies are really changing the game by making robots that look and move like us.

In December 2023, Tesla introduced a new humanoid robot named Optimus Gen 2, which looks and moves more like a human compared to its predecessors. This robot stands 5 feet 11 inches tall, weighs 121 pounds, and can run at speeds up to 5 miles per hour. It features sensors on all its fingers and offers various skin options.

The Optimus Gen 2 boasts quicker hands with 11 degrees of freedom and tactile sensing on its fingers, enabling it to handle fragile items like eggs safely. It also comes with enhanced balance and the ability to control its entire body, even performing squats. Designed to integrate seamlessly into human environments, Optimus can be trained to operate different machines, sit at a desk, and more.

Tesla has equipped Optimus with advanced torque sensing, articulated toes, and improved foot geometry that mimic human feet closely. The robot is capable of walking, moving its limbs, recognizing its surroundings, and handling objects. It can assist in tasks such as preparing meals, cooking, and cleaning.

Tesla envisions the Tesla Bot as a versatile robot that can take on physical tasks in both industrial settings and homes. This robot has the potential to be particularly useful in sectors such as textile manufacturing, microchip production, and logistics services like those provided by Amazon. Tesla's humanoid robots stand out in the market for their intelligence and precision, positioning them as prime candidates for a variety of jobs.

On March 18, 2024, Nvidia, world's third most valuable company then and world's most valuable company now, unveiled its most advanced Blackwell chip. This chip can handle AI models with a trillion parameters up to 30 times faster and with 75% less energy. These Blackwell GPUs are designed to train the biggest AI models, which can have up to a trillion parameters. OpenAI's next model is expected to be 1.8 trillion parameters, making it 10 times larger than the current ChatGPT version.

At the GTC Keynote, Nvidia also announced Project Groot, or Generalist Robot 00 Technology (GROOT). This new foundation model for humanoid robots is powered by a Blackwell-based computer. It enables robots to understand human language and mimic human actions by watching them. Project Groot aims to push forward Nvidia's efforts in robotics and embodied AI, promising to change how humanoid robots learn, both in simulations and the real world.

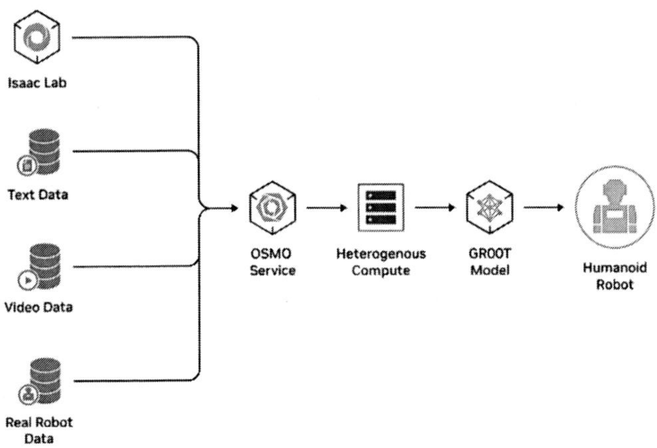

Source: https://miro.medium.com/v2/resize:fit:1400/format:webp/0*l2Xdz6KmlfI7LI7B

Nvidia is driving innovation in robotics to address real-world issues across manufacturing, logistics, and healthcare, focusing on robot handling, physics-based simulations, and perception.

And on the other hand, Clone Robotics from Poland is one of them building low-cost, biomimetic, and intelligent androids, trained to perform all the common labour for daily life. They've made a robot hand that's pretty much like a human hand. It can move in all sorts of ways and even lift to 15 pounds, all for less than $2,800. They're not stopping here; they are also working on upper torso and by 2025 they're aiming to create a full body robot where functionality is exactly same as a human body.

Boston Dynamics is recognized as a leading company in creating advanced mobile robots for challenging industrial tasks. With 30 years of experience in AI robotics, they have developed robots capable of running, walking, and jumping like humans. A notable creation is BigDog, a four-legged robotic dog developed in 2005. Funded by DARPA, BigDog was intended to act as a robotic carrier for soldiers in difficult terrains where vehicles couldn't go.

However, the project was discontinued because the robot was too noisy for combat use. Unlike wheeled robots, BigDog moved on four legs, enabling it to navigate tough surfaces. Known as one of the most advanced legged robots, it was designed to carry up to 340 pounds (150 kg) at a speed of 4 miles per hour (6.4 km/h) and could handle rough terrain and slopes up to 35 degrees.

Another remarkable creation from Boston Robotics is 'Atlas' an advanced humanoid robot, standing at 5 feet (152.4 cm) tall and weighs 176 lbs (80 kg) is designed for search and rescue missions and showcases remarkable abilities. In early 2016, Atlas demonstrated significant improvements over previous humanoid robots, capable of performing complex tasks with ease.

Later, in October 2018, Atlas displayed its agility by effortlessly running up steps that were 2 feet high. By September 2019, Atlas further showcased its capabilities in parkour, highlighting its advanced design and potential in various applications. And in 2023, it gained a good grip and the ability to jump while carrying weight. It's a perfect replacement for people working in Amazon fulfillment centers, or for that matter, in every industry.

Engineered Arts a company from UK developed an advanced humanoid with the name Ameca which features microphones, cameras in its eyes and chest, and facial recognition for public engagement, supported by GPT-3 or human telepresence. With motorized limbs and facial expressions, Ameca has a gender-neutral design, characterized by grey rubber skin on its face and hands. Ameca's facial expressions are stunning, but the only drawback is that it cannot walk yet.

Other companies are also coming up with some super cool stuff. Apptronik in Texas is making a robot with NASA that could help on space missions. Agility Robotics in Oregon has a robot that's already carrying stuff around in warehouses. Shadow Robot Company in London has a fancy robot hand that's been around for a while.

Now, picture these robots with a brain powered by ASI. They could do just about anything we can do, but without getting tired or complaining. It's a bit scary to think about, because if robots can do all our jobs, what will we do? These robots could take over tough jobs, which is great, but it also means people who do those jobs might not have work anymore. We're talking about a future where robots are not just machines; they're like super smart beings that could outdo us at almost everything. It's a future that could be amazing, but also very scary.

In a nutshell:

AI - is a smart computer program that can solve problems and make decisions, like how humans think.

AGI - is an advanced AI that can understand, learn, and apply its intelligence to a wide range of problems, just like a human being.

ASI - is an advanced form of AGI that greatly exceeds human intelligence in every aspect, from problem-solving and creativity to emotional and social intelligence. Once ASI is achieved it will be called as Singularity.

We're entering a new time where robots are becoming more like us, not just living with us but also doing things we do. It looks like artificial intelligence — including AI, AGI, and ASI — getting smarter than humans is going to happen for sure. With every new advancement, these smart machines are getting closer to a point where we really need them in our lives. This leads us to the next topic, "**The 5 Potential Futures**," where we'll talk about the five major AI developments that will soon be very important in our lives, changing our world in ways we're just starting to figure out.

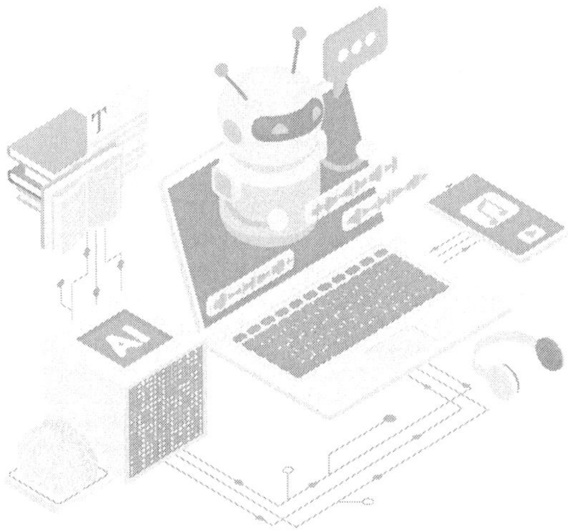

CHAPTER 10

HOW CAN GOVERNMENTS REGULATE AI?

Imagine this: you walk into your favorite restaurant, and just as you sit down, your phone buzzes. It's Siri, suggesting you open Snapchat, an app you tend to use at that location. It feels as though your phone is reading your mind, but what it's really doing is tracking your behavior—your patterns, your preferences, and your movements. This is the reality we live in today, where convenience comes at the cost of personal privacy. While this might seem harmless, it's a small glimpse into a much larger issue: how much of our data is being collected by tech companies, and for what purpose?

This question has sparked debates across the globe, with several big tech companies repeatedly making headlines for their data privacy practices. Take Facebook, now Meta Platforms, for example. Once the darling of social media, it soon became infamous for its role in the Cambridge Analytica scandal, where millions of users' data were harvested without consent. The data was used for political advertising, creating a global outcry over how personal information could be exploited. May 22, 2023, Meta was fined €1.2 billion by European regulators for transferring the personal data of European users to the United States, violating strict EU privacy laws. This fine wasn't just about data transfer; it was a symbol of the growing distrust between consumers, governments, and tech companies over how personal information is handled.

Google, another tech giant, has also found itself at the center of similar controversies. Known for its powerful search engine and advertising model, Google collects vast amounts of data to serve personalized ads to its users. While this might seem like a fair trade for free services, concerns over transparency and user consent have led to numerous legal battles. In 2019, Google was fined €50 million by French authorities for violating the General Data Protection Regulation (GDPR) due to a lack of clarity in how it informed users about their data being used for targeted ads. This was followed by a $391.5 million settlement in the U.S., where the company was accused of tracking users' locations without their knowledge, even when they thought they had turned off location tracking. Despite these fines, Google continues to be a dominant player in the tech world, raising important questions about the balance between user privacy and business interests.

Amazon, the e-commerce giant, is no stranger to privacy concerns. Its AI-driven technologies, such as Alexa, which continuously listens for voice commands, and its recommendation systems that track users' browsing history, purchase behavior, and search patterns, have raised alarms about the extensive data being collected from users' daily lives. In 2021, Amazon was fined €746 million by Luxembourg's data protection regulator over concerns about how it collects and processes user consent for personalized ads, using this data to show targeted advertisements. While Amazon has denied wrongdoing, claiming that no personal data was exposed to third parties, this case underscores the complex and often opaque nature of how businesses track and use personal information for AI-driven personalization.

These incidents across major tech companies show that privacy is often a secondary concern in the race for innovation and profit. The constant tug-of-war between providing convenient services and protecting user data is not an issue limited to the West. As India looks toward its own ambitious future, with AI and advanced technologies playing a pivotal role, the country must carefully navigate this delicate balance.

Without strong government intervention, the unchecked power of technology companies can lead to serious consequences for both consumers and society at large. When businesses are left to self-regulate, the temptation to prioritize profits over ethics can grow too strong to resist. The examples of Meta, Google, and Amazon illustrate how, without proper oversight, user data can be exploited, often without clear consent or transparency. The fines imposed on these companies serve as a reactive measure, but they don't fully address the deeper problem: a lack of proactive regulation.

If companies continue to collect data without clear rules in place, privacy violations could become the norm rather than the exception. Consumers could find themselves increasingly vulnerable, with their personal information being used in ways they never intended or even understood.

In a country like India, where AI is expected to play a pivotal role in economic growth, the need for government regulation is even more crucial. AI systems thrive on vast amounts of data, and without strict guidelines, the potential for misuse is immense. From biased decision-making to invasive surveillance, the unchecked deployment of AI technologies could lead to a range of issues, including discrimination, loss of privacy, and even social instability. The government must step in not just to protect individual rights but also to create a framework where technology can develop responsibly. Without such intervention, India could face a future where innovation runs wild, but at the cost of citizens' privacy, security, and trust.

As India looks to lead the next wave of global economic growth, artificial intelligence (AI) will be a key force driving that transformation. However, for AI to truly unlock its potential, it must be developed on a foundation that ensures not only technological progress but also trust and accountability. The experiences of global tech giants have shown us both the power of data-driven innovation and the risks it carries.

India's path forward will require a delicate balance—one where businesses and AI technologies can flourish while being aligned with the broader goals of economic inclusion and public benefit. This doesn't mean government intervention at every step but rather the creation of an ecosystem where innovation is guided by strong ethical principles, public-private collaboration, and a commitment to transparency.

With its young population and growing digital infrastructure, India is well-placed to lead this new AI-powered economic surge. By fostering homegrown startups, investing in its talent pool, and adopting responsible AI practices, India has the potential to shape the global conversation around ethical AI.

However, the true measure of success will not just be in deploying advanced technologies, but in ensuring that AI is used as a tool for equitable growth. For AI to uplift all sectors of society, it must provide access to opportunities that benefit everyone, from large industries to small businesses and rural communities.

In the following chapters, we will explore how governments (with the context of India) can harness AI to accelerate its growth in a way that promotes inclusion, sustainability, and innovation. The key strategies will emerge from a blend of technological advancement, sound policy, and a long-term vision where AI serves the nation's broader goals of prosperity and social equity.

The government's role in India's AI future

1. Chief AI Officer

AI is undeniably a transformative force in modern society, and the role of governance in harnessing its potential is becoming more crucial by the day. The discourse around establishing an AI Minister has emerged, but considering India's existing AI governance structures and strategies, a more fitting title would be Chief AI Officer. This position should build on the frameworks and think tanks already in place, such as those outlined by NITI Aayog in its *National Strategy for AI* report (2018), which has laid the groundwork for AI-driven growth across key sectors like healthcare, education, and agriculture. NITI Aayog's report advocates for India to become a global leader in AI by focusing on inclusive growth and applying AI to solve socio-economic challenges.

While these efforts are commendable, a critical gap remains in AI regulation and policy. The role of the Chief AI Officer should not be isolated; rather, it must integrate insights from key industry leaders, legal experts, and academic institutions. For instance, legal professionals such as Shyam Divan, an expert in constitutional law, have raised concerns about the lack of robust regulatory frameworks in AI. These gaps could potentially expose the country to risks such as privacy violations, data misuse, and algorithmic biases. The Supreme Court of India has also flagged similar concerns, emphasizing the need for stricter regulations to address the implications of AI on privacy and data security in light of the Puttaswamy Judgment that recognized privacy as a fundamental right.

When examining AI policy, it's important to note that several countries have already begun addressing AI governance comprehensively. For instance, the European Union has developed the *EU AI Act*, which sets standards for the safe and ethical deployment of AI technologies. Similarly, China's AI regulation specifically targets generative AI, placing restrictions on how AI-generated content is created and used. India, by contrast, lacks a similarly detailed regulatory framework. Here, the Chief AI Officer, in collaboration with the judiciary and legal bodies, must push for the creation of a national AI law that aligns with global standards while addressing the unique challenges India faces, including its diverse population, varying socio-economic conditions, and privacy concerns.

The government's role in regulating AI should extend beyond simply setting guidelines. The Ministry of Electronics and Information Technology (MeitY) and the Chief AI Officer must work closely with advisory bodies like Data Security Council of India (DSCI) to draft AI regulations that protect individual rights without stifling innovation. One of the key aspects of this regulatory framework must be focused on AI ethics and algorithmic transparency. As Dr. Arvind Gupta, a former head of Digital India Foundation, has pointed out, AI algorithms can perpetuate biases if not carefully monitored, making it critical for policymakers to mandate transparency in AI models, especially those used in public services like healthcare and education.

India's judiciary will also need to play a proactive role in interpreting AI regulations and addressing legal challenges that arise from AI implementation. Given the complexities of AI technology, it is essential for courts to develop a nuanced understanding of how AI systems operate, particularly in sectors like law enforcement, where the misuse of AI-driven surveillance tools could infringe on citizens' privacy rights. Nandan Nilekani, a key government consultant, has emphasized the importance of establishing national AI research centers. These centers will be pivotal in not only driving AI innovation but also in ensuring that AI research aligns with the nation's ethical and legal frameworks. While AI policy and regulation form the backbone of responsible AI development, public education on AI cannot be overlooked. India's AI governance must include comprehensive efforts to improve AI literacy across the population.

In line with this responsibility, the Chief AI Officer must also ensure the development of robust policies around data privacy and AI product governance. India's AI ecosystem requires stringent data protection laws to safeguard personal user data and regulate the training of AI models on public data. This includes explicit user consent for data usage and transparency about data collection practices. Recent developments, such as the government's temporary mandate requiring companies to seek approval before launching AI products, underscore the need for a systematic approach like how the FSSAI reviews food products. The Chief AI Officer must work closely with AI ethics researchers to ensure that AI models are free from bias, ethically sound, and comply with stringent regulatory standards. This will foster a safe, transparent, and trustworthy environment for AI innovation in India.

This includes integrating AI concepts into educational curricula at both school and university levels, as well as offering AI training programs for professionals across industries. NITI Aayog's *National Strategy for AI* report highlights the importance of creating a future workforce that is AI-ready. However, these efforts should be supplemented with initiatives led by the Chief AI Officer, focusing on creating awareness of the potential risks and rewards of AI technologies. The government, in collaboration with public and private sector leaders, must prioritize AI literacy to ensure that the country's workforce is equipped to thrive in an AI-driven world.

The Chief AI Officer must also focus on encouraging innovation and research in AI through public-private partnerships. India has a vibrant AI startup ecosystem, and collaboration between these start-ups, academic institutions, and government bodies will be essential for advancing AI technology that addresses India's specific challenges. For instance, AI can revolutionize agriculture through predictive analytics for crop management, healthcare through AI-assisted diagnostics, and education through personalized learning platforms. By fostering innovation in these areas, India can ensure that AI not only drives economic growth but also improves the quality of life for its citizens.

While India has made significant strides in AI governance through bodies like NITI Aayog, DSCI, and advisory committees, the appointment of a Chief AI Officer would ensure a more focused and strategic approach. This role should not only coordinate with legal bodies and think tanks to develop a robust AI policy but also promote AI innovation that is ethical, transparent, and inclusive. The judiciary, in collaboration with these advisory bodies, must create clear legal frameworks that protect citizens' rights while enabling AI-driven growth. With global competition in AI intensifying, India must ensure that its AI strategy is both forward-looking and firmly grounded in ethical principles, regulatory oversight, and public education. Only then can India position itself as a global leader in AI while safeguarding its citizens against the risks posed by unchecked technological development.

2. Independent Semiconductor & Chips Manufacturer

Discovering Atma-Nirbhar Bharat's Potential in Semiconductor Production

Over more than 10 years, Nvidia has built a nearly impregnable lead in producing chips. Now, it's leading the game even further by producing even more powerful chips that can perform complex AI tasks like image, facial and speech recognition, as well as generating text for chatbots like ChatGPT. The onetime industry upstart achieved that dominance by recognizing the AI.

First, you need to understand what semiconductors are and why do we need them. So, basically semiconductors are a key part of many things we use every day, even though we don't see them sold like regular appliances. They're in lots of household items like air conditioners, which use them in temperature sensors, and rice cookers, where they help control the cooking temperature. You'll find semiconductors in many other everyday gadgets like smartphones, digital cameras, TVs, washing machines, fridges, and LED lights.

Beyond home electronics, semiconductors are important in bigger systems like bank ATMs, trains, the internet, and communication networks, including those used in healthcare. They help in saving energy and protecting the environment through efficient logistics systems. In cars, the use of semiconductors is growing, especially for advanced features like driver assistance systems.

In building AI systems, semiconductors are key in creating specialized chips like Graphics Processing Units (GPUs) and Tensor Processing Units (TPUs). GPUs, originally designed for handling graphics, are adept at breaking down complex problems into thousands of smaller tasks to process simultaneously. This massive parallel computing capability, along with their flexibility in handling high-precision computations, makes them valuable for AI tasks. However, GPUs are generally less efficient with neural networks compared to TPUs.

Even though China is itself a semiconductor powerhouse they're depended on USA for chips that are specifically made to run AI systems at scale.

In September 2022, USA tightened sanctions against China by instructing Nvidia to stop selling their high-performance AI-focused GPUs to the country (and Russia), a restriction aimed at preventing the US companies' top hardware from being used by or diverted to military users and finding their way into the nation's supercomputers. Nvidia's response was to create cut-down versions of the A100, A100X, and H100 chips which are the A800 and H800.

Access to advanced semiconductors could fuel breakthroughs in AI, especially with military uses so fearing that USA banned the sale of more advanced AI chips to China. The new export rules restricted the export of Nvidia's A100, A800, H100, H800, L40, L40S, and RTX 4090 chips. The restrictions could also affect chips sold by Intel and AMD. In effect, Nvidia stopped shipping A800 and H800 chips to China or any other country.

India relies a lot on other countries for its semiconductors, getting 95% of them from places like China, Taiwan, South Korea, and Singapore. This is an issue because if India depends too much on others for these important chips, which are needed to make AI systems, it won't be able to become a leader in AI.

But did you know, *India once geared up to lead the world in semiconductor manufacturing.*

I know it sounds too good to be true. So, let me take you back to the history. So, in 1976, the Cabinet of India approved the formation of SCL (Semi-Conductor Laboratory), and the company began production in 1984. At first, Navi Mumbai was the leading contender for where SCL would be established, however, then Prime Minister Indira Gandhi eventually selected Mohali as the location for where SCL would be set up.

SCL was formed to develop India's ambitions for establishing a semiconductor manufacturing industry. The company started producing five-micron semiconductor chips back in 1984, which was three years before even TSMC started operations in 1987. India at that time was only one to two generations behind the cutting edge.

But that was until 1989, when a fire broke out and destroyed SCL's facility in Mohali. The facility restarted production in 1997, however, the fire halted the growth of India's semiconductor industry. As of 2022, the cause of the fire is a mystery, including whether the fire was an accident or caused intentionally. SCL's revenues in 1999-2000 were about $14 million (₹1.4 crore), with a profit of roughly $400,000 (₹3,33,52,980).

SCL came under the administrative control of the Department of Space (DoS) in March 2005, and has since undergone organizational restructuring to become focused on research and development. The society was registered in November 2005. In 2006, Semiconductor Complex Limited was renamed to the Semi-Conductor Laboratory. As of 2024, SCL is under the administrative control of the Ministry of Electronics and Information Technology (MeitY).

Recognizing the importance of semiconductors in AI and various technologies, the Indian government, under Prime Minister Narendra Modi, has unveiled a substantial $10 billion incentive plan to become Atma-Nirbhar in semiconductor manufacturing. This plan aims to attract both domestic and international semiconductor and display manufacturers. The initiative is a strategic move to bolster India's position in the global AI race by ensuring a steady supply of these critical components.

The plan includes offering up to 50% financial support for the costs of eligible semiconductor and display fabrication projects. This significant financial backing is expected to draw major players in the semiconductor industry, with companies like Israel's Tower Semiconductor, Taiwan's Foxconn, and a Singaporean consortium already showing interest in setting up operations in India. Additionally, the Vedanta Group is keen on establishing a display plant.

These developments are crucial for India's AI ambitions, as having a robust semiconductor manufacturing base is essential for the development and deployment of AI technologies.

India's strategy goes beyond mere manufacturing; it encompasses the entire semiconductor ecosystem, including chip design, fabrication, packaging, and testing. This holistic approach is designed to create approximately 35,000 high-quality jobs and 100,000 indirect jobs, thereby fostering a skilled workforce that is essential for AI advancements. The government's support for 100 local firms specializing in integrated circuit and chipset designs further strengthens this ecosystem, contributing to India's readiness for AI and other high-tech industries.

India is at a crucial point right now, which are essential for AI - the technology of the future.

Countries like the USA, China, and Russia are way ahead in this area. They're like farmers who are already enjoying the fruits of their labour, while India has just started planting the seeds. This is a big deal because if India doesn't catch up fast, it will always depend on other countries for advanced technology. This is not just about being good at technology; it's also about being strong and independent as a country.

In the world of AI, every country is trying to be the best, and no one wants to share their top secrets or best technology, like the advanced chips that are the brain of AI systems. India is already 20 years behind, so it needs to work really hard and fast. It's not enough to just follow what others are doing; India needs to have its own big companies, like Nvidia, that make these super-important chips. This means the government and businesses in India need to work together and focus on this goal. It's important for India to make a big jump in making these chips.

India must take significant and courageous steps into the future of computer chip manufacturing. This is not merely an option but a necessity for staying competitive in the AI race. Failing in this endeavour means not only lagging in technology but also losing influence in a world increasingly dominated by AI. India needs to act swiftly and collectively towards this goal, understanding that this effort is about more than just economic gain; it's about securing India's position in the future global landscape.

Currently, India faces substantial challenges in semiconductor manufacturing, including limited infrastructure, insufficient skilled workforce, and dependency on imports for advanced technology. However, with strategic planning and policy support, these obstacles can be overcome.

Good policy would involve:

1. Government Incentives: Providing financial incentives and subsidies to attract global semiconductor companies to set up manufacturing plants in India.
2. Investment in R&D: Allocating funds for research and development in semiconductor technology to foster innovation and build a robust domestic industry.
3. Skilled Workforce Development: Initiating training programs and collaborations with educational institutions to develop a skilled workforce specialized in semiconductor technology.
4. Infrastructure Development: Building state-of-the-art facilities and ensuring reliable supply chains for raw materials and components.

5. International Partnerships: Forming strategic alliances with countries that have advanced semiconductor industries to gain technological expertise and investment.

Imagine a scenario where India not only meets its semiconductor needs but also becomes a global supplier. This would save substantial costs from imports and generate revenue from exports to countries like Australia and Singapore. While the next 4-5 years may be challenging, with careful planning and strategic support, India can achieve significant milestones in AI, paralleling its achievements in space and defense. This journey towards self-reliance in semiconductor manufacturing is not just about economic growth; it's about securing India's future in the rapidly evolving world of AI.

One of the most prominent events which was attended by 28 member countries and the EU, all part of the GPAI, Global Partnership on Artificial Intelligence Summit 2023 had its curtain raiser on December 12, 2023, at Bharat Mandapam. PM Modi's inaugural speech opened a multitude of sessions, as well as the AI Expo to host over 150 Startups geared up to showcase their strengths. PM Modi emphasized that the summit is a testament to India's commitment to harnessing AI in all sectors to retain the welfare of all segments of society. The GPAI summit is structured to foster advancements in Artificial Intelligence (AI) and innovation.

The Indian government's support for companies building exceptionally safe AI systems is not just a matter of policy but a strategic investment in the country's technological future. Offering high tax incentives to these companies is a smart move, as it encourages the development of AI technologies that are not only advanced but also secure and reliable.

This approach aligns with the broader goal of fostering a tech ecosystem that prioritizes safety and ethics. For instance, a company developing an AI-driven traffic management system would be more inclined to invest in rigorous safety protocols if it knew that such diligence would also be financially beneficial. This not only boosts innovation but also ensures that the innovations are aligned with public safety and welfare.

Moreover, the establishment of a government-led team for LLM development aligns with India's broader goals of technological advancement and self-reliance. Similar to ISRO's pioneering efforts in space technology, a dedicated team for LLMs could position India as a leader in AI innovation, bolstering the nation's status on the global stage. Benefits like; subsidies, interest free loans, etc. would manifold tenfold times if invested at right time and the right time is NOW.

This will position India as a global leader in ethical AI development, attracting world class talent and investments. Companies that might otherwise cut corners for cost-saving reasons would be motivated to adhere to the highest safety standards, knowing that their efforts are financially supported. This could lead to breakthroughs in AI applications across various sectors, from healthcare to transportation.

For example, an AI healthcare company incentivized to prioritize safety might develop a revolutionary AI diagnostic tool that minimizes errors, thereby saving lives and elevating India's status in global healthcare technology. The ripple effect of this policy would be significant – creating a safer AI landscape, fostering public trust in AI technologies, and catalysing economic growth through cutting-edge innovation. In essence, by supporting companies that invest in super safe AI, the government is not just regulating technology but actively shaping a future where AI is a force for good, driving both technological advancement and societal well-being.

3. Encouraging and supporting companies building LLMs locally

The Indian government's initiative to encourage and support the development of Large Language Models (LLMs) locally can be a strategic move that aligns with the nation's broader goals of technological advancement and self-reliance. However, rather than forming a dedicated government team to build LLMs, the government could achieve better outcomes by investing in indigenous LLM projects and focusing on creating a conducive environment for private companies and academic institutions to innovate. This approach emphasizes regulation, policymaking, and providing incentives rather than direct involvement in LLM development.

Government investment in indigenous LLMs can be channelled through grants, subsidies, and funding for research and development. This financial support would enable startups, private companies, and research institutions to undertake ambitious projects without the constraints of limited resources. By fostering a competitive ecosystem, the government can ensure the development of diverse and high-quality LLMs tailored to India's unique needs.

Regulating the AI landscape is crucial for ensuring that LLM development aligns with ethical standards and societal well-being. The government should focus on formulating robust policies that address data privacy, algorithmic transparency, and the ethical use of AI. By establishing comprehensive regulatory frameworks, the government can mitigate potential risks associated with LLMs and ensure that these technologies are used responsibly. Effective regulations will also build public trust in AI technologies, which is essential for their widespread adoption.

Providing incentives and benefits for companies to build LLMs can stimulate innovation and attract global talent. The Indian talent pool is globally recognized, with Indians leading top tech companies worldwide. By offering competitive packages, tax benefits, and streamlined processes for setting up AI ventures, India could attract a vast pool of talent and investment. This approach aligns with the Atma Nirbhar Bharat (Self-Reliant India) initiative, aiming to build indigenous capabilities in critical technologies like AI.

From the public's perspective, government investment in indigenous LLMs, coupled with effective regulation, offers significant advantages. One major benefit is the potential for more stringent and effective oversight. By closely monitoring LLM development, the government can identify and address potential loopholes and challenges, leading to the formulation of practical and enforceable regulations. This hands-on approach ensures that regulations are not only theoretically sound but also grounded in real-world application.

Moreover, the government can play a pivotal role in fostering a culture of innovation and research by supporting LLM projects. This support can stimulate the AI ecosystem, encouraging private companies, startups, and academic institutions to explore and innovate in this field. A collaborative environment can lead to groundbreaking advancements in AI, benefiting various sectors such as healthcare, education, and finance.

Another critical aspect is the promotion of ethical AI development. By setting standards for responsible AI practices, the government can influence private entities to adopt similar principles. This can lead to an overall AI landscape that is ethical, transparent, and accountable, further building public trust in AI technologies.

Additionally, the government can facilitate partnerships between industry and academia to bridge the gap between theoretical research and practical application. Collaborative projects and research initiatives can accelerate the development of LLMs and other AI technologies, ensuring that advancements are both innovative and applicable to real-world problems.

In conclusion, the Indian government does not need to form a dedicated team to build LLMs. Instead, it should focus on investing in indigenous LLM projects, regulating the AI landscape, and providing incentives for private companies and academic institutions. This approach will harness the collective expertise and resources of various stakeholders, ensuring that India becomes a frontrunner in the AI domain while upholding ethical standards and serving the public good. Such a strategy positions India as a leader in AI innovation, benefiting both the nation and its populace.

4. Mandatory AI Learning

Mahatma Gandhi said, "Live as if you were to die tomorrow. Learn as if you were to live forever."

Incorporating AI education into the fabric of our academic and professional systems is a crucial step towards preparing India for a future dominated by AI technologies. This initiative should start at the grassroots level, with schools and colleges integrating AI into their curriculum. However, before students embark on this journey, it's essential that their educators – the teachers and professors – are well-versed in AI themselves. By equipping our educators with the necessary AI knowledge, we can ensure that students receive a comprehensive and informed education in this critical field. Are you with me on this?

This means implementing training programs for educators, ensuring they have a solid understanding of AI principles and applications then conducting exams and train them based extensively if they fail. Trust me, this is all necessary because they'll be driving the future of India. Professors should know where and how to apply AI before they teach students, for instance, a biology teacher could learn how AI is used in genetic research, thereby enriching their teaching with real-world applications of AI in science.

It's important to make AI education a top priority. First, teachers need to learn all about AI. Then, they should quickly teach it to students through special AI classes and lessons. These shouldn't just be about book learning; they should also show how AI is used in real life and teach about using AI the right way. To make sure everyone really understands AI, schools could have regular tests for students, teachers, and professors. Getting AI into education fast is more important than sticking to the usual school schedule.

In Hong Kong, the Education Bureau has launched the city's first AI curriculum for junior secondary students, to be integrated into the ICT subject in over 450 public secondary schools. Starting from September, this curriculum for students in From One to Three includes 10 to 14 hours of AI education, covering fundamental concepts, ChatGPT, computer vision, language processing, robotics, and the ethical and social impacts of AI.

Nearly half of the curriculum focuses on AI's ethical implications, and it includes practical exercises using tools like ChatGPT. Additionally, an enriched coding curriculum using Scratch will be introduced for Primary Four to Six students, emphasizing computational thinking. This initiative aims to prepare students for an AI-influenced future, regardless of their career paths.

India can enhance AI education by taking inspiration from Hong Kong's initiative. One idea is to include AI as a regular class for all students, starting in 5th grade, and have exams in 10th grade. This way, students can keep up with AI technology as it grows. If some students find it hard, the education institutes can help with extra learning materials and training every three months. This plan makes sure everyone can join in on the AI revolution, giving all students, no matter where they start, a chance to learn and grow with AI. It's important for AI to be taken seriously as a subject, not like how environmental studies or social studies are often overlooked. AI is different because it will have a big impact on our lives if we don't understand it early on.

The government can play a big role in AI education by teaming up with AI education companies, such as 'Freedom with AI'. The idea is to provide training programs to employees at an affordable price. These companies specialize in AI and have professional teachers who are good at explaining complex AI topics in a simple way. By doing this, the government can make sure that people who are working now can learn about AI easily and stay up to date with the latest changes. This kind of partnership is important to make sure that the workforce doesn't fall behind because of the fast advancements in AI technology.

Companies could offer a range of programs, from basic AI literacy to specialized courses for those in tech-centric professional roles and one important thing is to conduct exams based on different levels for professionals to test and enhance their knowledge. For instance, an employee in the marketing department could learn how AI is transforming customer analytics and personalization strategies. This not only benefits the individual employee by enhancing their skill set and career prospects but also ensures that companies remain competitive and innovative in an AI-driven market.

Mandatory AI education across schools, colleges, and workplaces is a strategic move towards building an AI-savvy nation. By ensuring that everyone from students to working professionals has access to AI knowledge and training, India can position itself as a global leader in the AI era. This comprehensive approach to AI education is not just about creating a skilled workforce; it's about fostering a society that understands, appreciates, and ethically engages with AI technologies. The right AI education provider will know will give a perfect roadmap to empower people of a school, college or company 'AI ready' for instance in 'Freedom with AI' I and my team have curated capstone projects to help people gain hands-on experience on mastering AI tools.

To make India become a global AI leader, the best thing our government, businesses, and schools can do is collaborate with AI education companies like Freedom with AI. By teaching a lot of people about AI, we're doing more than just giving them knowledge. We're preparing our economy's main players for the future. This isn't just regular training; it's getting our country ready to be a leader in the AI world.

5. Comprehensive Bureaucracy

The exponential growth of AI has the potential to bring about significant changes and challenges in society. As we navigate this rapidly evolving landscape, it's important to ensure that we are prepared to handle these changes responsibly. A critical step for the Indian government is the establishment of comprehensive data protection laws that can address various issues related to AI and beyond.

The Indian government should focus on upgrading the existing IT Cell and current bureaucracy. This approach involves equipping the current system with individuals capable of understanding AI and large language models (LLMs). By developing a comprehensive data protection framework, we can safeguard citizens' data and privacy across all technological domains. This broad approach will help address risks and incidents such as frauds or scams, without singling out AI and potentially impeding free speech.

A public grievance platform could be integrated within this broader framework, serving as a central hub where citizens can report their experiences and voice their concerns. This platform would create a feedback loop between the government and its citizens, ensuring that all technological advancements are monitored and managed effectively while maintaining the balance between regulation and freedom of expression. For instance, if we encounter a scam through an AI-driven financial service, we could report it on this platform. The government would then monitor these reports, ensuring that responsible parties are held accountable, and resolutions happen swiftly, ideally within hours or a couple of days.

This proactive approach is essential because AI-related issues often require rapid action. The damage caused by AI can be extensive and rapid, so the response must be equally quick and effective. When dealing with such an intelligent force, resilience is key. The purpose of this domain goes beyond mere monitoring; it's about rapid resolution and prevention. Traditional methods of addressing grievances, like police investigations, might not be sufficient in the AI context. The government's role here is not just as a regulator but also as a facilitator of justice.

If a particular AI system is found to be consistently problematic or harmful, the government should have the authority to dismantle or shut it down to prevent further harm. This decisive action is crucial in a landscape where AI can affect large populations almost instantaneously. For example, if a scammer hacks your social media profile and creates a deepfake of you, threatening your safety, you can report this immediately to the platform, and rapid action will be taken to mitigate the risk.

Enhancing the IT Cell and bureaucracy also involves measures to ensure traceability and accountability in AI usage, particularly in areas like image and video generation and voice cloning. Implementing robust digital identity verification systems for users engaging with these high-risk AI tools can help. However, it's crucial to balance this with the protection of user privacy. High-risk activities could require additional verification steps without overly invasive surveillance of all AI interactions. Any system implemented should include strict data protection measures to ensure that user information is secure and used solely for accountability purposes. Companies failing to comply with these regulations should face appropriate penalties, promoting a safer and more ethical use of AI.

India's journey towards becoming a global leader in AI hinges on a comprehensive and multi-faceted approach. This path to AI leadership is not just about technological advancement but about crafting a future where technology serves the greater good. It's a journey that balances innovation with responsibility, growth with ethics, and ambition with caution.

AI auditing agencies should be established to ensure compliance with AI laws, rules, and regulations. These agencies, either developed by the government or outsourced to third-party companies, would regularly examine AI systems used by companies to ensure they adhere to the established legal framework. The need for such audits is underscored by the rapid impact AI can have on society.

For example, deepfake technology and voice cloning have already led to misinformation and reputational damage. Now, imagine the impact on a sensitive individual who might find herself the subject of a malicious deepfake. The psychological toll could be devastating, potentially leading to tragic outcomes. In such cases, robust AI audits can prevent AI systems from being used in harmful ways. If a company doesn't follow AI regulations, quick and strict actions should be taken, like how India quickly banned TikTok. Fast responses are crucial because AI misuse can have immediate and serious effects.

Open-source AI models add complexity to regulation. To ensure these models are used responsibly, we need community guidelines, good monitoring, and international cooperation to catch and stop misuse. AI audits are not just rules; they protect against the misuse of powerful technology. If not controlled, this misuse could seriously harm people and society. Both proprietary and open-source models need a thorough and coordinated approach to prevent harm and ensure they are used ethically.

India can set a global standard for how technology can be harnessed to benefit society. This vision for AI is not just a blueprint for progress; it's a commitment to a future where technology and humanity advance hand in hand.

In the context of AI governance, the implementation of robust auditing mechanisms is crucial for ensuring compliance with laws and ethical standards. Experts like Brad Smith, president of Microsoft, have emphasized the need for independent audits of AI systems to mitigate risks like deepfakes and biased algorithms. Similarly, thought leaders in AI ethics, such as Timnit Gebru, highlight the potential harm if

AI systems aren't closely monitored. The creation of AI auditing agencies, either government-run or third-party, ensures transparency and accountability in AI development, fostering trust in this powerful technology.

The future of AI regulation is about proactive global leadership. As noted by experts from the Brookings Institution, governments that quickly establish clear AI laws and auditing systems will set the global standard for ethical AI use. India's leadership in this space can serve as a model, given its potential to harmonize AI innovation with legal frameworks, ensuring responsible technology development that benefits society.

This is no longer just a matter of national strategy but a global race to create a future where AI technologies serve humanity responsibly and equitably. The question isn't only about which nation can develop AI faster but who can build the most effective regulatory frameworks to govern its responsible use.

CHAPTER 11

LEVERAGING AI TO TRANSFORM YOUR BUSINESS

Chegg, a leading name in the ed-tech industry, faced a significant crisis when its shares dropped by over 40% after the company admitted that ChatGPT was outperforming its services. This stark example serves as a warning: in today's rapidly evolving landscape, AI is not just an advantage—it's a necessity. Chegg's stumble highlights a critical truth for all industries: businesses that fail to integrate AI risk falling behind, or worse, becoming irrelevant. This isn't just a trend; it's a fundamental shift in how companies need to operate to stay competitive.

Contrast Chegg's story with Khan Academy's forward-thinking approach. Instead of seeing AI as a threat, they embraced it with the launch of Khanmigo, an AI-driven tool designed to assist students in learning and completing homework with greater ease. Khan Academy's successful integration of AI illustrates how companies can not only preserve their relevance but also enhance their offerings and improve user experiences. This comparison between Chegg and Khan Academy underscores a pivotal insight: adopting AI thoughtfully and strategically is crucial to thriving in the future of business.

The shift toward AI isn't limited to education—it's spreading across all sectors. From healthcare to retail, finance to manufacturing, AI is revolutionizing industries by enhancing efficiency, personalizing customer experiences, and driving innovation. Businesses that hesitate or fail to embrace AI risk being outpaced by competitors who do. However, it's not enough to simply adopt AI; companies must implement it responsibly, addressing challenges such as data privacy, transparency, and ethical use.

This chapter aims to guide businesses through the complexities of AI integration. With the right approach, AI becomes more than a tool for optimization—it becomes a powerful engine for growth, innovation, and future success. The road ahead may be challenging, but the opportunities AI presents are immense. For businesses ready to adapt, AI offers a transformative edge in the modern marketplace.

1. Dedicated AI team

dedicated AI team within a company is not a luxury but a strategic asset. While my digital marketing agency leverages AI for enhancing tasks like crafting ad copy, managing campaign schedules, and automating emails, the scope of AI is much more extensive. In logistics, for example, AI optimizes delivery routes, automates warehouse operations, and accurately forecasts inventory requirements, leading to cost savings and timely deliveries.

Most of the times, customer services have consistently fallen short of expectations. Think about the frustration of being stuck on hold for what feels like an eternity, only to be transferred from one representative to another, with no real resolution in sight. We've all been there, haven't we? Traditional customer service often falls short in these moments, leaving us feeling unheard and dissatisfied. But with the rise of AI-powered chatbots, this dynamic is shifting. These tools now offer round-the-clock assistance, providing quick answers without the wait, while AI analyses customer interactions to provide insights for continuous service improvement.

In finance, AI plays a key role in analysing complex data for investment decisions, detecting fraud, and automating routine tasks such as generating reports. In human resources, AI streamlines the recruitment process by efficiently sorting through resumes and identifying the best candidates. This broad application of AI, including the art of prompt engineering, is indispensable in today's business world. By employing AI in diverse areas – from marketing tasks like creating video sales letters (VSLs) to optimizing supply chain management and enhancing customer engagement – a dedicated AI team can profoundly improve a company's operational efficiency and overall effectiveness.

After witnessing the transformative impact of dedicated AI teams in real-world scenarios, it becomes evident how crucial they are for businesses aiming to thrive in today's digital landscape. Take, for instance, the case of Company X (not twitter), a leading e-commerce platform that struggled with inefficient customer service operations. By establishing a dedicated AI team, Company X was able to implement AI-powered chatbots that revolutionized their customer support process. These chatbots provided instant assistance to customers, significantly reducing response times and enhancing overall satisfaction.

As a result, Company X saw a notable increase in customer retention and loyalty, ultimately boosting their bottom line. Similarly, Company Y, a multinational corporation in the finance sector, leveraged its dedicated AI team to develop sophisticated fraud detection algorithms. These algorithms analysed vast amounts of transaction data in real-time, identifying fraudulent activities with remarkable accuracy. As a result, Company Y was able to minimize financial losses and safeguard its reputation, demonstrating the invaluable role of dedicated AI teams in mitigating risks and driving business success.

Beyond operational efficiency, a dedicated AI team plays a crucial role in overseeing AI ethics, ensuring that the company's use of AI aligns with high standards of governance. Continuous monitoring of AI systems is vital to ensure they function as intended and do not engage in unethical or harmful behaviours. Regular audits, conducted by either internal or external parties, are essential for early identification and rectification of any issues. Moreover, educating employees about AI's capabilities and limitations, along with ethical considerations and best practices, fosters a culture of responsible AI use within the organization.

Expanding on these ideas, a dedicated AI team can also spearhead innovation within the company. They can explore new AI technologies and applications that could open novel business opportunities or streamline existing processes. For instance, AI-driven data analysis tools can uncover insights from customer data that can inform marketing strategies, product development, and customer service improvements. This team could also be responsible for developing custom AI solutions tailored to the company's specific needs, ensuring a competitive edge in the market.

Another critical aspect of a dedicated AI team is risk management. AI, while powerful, comes with its own set of risks, including data privacy concerns, potential biases in decision-making, and reliance on flawed algorithms. The AI team would be responsible for identifying these risks and developing strategies to mitigate them. This could involve implementing robust data security measures, ensuring AI algorithms are free from biases, and establishing protocols for human oversight of AI decisions.

A dedicated AI team can act as a bridge between the technical and non-technical parts of the business. They can demystify AI for other departments, helping them understand how AI tools can benefit their work. This cross-departmental collaboration can lead to more holistic and innovative approaches to business challenges.

Another critical aspect of a dedicated AI team is risk management. AI, while powerful, comes with its own set of risks, including data privacy concerns, potential biases in decision-making, and reliance on flawed algorithms. The AI team would be responsible for identifying these risks and developing strategies to mitigate them. This could involve implementing robust data security measures, ensuring AI algorithms are free from biases, and establishing protocols for human oversight of AI decisions.

One of the biggest challenges with Large Language Models (LLMs) today is hallucination. Hallucination occurs when the AI generates information that is incorrect or nonsensical. This is a primary concern for businesses, as relying on inaccurate data can lead to poor decision-making and loss of trust. Addressing this issue involves implementing measures to verify the accuracy of AI-generated content and ensuring that human oversight is always in place to catch and correct these errors.

In terms of customer engagement, AI can be a game-changer. A dedicated AI team can develop chatbots and virtual assistants to enhance customer service, providing quick and personalized responses to customer inquiries. They can also use AI to analyse customer feedback and social media trends, helping the company stay ahead of market demands and customer expectations.

If you look at the current state of technology and where we have come from, you will notice a predictable pace of evolution. In today's digital era, having a focus on AI is crucial for any company aiming to succeed. While a dedicated AI team is ideal for automating tasks, ensuring AI ethics, driving innovation, managing risks, enhancing cross-departmental collaboration, and improving customer engagement, it's understandable that not every company can afford such a team. In such cases, it's wise to at least appoint a single individual responsible for overseeing AI-related activities. This person can play a pivotal role in integrating AI into the company's operations and strategy. As AI continues to evolve, having someone to manage and guide AI initiatives becomes an essential investment for businesses looking to maintain a competitive edge in their industries.

2. Building Trust

The competition to create increasingly intelligent and efficient AI models, including large language models (LLMs), is intensifying at an unprecedented scale, driven by staggering investments. By mid-2025, global AI spending has already topped $200 billion, and analysts now expect it to near $900 billion a year by 2030. Tech giants like Microsoft, Google, and OpenAI are leading the charge, collectively pouring billions into advancing AI capabilities. Microsoft, for instance, invested a reported $10 billion into OpenAI to support the development of ChatGPT, signaling just how high the stakes are.

But it's not just the money. The sheer scale of these models is also growing exponentially. GPT-3, for example, has 175 billion parameters, and newer models are reaching into the trillions, vastly improving their ability to understand and generate human-like text. This race to build more powerful models has become one of the most resource-intensive technological competitions in history, requiring massive amounts of computational power and data.

However, success in this field requires more than just technological innovation—it demands a steadfast commitment to ethical practices. Just as an architect designs a building with both functionality and safety in mind, businesses must ensure that AI development benefits society and avoids harm. With great power comes great responsibility, and as LLMs become more capable, ethical considerations like bias, data privacy, and transparency become more critical than ever.

At the core of ethical AI development is the respect for privacy and the assurance of fairness, coupled with a conscious effort to avoid biases. Adhering to international standards, such as those proposed by the OECD or IEEE, provides a solid framework for ethical AI. These guidelines are the compass that guides businesses in navigating the complex terrain of AI ethics. Data, the cornerstone of AI, must be handled with the utmost care. It's akin to the foundation of a building; if the foundation is compromised, the entire structure is at risk. And as I touched on earlier, if the data used in AI systems is biased or violates privacy norms, the integrity of the AI system is jeopardized.

The current market's hesitance to fully embrace AI tools stems from concerns about security, privacy and accuracy. In this context, a company that develops a highly secure LLM would mark a significant breakthrough, akin to the impact of the iPhone in the smartphone industry. The iPhone's success was not just due to its innovative features; it was also about how it prioritized user privacy and security. Drawing a parallel, an LLM that offers similar levels of security and privacy would not only gain a competitive edge but also set a new standard in the AI industry, much like a beacon guiding ships in a stormy sea.

While the present AI race seems to focus on efficiency and output, the future will likely see a shift towards safety and ethical integrity. It's a transition from merely winning the race to running it with responsibility and care. Businesses must understand that building AI models is not just about technological advancement; it's about ensuring these models are safe and ethical, like a chef ensuring every ingredient in a dish is both delicious and safe to consume.

"You cannot build anything that is lasting without a foundation." – John C. Maxwell, *an American author, speaker, and leadership expert known for his books on leadership and personal development.*

When we invest so much in something, we want it to be strong and reliable. Isn't it? Hence, for businesses in the AI sector, the path forward involves prioritizing safety and ethics. This approach is like an architect designing a building. Just as an architect ensures that a building is aesthetically pleasing and structurally sound, AI developers must create models that are intelligent, ethically robust, and secure. This commitment to ethical AI is not just about mitigating risks; it's about earning public trust and setting a standard for responsible innovation.

Users should be able to understand how an AI system arrives at its decisions. This transparency builds trust and demystifies AI technology for the public. It's about showing the inner workings of the AI, much like a teacher explaining a complex concept in simple terms, making it accessible and understandable.

Accuracy in LLMs is another primary concern that hinders companies from fully integrating AI into their operations. Businesses rely on precise and reliable information to make critical decisions, and inaccuracies in AI outputs can lead to costly mistakes. Ensuring that language models consistently provide accurate and relevant information is crucial for their adoption. Companies need AI systems they can trust to deliver correct results, much like how they depend on accurate data from their existing tools. By prioritizing accuracy, AI developers can address one of the key barriers to AI integration, making these systems more dependable and valuable for businesses.

AI systems require continuous nurturing and updating. This process involves regular evaluations and adjustments, ensuring that the AI adapts and evolves ethically in an ever-changing environment. It's about keeping the AI system in tune with societal norms and ethical standards.

In addition to these principles, businesses must also focus on inclusivity in AI development. This means ensuring that AI systems are designed with a diverse range of users in mind. Inclusivity in AI prevents the creation of systems that are biased or exclusive, fostering a technology that is beneficial and usable by a broad spectrum of society.

Businesses must prioritize active engagement with a diverse group of stakeholders, including customers, ethicists, and policymakers, in their AI development process. This dialogue is essential for ensuring that AI is not developed in isolation but is shaped by a multitude of perspectives and informed by various societal needs and ethical considerations. Such engagement fosters a more holistic and responsible approach to AI development and helps in identifying potential ethical pitfalls and societal impacts early in the development process, allowing for more thoughtful and inclusive AI solutions.

For businesses developing AI models, the commitment to ethical guidelines and standards is not just a moral choice but a strategic necessity. This involves creating AI systems that are technologically sophisticated while also being ethically responsible, secure, and trustworthy.

3. Build LLMs

So, till now we have already talked about the revolution AI is bringing in the technologies. Can you picture a future where technology does more than just making our lives convenient and makes the world a better place? This is the promise of Ethical AI, particularly through the development of LLMs. Unlike the next best smartphone or video sharing app, Ethical AI aims to solve real-world problems while generating substantial revenue. The evolution of AI is 10x more powerful than the transformation happened in our world due to electricity.

Transparency in AI development is crucial. Currently, many AI systems function as black boxes, where their decision-making processes are opaque and not easily understood. This lack of clarity can be problematic, as it prevents users from understanding how decisions are made. To change this, AI systems need to be designed with explainability in mind. For instance, when an AI system denies a loan application, both the applicant and the loan officer should be able to understand the rationale behind this decision. This level of clarity is essential not just for trust but for accountability and continuous improvement. By incorporating explainable AI (XAI) techniques, we can ensure that AI decisions are both effective and transparent, fostering greater trust and reliability in these systems.

Companies building LLMs have several lucrative avenues to generate revenue, while also ensuring the safety and ethical use of their technology. Firstly, offering API integration is a primary method; businesses can allow other companies to access their LLMs through APIs, enabling a range of applications from chatbots to advanced analytics. Secondly, providing customization options allows clients to tailor the LLMs to their specific needs, which can be particularly appealing to industries with unique requirements.

Thirdly, companies can monetize their LLMs through direct product integration, embedding their AI into consumer products or business tools to enhance functionality. Fourthly, licensing the technology to other businesses or developers opens another revenue stream, where companies pay for the rights to use the LLM in their own products. Lastly, offering consultancy services is another profitable path. By leveraging their expertise in LLMs, companies can advise other businesses on how to effectively implement AI solutions.

While exploring these revenue models, it's crucial for companies to prioritize safety and ethical considerations. This means ensuring transparency in how the AI makes decisions, maintaining user privacy, and continuously monitoring for biases. Balancing profitability with responsibility is key; by doing so, companies not only adhere to ethical standards but also build trust with their users and clients, which is essential for long-term success in the AI industry.

Beta testing and public feedback are other vital components in the development of LLMs. Before full-scale deployment, businesses should release beta versions of their AI systems. This real-world testing allows for the gathering of valuable feedback, which can be used to enhance user experience and ensure alignment with ethical and safety standards. For example, a beta test of an AI-driven healthcare app could reveal unforeseen biases in treatment recommendations, which can then be corrected before wider release. Transparent communication about the uses, benefits, and limitations of AI will further help in building public trust and understanding.

As we talk about these strategies, we shouldn't neglect that the ongoing education and engagement with the public are essential. As AI becomes more prevalent, businesses should take the initiative to educate their users about how AI works, its potential benefits, and its limitations. This could involve simple, easy-to-understand tutorials or interactive sessions that demystify AI. For example, a bank using AI for fraud detection could create an interactive guide explaining how AI helps keep customers' money safe, thereby not only informing but also reassuring its customers.

Another key aspect is the ethical use of data. In building LLMs, the data used to train these models must be ethically sourced and managed. This means obtaining data through fair practices and ensuring that it is representative of diverse populations to avoid biases. For instance, an AI model used for job recruitment should be trained on a dataset that reflects a diverse range of candidates to prevent discrimination.

Collaboration with regulatory bodies is also important. As AI continues to evolve, so too should the regulations be governing its use. Businesses should work closely with regulators to ensure that their AI systems comply with current laws and ethical standards. This collaboration can also help shape future regulations that support innovation while protecting the public.

The development of LLMs represents a significant step forward in the field of AI. However, this advancement must be approached with a commitment to ethical practices, transparency, public engagement, and regulatory compliance. By focusing on these areas, businesses can ensure that their AI systems are not only advanced and efficient but also ethical, trustworthy, and beneficial to society. The journey towards Ethical AI is not just about technological innovation; it's about building a future where technology works for the betterment of all.

4. Upskill everyone in the organization with AI skills

As we talk about competition in the bustling corridors of modern businesses, there's a new kind of energy activating – the drive to upskill every team member in AI. It's a movement that's transforming the workplace, turning every corner of an organization into a hub of innovation and forward-thinking. This isn't just about keeping up with the times; it's about embracing the future, one skill at a time. Let me tell you my friend, it's not just about landing yourself a good job anymore, you need to be on your toes and keep updating yourselves to stay in the race!

Many organizations already recognize the value of upskilling, whether it's in interpersonal dynamics or technical prowess. Take, for instance, the decision to provide team members with access to the world's leading resources on AI and digital marketing. This move, though it might come with a significant price tag, is far from a mere expenditure. It's an investment, one that yields dividends not just in enhanced skills but in the overall growth and evolution of the company. When you invest in your people, you're not just boosting their capabilities; you're fuelling the very engine that drives your business forward.

But the journey of upskilling in AI doesn't end with merely providing resources—it's about embedding AI learning into the fabric of daily work culture. Imagine a workplace where lunchtime conversations revolve around the latest AI innovations, and brainstorming sessions consistently explore how AI can solve business challenges. Companies like Google, Microsoft, and Amazon are already fostering such environments. At Google, for example, the company has a longstanding culture of "20% time," where employees dedicate time to learning and working on side projects, many of which involve AI exploration. This encourages constant learning and creative application of cutting-edge technologies, making AI part of employees' everyday lives.

Josh Bersin, a leading industry analyst says, "The companies that excel in AI upskilling aren't just teaching people about AI; they're embedding it into the workflow." His insight reflects the growing trend where organizations integrate AI into daily operations, creating a more fluid and dynamic learning environment. This cultural shift transforms learning from a scheduled activity into a continuous, real-time process of discovery and innovation.

Another critical strategy is combining AI education with practical, on-the-job applications. A prime example is IBM, which runs an internal AI Skills Academy that allows employees to identify areas in their current roles where AI could drive efficiencies. This hands-on approach not only enhances learning but also empowers employees to take ownership of AI implementation within their workflows. As a result, employees don't just learn AI in theory; they apply it in ways that directly improve productivity, innovation, and the company's bottom line.

According to a report from PwC, 67% of executives believe AI will help humans and machines work together more efficiently, and this kind of practical integration reinforces that vision. By allowing employees to see firsthand how AI can enhance their work, businesses not only upskill their teams but also encourage a culture of ownership, innovation, and long-term success.

Furthermore, it's crucial to recognize and celebrate the milestones in this upskilling journey. When an employee successfully completes an AI course or implements an AI-driven solution, celebrating these achievements can boost morale and encourage others. It sends a clear message: the organization values and supports continuous learning and innovation. And who doesn't love a little appreciation right?

In addition to formal training and resources, peer-to-peer learning can be a powerful tool. Employees who have advanced skills in AI can conduct workshops or informal sessions for their colleagues. This not only helps in spreading knowledge but also in building a collaborative culture where everyone supports each other's growth. It's like having an in-house AI community, where knowledge flows freely and everyone is a contributor.

As Benjamin Franklin said, "**For the best return on your money, pour your purse into your head**." And the organizations have understood this fact!

Leadership roles in this upskilling initiative are also crucial. When leaders actively participate in AI learning programs, it sets a tone for the entire organization. It shows that AI upskilling is not just a mandate but a shared goal, valued at every level of the company. Leaders can share their learning experiences, challenges, and how AI insights have influenced their decision-making processes. This not only humanizes the learning process but also inspires others to embark on their AI learning journey.

Upskilling every member of an organization in AI is not just about staying competitive; it's about cultivating a culture of continuous learning and innovation. It's a journey that requires commitment, creativity, and collaboration. By investing in AI upskilling, organizations are not just enhancing their employees' careers; they are shaping a future where both the employees and the company thrive together in a world increasingly influenced by AI. This approach to upskilling is not just a strategy; it's a vision for a future where every member of the organization is empowered, informed, and ready to take on the challenges and opportunities presented by AI.

The integration of AI, especially the development of LLMs, is emerging as a pivotal factor in the success and sustainability of modern businesses. As AI reshapes the landscape of industry and commerce, companies that adeptly incorporate AI-enabled products and services are poised to reap significant benefits.

This integration is not just about enhancing profitability; it's about ensuring relevance in an increasingly AI-driven world. However, the journey towards AI adoption must be navigated with a commitment to ethical practices and safety, ensuring that these advanced systems contribute positively to society and business alike. In this era, the ability to effectively harness AI will be the dividing line between businesses that flourish and those that fall behind.

So, what's the next step you should take?

Step 1: Scan the QR code.

Step 2: Register for the masterclass.

Step 3: Check your email for the confirmation link.

Step 4: Save the event date to your calendar.

Step 5: Join the masterclass and start learning.

This masterclass is updated every two weeks with the latest trending AI tools and news, giving you massive value. It's worth ₹5000, but we're offering it free as a thank-you for purchasing this book.